PRAISE FOR
JOINT VENTURE

This is not another how-to-be-spiritual book, but a treasury of hard-earned wisdom from a Christian life well lived. Jeanie Miley is a first-rate spiritual guide, and in this text she tells us in intimate and open narrative her own pilgrimage, how she came through, and where she found bread for the journey. This comparison no doubt embarrasses her, but *Joint Venture* is in a way like Augustine's *Confessions*—it takes one life deeply committed to the quest for Christian wholeness and makes it a rich resource for other seekers. Take and read. Here find wisdom.

—LOYD ALLEN
Sylvan Hills Chair of Baptist Heritage and
Professor of Church History and Spiritual Formation
McAfee School of Theology

Joint Venture is a sensitive and honest memoir of a woman's response to the call of her inner authentic self to be set free, not as an egotistical venture, but as a sacred responsibility and a partnership effort with God. Reading Jeanie Miley's experience of her search encourages me to continue on my own "joint venture" with God—with an inspiring sense of the companionship of a sister in Christ on a similar pilgrimage.

—ANDREA WELLS MILLER
Author, *BodyCare*
Co-author (with Pia Mellody and J. Keith Miller), *Facing Codependence*

With non-brittle, loving honesty and practicality, Jeanie Miley describes the journey of discovery and release of the loving, creative person in each of us who has been wrapped in the invisible grave clothes of denial and out-of-touch religious and social conventions. This is a strong, clear message that I believe can help thousands of women and men break through the frustrating fear of discovering and becoming who (and what) God made us to be. I strongly recommend this book.

—KEITH MILLER
Author, *The Taste of New Wine*
and *A Hunger for Healing*

Smyth & Helwys Publishing, Inc.
6316 Peake Road
Macon, Georgia 31210-3960
1-800-747-3016
©2011 by Smyth & Helwys Publishing
All rights reserved.
Printed in the United States of America.

The paper used in this publication meets the minimum requirements of
American National Standard for Information Sciences—
Permanence of Paper for Printed Library Materials.
ANSI Z39.48–1984. (alk. paper)

Library of Congress Cataloging-in-Publication Data

Miley, Jeanie.
Joint venture : practical spirituality for everyday pilgrims / By Jeanie Miley.
p. cm.
Includes bibliographical references and index.
ISBN 978-1-57312-581-9 (pbk. : alk. paper)
1. Christian life.
2. Spirituality. I. Title.
BV4501.3.M557 2011
270.8'2—dc22

2011012424

JOINT VENTURE

PRACTICAL SPIRITUALITY
FOR EVERYDAY PILGRIMS

Jeanie Miley

ALSO BY JEANIE MILEY

To my grandchildren, in whom I delight . . .

Abby Elizabeth Doss
Madeleine Grace Schlegel
Matthew Miley Doss
Lucas William Everett
Samuel Miley Everett
Dylan Andrew Schlegel
Ryan Alexander Schlegel

May you sing freely the song that is in you—
May you always know how deeply you are loved—
May you love well and laugh much—
May you know God, who dwells within you.

ACKNOWLEDGMENTS

With deepest gratitude to my teachers, mentors and guides in this joint venture called life. Because of you . . . how *can* I keep from singing?

Martus Miley, my husband
Louis Ball, my father
Helen Smith Ball, my mother
Michelle Miley, my daughter
Julie Miley Schlegel, my daughter
Amy Miley Everett, my daughter
John Claypool
Hardy Clemons
Sister Mary Dennison
James Hollis
Fr. Keith Hosey
Carole Hovde
Howard Hovde
Sandra Hulse
Thomas Keating
Pat Johnson
Pittman McGehee
Ann Miller
Keith Miller
Bishop Michael Pfeifer
Elaine Rohr
Floyd Thatcher

The Monks at St. Benedict's Monastery, Snowmass, Colorado
To the writers, poets, artists and musicians who have enriched my mind, my heart and my soul . . . thank you.

To the many friends who have blessed me, to those who have challenged me, to those who have trusted me with your stories and to those in my classes through the years . . . thank you.

Thanks be to God for these instruments of God's grace,

Jeanie Miley
September 1, 2010

CONTENTS

FOREWORD

Jeanie Miley begins *Joint Venture* with words from Mary Oliver's poem "Summer Day": "Tell me, what is it you plan to do with your one wild and precious life?"

From this simple question, Jeanie takes us on a journey. I use the word "journey" deliberately. Several times while reading how Jeanie sees and has experienced the "joint venture" between God and us, I kept remembering how I felt reading Geoffrey Chaucer's *The Canterbury Tales* many years ago. I can remember the day that I felt like I was on the road to Canterbury with those pilgrims and that our life with God and toward God is indeed a journey. As we walk this path, this joint venture, we need each other, and as we share our tales we come to know not only each other but also the way God has blessed us and changed us and made us His own.

Jeanie shares the tales of her life from growing up in a Baptist parsonage to marrying a preacher of the same denomination to having babies and then grandbabies. I felt like I came to know not only her but also all the other people who have led her and mentored her and sometimes given her just the moment of love and grace and encouragement she needed.

Growing up, Jeanie worried that she would be called to be a missionary, which would entail giving up ever getting married or having children as she sacrificed her life in "deepest Africa." As one travels with Jeanie in what she calls the joint venture of her life, one comes to see that she is both a missionary and an evangelist. Although she did not travel to darkest Africa, she travels to some pretty dark spots in her own life and she returns from those dark places with a message of hope. There is no darkness that the Lord Jesus does not know. There is no darkness that He will not share with us. There is no darkness where His light cannot penetrate. She is an evangelist, not using a program but using her life. She is the best kind of missionary and evangelist. She does not scold or threaten, and she never resorts to trying to frighten people into the Kingdom. There is nothing canned or pedantic in her reflections. But she knows good news and she shares good news by coming alongside of us in the everyday, ordinary stuff of our lives.

Jeanie says that at one time in her life John 15 became her favorite passage of Scripture with its guidance that we are to "abide in Christ." Our abiding in Christ, as the passage says, is not just for our own comfort and nourishment but also that we may bear "much fruit." This book is about her abiding in Christ in myriad ways, and about fruit that Christ has borne in her, fruit that she is now sharing with us.

The list of things that worked for me in Joint Venture are many; the list of things that did not are . . . well . . . nearly non-existent. I do think there are moments when Jeanie may be a little too self-deprecating. Of course, she is trying to be humble. Of course, she is coming to God "just as [she is] without one plea." But my guess is that she might still be recovering from some of the messages, spiritual and otherwise, that she received along the way. She says that if we are "looking for an authority, [that we] won't find it in [her]." Although I can understand her objection, I do not agree. She is, I believe, an authority on things spiritual and on what she calls the Joint Venture, because she knows the Author of Life and the Giver of Salvation and the Inspirer of our Souls and Lives. She is an authority on matters of the heart and our walk with God because she has prayed without ceasing and traveled the world from without and from within for truth. She has walked with many fellow pilgrims and has taken the wounds of her life—the wounds that we all have to a greater or lesser degree—and she has with conviction and honesty taken us to the scarred but redemptive hands of Jesus. She has shown us how grace leaks out of the brokenness of our lives, and that we not only need God but each other in the Joint Venture of grace.

When I finished the book the words that came to me were these: "Well done, good and faithful servant." Well done. Jeanie's stories are not unlike the stories of Jesus feeding the 4,000 or 5,000—only in reverse. In those feeding stories, Jesus feeds the people and then he asks for the fragments to be collected. In her own story, Jeanie has collected the fragments of her life, and then she feeds us.

Reading this book is a feast. Come to the table and be fed.

—*James W. Nutter*
Rector, Palmer Memorial Episcopal Church
February 2011

INTRODUCTION

*Tell me, what is it you plan to do with
your one wild and precious life?*

—MARY OLIVER, "THE SUMMER DAY"

"Do you wish you had waited until you were out of residency to have a baby?" I asked my daughter.

It was Christmas Eve, and our daughter Julie had just arrived at our house after a thirty-hour rotation at Texas Children's Hospital. Exhausted from a particularly stressful night, she immediately changed clothes, washed her hands, retrieved four-month-old Madeleine from an adoring aunt, and fell into the nearest chair in our den with her baby in her arms. As she nursed her hungry infant, they both fell asleep.

Later, after she had rested and showered, Julie came back downstairs to join the family. She was obviously refreshed, but fatigue was etched all over her face. It was then that I asked my question with the intent to communicate empathy for Julie's stress and strain in balancing the last year of her pediatric residency and the demands of motherhood.

Julie whirled around, aghast.

"Mom," she exclaimed, "if we had waited, *it wouldn't have been Madeleine!*"

Think about it! Of all the possible combinations of genes that could have come together in the mysterious process of conception, Madeleine was born.

At another moment in time, who might have been conceived?

Celtic spirituality holds the idea that every time we look into the face of a newborn infant, we look into the face of God. I know for sure that every time we look into the face of an infant, we look into the face of mystery and of infinite potential that is ours to discover.

I tell this story often to introduce the concepts I share in this book, whether in the sacred space of individual spiritual direction or in a group setting. Whenever I tell it, there is instantaneous resonance. Some people gasp quietly, and someone always cries. Others suck in their breath and smile, and now and then, someone has to leave to go cry alone.

The very idea of one's unique life is staggering to ponder!

How fortunate for a child to be welcomed into the world as she or he is by the people who birth that child. However, many people bear the burden of being born at an inconvenient time or being unwanted, either for who they are or are not.

Countless people have so conformed and adapted to others' expectations that they have lost the sense of their wild and precious lives. For people who have spent a lifetime trying to be someone they aren't, the story of my daughter and granddaughter somehow connects them to a deep inner wisdom that affirms, "Who I am matters." A blessing and an inner awareness of one's intrinsic worth and value is the birthright of every child.

In the first half of life, we must learn to adapt and conform to prescribed role constraints or the belief that it is our job to be who other people want us to be, do what others decide we should do, or play a role in someone else's drama or life script. We learn early to ignore our authentic selves. Many people silence their own beings for so long that they lose the ability to hear the nudging of the still, small voice at the core of who they are.

Just because we cannot hear or see the True Self within us doesn't mean it is silent. At some point, our True Self—the one wild and precious life inscribed in every cell of our beings—comes calling and demands to be set free.

Whether it is fact or legend, I am fascinated by the story of Michelangelo's being ridiculed for bringing a particular piece of marble down from the quarry. "Why did you go to all this trouble to get that ugly piece of rock?' he was asked. "There's an angel in here that wants to get out," he replied.

On my first trip to Europe, I carried a paperback copy of Irving Stone's *The Agony and the Ecstasy*.[1] Traveling through sunflower fields in Italy toward Florence, I was deep into the life of Michelangelo. I walked into the Accademia Gallery in Florence, Italy, and my excitement over finally seeing the magnificent sculpture, the *David*, had me almost breathless with anticipation.

So it was that I stood speechless with awe before the statue of David, overwhelmed by the beauty of it, but also by the reality that another human being could have evoked such magnificence from a block of marble.

Apparently, Michelangelo's genius and artistry were guided by the belief that the form was already in the stone, imprisoned and waiting for the artist to release it.

I remembered reading that someone asked Michelangelo how he could sculpt such magnificent pieces. "I see what is in it," he said, "and I just start chipping away at what doesn't belong until the piece is free."

That idea has become my metaphor for the process of spiritual growth. It takes nerve and courage to put oneself under the sculptor's tools or to be a partner in the process of chipping away what binds the angel or the True Self. Fortunate and blessed is the human being whose True Self is recognized and acknowledged by another human being, for to be known as one truly is allows one to be set free from everything that constrains the True Self.

As I left the gallery and got back on the tour bus, another image pushed the David sculpture out of my mind. The image has haunted me for twenty years since that day in Florence.

Walking through the Prisoners' Gallery that leads to the statue of David, I was stunned to see unfinished works of the great sculptor lining the wall of that long hallway. With the glorious David in view at the far end, these figures seemed half-finished, trapped in the marble.

As we rushed purposefully toward the *David*, my sister had commented on those unfinished pieces, but I was so eager to see the completed statue, the glorious, famous, *finished* product we had traveled thousands of miles to see, that I didn't stop to ponder the mind-jolting symbolism of the "prisoners."

Haunted by those trapped figures, I read later that Michelangelo believed that just as it was his job to release what was already in the marble, the human soul is a prisoner who strives to be released from its bodily form. Those prisoners in his gallery remind me some of us live out our lives trapped, unfinished, and incomplete.

Michelangelo's figures appear to be struggling to free themselves, but they are forever enslaved in something from which they cannot be released. The image of the unfinished figures reminds me that it is an arduous task for the True Self to break free from the rigidity of the ego, cultural demands, role expectations, and the various complexes that operate from the basement of our unconscious.

I described those prisoners many times in my teaching and speaking, and finally a friend brought me back a ten-inch model of one of Michelangelo's unfinished prisoners, trapped in a block of white plaster with an arm over one eye as if in agony. As I write, that model occupies a place on the bookshelf in front of my desk to remind me of the struggle both to be free and to allow oneself to be freed. I am encouraged and challenged by the idea that the soul or the True Self is relentless, working from within the depths of a person to be and to become what is intended for it.

I've come to understand that the uniqueness of each person is programmed within that person. *That* is the inner drumbeat I have heard all of my life. Call it the *imago Dei*, the image of God that is inscribed within each person. Call it the True Self or the soul. I believe God dwells within every person, and I believe every human being carries a spark of the Divine that longs to be expressed in the uniqueness of the individual.

The True Self, the *imago Dei*, the soul, Christ within—however you name that part of the human being where God resides—is utterly relentless and infinitely creative in accomplishing its purpose.

The True Self will do whatever is necessary to push a person to becoming who she is meant to be, even to the point of creating crisis externally to free the soul internally.

The True Self is not concerned with how uncomfortable the poor, pathetic ego may become, and every triumph of the Self is experienced as a defeat for the ego.

Like every other child, my granddaughter Madeleine is *intended* to be and become her true, authentic, real Self. She is meant to become who she was designed to be by the One who made her, just as I am intended to be who I was created to be.

It sounds simple, doesn't it?

It is simple. But it isn't easy.

Poet Mary Oliver's wildness is the wildness of our natural selves, the unique individuals God designed us to be.[2] It is the wildness of the virgin forest, the unspoiled, uncontaminated nature that now exists only in remote parts of our planet. It is the part of us that is unlike any other human being that has ever been, the part that is still free and untainted by outer-worldly constraints.

In Jesus' attempts to define and describe "the kingdom of heaven," it is recorded in Matthew 13:44 that he likened that mysterious reality to a fine pearl for which a merchant sold everything he had.

The True Self at the core of each of us is precious beyond description. I understand this authentic Self to be the pearl of great price for which we yearn. The journey to find what is already within us is both costly and rewarding.

This book is about the process of finding that pearl. It is about salvation in the context of the full meaning of the word. It is about becoming whole and healthy, and that process takes a lifetime. It is about living the life we are meant to live now; it is about quality of life and not just length of life. It is about fulfilling the purpose for which we were made on this earthly plane.

Just as the angels in Michelangelo's marble had to be released through the sculptor's efforts, so the True Self that is in us, the pearl of great price, is released through a joint venture. I believe God, the great and skilled artist, has a huge role in this venture, and sometimes we cannot understand what is happening to us. Life impinges on us, doing its part through our relationships, those we enjoy and those that annoy us and even wound us, and we can do our part to help God sculpt us into who we are intended to be. We do our part by becoming conscious and pliable and by taking responsibility for our lives.

When the human Jesus walked and talked among other humans, he did four things that affected their lives on earth. He healed, transformed, liberated, and empowered individuals. I believe it is possible for Jesus to affect us in the same way today. I believe there is a mysterious and wondrous joint venture, a dynamic and intentional process, available to us in which we partner with the Living Christ and work out our own salvation.

This book is about how God uses people, processes, experiences, and trials as tools to help us free the angel (the True Self) in each of us. It is about how God meets us in the everyday, ordinary *stuff* of life, working creatively and redemptively in a joint venture with us to liberate the authentic and unique part of us. Salvation is both an event and a process, and we are to work out our salvation just as the apostle Paul said, with fear and trembling in practical and mundane ways, day by day (Phil 2:12).

The uniqueness of each human being must be protected. Adults, privileged to be entrusted with children, are to help them learn how to live their own wild and precious lives freely within various communities and systems *and* to live as members of a community without losing their individuality. Perhaps one of the best gifts we can give to others is our authentic Self.

The drumbeat of the soul (another synonym in this book for the True Self), the voice of God speaking from within a person, is relentless. The drumbeat is steady, persistent, and sometimes troublesome, but it will be heard one way or another. The drumbeat is the voice of love, first and fore-most, and the drummer is the Lover of our souls.

This joint venture is a love story, and I have come to believe that our personal stories are love stories too—stories of God's yearning to love us and set us free to be all we can be and to do what we were sent here to do. It takes a joint venture of love to bring forth all that is within each one of us, no matter how old we are.

If you are looking for "the answer" or easy answers, you won't find them in this book. If you're looking for an authority, you won't find it in me.

If, on the other hand, you want to ask questions about life and God and reflect deeply on your wild and precious life, I can share with you what other seekers along the way have shared with me.

It is my experience that the One who made each of us somehow meets us at the precise point of our need, so there is no one-size-fits-all spiritual growth plan. The Creator is infinitely creative in finding ways to evoke, nur-ture, and sustain the created life. While I do not believe we are puppets, controlled and manipulated by a Big Puppeteer, it does seem to me that through the mysterious ways of coincidence and synchronicity, the Companion brings into our lives the resources we need to become whole and healthy. The books, the people, the opportunities, and, strangely, the prob-lems we encounter appear to point the way forward.

So it is that we are sojourners together on this venture we call life. We are fortunate when there are human companions along the way who under-stand that it is possible to experience the kingdom coming on this earth among our daily schedules and routines. The Eleventh Step of Alcoholics Anonymous encourages participants to "seek to maintain conscious contact with God." If we take this step in the common, everyday, mundane events of life, we will experience life in a richer, more meaningful way.

I have included the following words of poet Rainer Maria Rilke in a pre-vious book. They continue to comfort and inspire me, and they are pertinent to this journey I'm calling a joint venture, a journey into the depths of our lives.

> Have patience with everything unresolved in your heart and try to love the
> questions themselves as if they were locked rooms or books written in a
> very foreign language. Don't search for the answers, which could not be
> given to you now, because you would not be able to live them. And the

point is to live everything. Live the questions now. Perhaps then, someday far in the future, you will gradually, without even noticing it, live your way into the answer.[3]

This book is about living into the deep questions that matter.

NOTES

1. Irving Stone, *The Agony and the Ecstasy* (Garden City NY: Doubleday, 1961).

2. Mary Oliver, "The Summer Day," *New and Selected Poems* (Boston: Beacon Press, 1992).

3. Ranier Maria Rilke, *Letters to a Young Poet* (Novato CA: New World Library, 2000).

Chapter 1

SPIRITUAL . . .
OR RELIGIOUS?

Life has not turned out as I thought it would.

"We've lost the public schools and the mainline denominations!" I exclaimed to my husband, venting my angst about the turmoil in both institutions. I was, admittedly, overdramatic. "If the post office goes, I'll know that life as I have known it is over."

The next day, the *Houston Chronicle* ran an article about the closing of two of the post offices in our area and the sale of the property where each has stood for decades.

Perhaps my outburst was hyperbole. Maybe not. There's no question that the institutions that have given stability and structure to us are in radical transition. Perhaps, too, I was still feeling the effects of Hurricane Ike, the devastating storm that had wreaked havoc along the Gulf Coast, sending its effects as far north as Missouri and influencing gas prices and airline scheduling from the Gulf Coast to Atlanta and beyond.

Driving through nearby neighborhoods in those weeks following Ike's violent onslaught, I saw large, old oak trees lying on their sides with their roots exposed. They were a disturbing symbol of impermanence. Classified initially as a Category 3 hurricane, Ike was so enormous in its scope and lasted so long that the way of categorizing hurricanes is now being studied and adapted to the realities of such a devastating "act of God." Contemporary cultural changes have been going on for my entire adult life; those changes have now begun to disrupt everyday life, and that disruption has a subtle, ever-increasing effect on us as individuals.

As we gathered around a table at Café Express last night, friends who attend the Bible study I teach at St. Luke's United Methodist Church talked with me about the rapids of change. Laurie Coleman summed up the cultural shifts when she said, "In my family there were three daughters spanning eleven years. My parents always said that they hoped my older sister would get out of high school without getting pregnant, that I would get out without getting on drugs, and that my younger sister would get out alive." As we sat there taking it all in, she added, "We all met our parents' goals."

Lying awake at night during the weeks when we in the Gulf Coast area were consumed with restoring order in our corner of the world, I recalled the night that John F. Kennedy was killed. Shocked that such a thing could happen in Dallas, the city where my family lived, my parents drove us downtown to the site of the assassination. We milled around the crime scene with others who were trying to integrate the hard, cold, brutal reality that would mark our city and our lives for generations. Today we would not have been allowed to walk that site as freely as we did that cold November night.

Recently, when my husband and I walked past our federal buildings in Washington, D.C., I felt the constant eyes of cameras and guards. Later, we stood in the street beside our hotel and observed the elaborate process of getting the president down the street to the Lincoln Theatre. The cars in his motorcade zigzagged down the street to confuse or disorient possible assassins. Armed guards were on every roof around the area, their guns aimed in all directions.

Watching the drama, we talked about how the "security" reminded us that we were less safe and more anxious than ever. I recalled an axiom I have debated for decades: *In my defenselessness my safety lies.* I want to believe that. Do I dare believe it?

Was it Kennedy's assassination that signaled the end of innocence for this country, or was it Watergate or Viet Nam? If those events were not enough to strip us of illusions about invincibility and who we are as a nation, surely the tragedy of 9/11 was.

It isn't only outer, cataclysmic events that push harsh realities into our faces. Even if the riptides of change do not turn our culture upside down, there is no way our world will conform to some of the simplistic, happily-ever-after movies and sitcoms we watch. The idealism of youth has a way of caving in. I recall a friend's wry humor: "You want to make God laugh? Tell him your plans."

For some, life is richer and better than they could have foreseen or imagined. Some people get lucky, or so it seems, and some people make their own luck. For others, life brings challenges and heartaches so wrenching that one has to step back in horror and ask, "How could this happen to a human being?" and "How can a human being survive such pain?" For all, if there is any level of honesty, life turns out to be a mixed bag of imperfections, unanswered riddles, and incomplete projects.

I have lived a rich life. I have been blessed in countless ways, and I am fortunate beyond belief. I am profoundly grateful for the grace and mercy I have been given and for the gifts of life I enjoy. I

We are not human beings on a spiritual journey. We are spiritual beings on a human journey.

—STEPHEN COVEY

have also had my share of losses and disappointments, and I have had my own "Job" experience when I wrestled with God on the ash heap of suffering.

Upon starting out her life, what person can imagine what she will be required to live?

Who would have the courage to venture forth in the world if he knew what was ahead? Who could be bold enough to begin, to marry, to have children, to pursue a dream while knowing the risks?

"Life is neither black nor white," I tell my daughters, "but plaid. There are dark and light hues in the fabric of each day, and, now and then, a golden thread."

And sometimes the fabric is frayed in places.

Our job is to live the one wild and precious life that is ours to live.

The rules, guidelines, ways, and means I learned as a child are not adequate for the challenges of today.

Walking home from school on a crisp fall day in Roswell, New Mexico, I opened the door to our house, the church parsonage, and the tantalizing aromas of apples and cinnamon drew me straight to my mother's kitchen.

Mother, always the queen of her kitchen, was bustling around with a pot of apple butter bubbling on one burner and a pan of apple jelly on another. In the oven was an apple pie, her masterpiece.

My mother prided herself on the fact that her jellies contained no preservatives and that she could get them to gel without any help from commercial products. In fact, she disdained anyone who had to rely on such crutches. Whether the jelly was blackberry, plum, grape, or apple, it was the purest jelly ever. How we loved those jellies on her legendary hot rolls, and her fruit pies and cobblers were the envy of her friends.

"Look at this!" Mother would exclaim, holding each jar up to the light so that we could see how clear and lovely it was. Jewel-like, her jellies all but glowed. I assumed then that I would follow in her footsteps and make a home and run a kitchen like she did. I could not have imagined when I was ten years old the changes in the family that would occur between my mother's generation and mine, and certainly I could not have foreseen the changes my daughters and their children would experience.

How simple and uncomplicated the world seemed from my mother's kitchen. My future plans that stretched out before me were as clear and pure as her jellies with the New Mexico sun shining through them.

Born into the home of a Baptist minister in Texas, I learned the rules for life by osmosis and by directives and didactic teaching. Those rules and the roles I was expected to play helped me be a compliant preacher's kid, but they have not worked so well in living out of the other parts of my life.

In my childhood, I formed the belief that being a good Christian would somehow pave the way for an easier life. I thought that if I followed the rules my Sunday school teachers presented, I would go to heaven when I died, but I would also gain earthly rewards and privileges and avoid the troubles and punishment of people who didn't follow those rules. Most likely, I assumed that as a Christian, I was one of God's special pets, as priest and writer John Claypool liked to say, immune to the vicissitudes and troubles of those who didn't believe as I did. I shudder now to think that my childhood fantasies about who I was included such arrogance, but it was an arrogance born of childish ignorance and innocence.

Good, faithful Christians get cancer just like everyone else. Troubling statistics reveal a higher divorce rate among evangelical Christians than the rest of the population, and good kids from good Christian families get into serious trouble. Bad things happen to good people and, contrary to what I was taught, good things happen to bad people. Those rules I learned when I was a child didn't cover everything, and I'm still learning that knowing who is good and who is bad is not as easy as I once thought!

While I thought the people who were the authorities in my life held the answers to life's riddles, I have discovered that their answers sometimes did not fit my questions. I've also noticed that the sure *certainty* of some was a defense mechanism formed to avoid painful realities. I have followed various guides through life only to discover that they didn't know where they were going any more than I did or that where they were going was not where I was intended to go. Life is much too complicated to fit into the simplistic or sentimental religious system of my childhood and adolescence.

Growing up in Lamesa, Texas, and Albuquerque and Roswell, New Mexico, how could I have anticipated the changes in the world and in my personal world? As an adolescent girl in Dallas, Texas, in the early 1960s, how could I have imagined this global village we inhabit today? this pluralistic society? this magnificent venture called life?

Almost swooning with the force of the sweet fragrances in my mother's kitchen, how could I have known how to handle the rapid changes of technology, the wonders and failures of modern medicine, the trips to the moon, and instant global communication? My friend tells her son, a technology wizard, "I will learn one new thing about technology a week, but only one." In my book, she's ambitious.

What could my father have taught me that would have prepared me, a keeper of the religious traditions, for the mega-church phenomenon, preachers who are beamed to remote locations as holograms, the emergent church, and postmodern thought? How would his simple and deep faith have weathered the wave of the denominational scandals and breakdowns, the culturally accepted agnosticism and atheism, the changing morals and mores, the prevailing and sanctioned narcissism and hedonism?

What could my mother have told me from her lived experience that would have equipped me to ride the rapids of change in the family? in my own family?

Indeed, I am one of the fortunate ones in the world, and I know it. I have a sense of purpose that energizes and motivates me. I have had opportunities that have challenged me and given me deep pleasure and joy, and yet, my life has not been as I thought it would be, and the map I had, albeit at an unconscious level, has not been adequate for the territory I've traveled. Armed with simplistic answers, arrogant certainty, and the confidence of youth, I've had to learn the hard way that the answers of yesterday are not adequate for the complexities of today. The rules I thought would protect me often don't work in the hard places of this postmodern world, and the easy answers I could apply so swiftly in young adulthood, confident and unconscious in my either/or world, simply fall flat, felled by their inadequacies.

Salvation is about more than staying out of hell and getting into heaven.

Salvation is more than a one-time event; it is a lifelong process, a dynamic joint venture with God and with life.

For me, much of the journey of salvation has been learning what Jesus meant when he said, "Follow me," and then trying to do just that.

I gave my heart to Jesus when I was nine years old.

With my childhood innocence, I gave as much as I knew of myself to as much as I knew of God. That was what we did in my tradition, and while I look back on that moment with the realization of how little I knew about what I was doing, I believe that decision was authentic and real for me at that time in my life.

My decision was only a beginning, a first step in a faith journey that would take me into places I couldn't have imagined at age nine. My sassy question to my mother in front of her friends, "If Jesus is the answer, what are the questions?" has followed me around, pushing me out of my comfort zone and into other questions that have kept me challenging the things that don't make sense to me and standing up to the processes that stifle my faith and spirit rather than enlarge them.

Come to me, all you who are weary, and I will give you rest. Take my yoke upon you and learn of me, for my yoke is easy and my burden is light.

—MATTHEW 11:28-30

At the time, some of my Sunday school teachers in the church where my father was pastor expressed concern to him about my not having "walked the aisle" sooner. After all, I was the preacher's kid, and it didn't look good for their teaching or my father's preaching that my response was delayed.

I will forever treasure the fact that my dad was irritated by the interference in his family, and he came to my defense like a good father would. I remember my father's insistence that the decision I made would be my decision and not a conformity to the women who were worried about my eternal salvation. It was a sweet moment when he informed them that he could handle this issue, and I loved him for standing up for me.

I did not feel pressure to join the church to accommodate the ladies or because I was afraid I would go to hell when I died if I was not "saved." My father was opposed to using manipulation or scare tactics to push people into the kingdom of God or onto the rolls of the churches he pastored, and I am forever grateful to him for that.

However, when I did decide to walk down the aisle, who knows what kinds of pressures I felt because I wanted to please my parents? Knowing myself as I do now, I'm confident that part of my motivation was to protect my dad from having to answer to the church ladies about my salvation; I am equally confident that the God who made me honored my childish, naïve, and innocent decision with his great love and mercy.

As I look back on the things that formed or deformed me in my childhood, I realize that I learned to lie in Sunday school. It happened like this.

In Sunday school each week, we put our offerings in an envelope printed with what was called the "Eight-point Record System." We were to grade ourselves, checking off that we were there and on time.

We got points for being present and punctual, studying the Sunday school lesson, bringing our Bibles and an offering, bringing a guest, staying for worship, and having made a contact during the week. Checking these boxes each week, we could measure our faith, or maybe our holiness and righteousness.

Because I was the preacher's daughter, I dared not make less than 100 percent, and so it took me no time at all to check all the little black boxes, add my grade up to 100, and turn in the envelope. I felt guilty about it, but I think I'm more drawn to the idea that at some level I knew the system was profoundly flawed, that it did not measure spirituality, and that in the long run, my performance and that grade did not matter!

I don't know that my childish rebellion was a good thing, but it may have saved my life. Maybe it kept the church ladies from reporting my deficiencies to my father.

Somehow, though, there was within me a deep connection with God at a heart-and-soul level, a connection not based on outward performance, a connection that kept drumming away in me. I wanted to be good, but I also wanted to break free of the old constraints and do something that truly made a difference in my everyday, ordinary life and in the lives of others.

The disconnect between what happened on Sunday and what happened the rest of the week bothered me when I was a child, and it still bothers me when I see it in myself. The ways "Christians" would treat each other, the inability or unwillingness to face hard issues honestly, and the narrow, constricted, pursed, and sometimes priggish Puritanism that pervaded my world felt like death wrappings, smothering the vital life force that clamored within me. Later, it bothered me to live with the lies of denial, the pretenses that everything was okay when it wasn't, and the presumptions of righteousness.

I am convinced that salvation is about living healthy and meaningful lives in the present moment. It is about recovery from the things that enslave us, the dysfunctional patterns that wound us, and the various misunderstandings about life and God and ourselves that keep us stuck in self-defeating patterns.

Salvation is about living now. It is not about escaping life, but about entering fully into life. It is about becoming who we are and doing what we're intended to do while we are on this earthly plane.

Living with God and following Christ is more than keeping religious holidays or rituals, reciting creeds, formulae, or even Scriptures, assenting to the right doctrine or theology, or being a good person. Religion may be the outer expression of an inward condition, and it may be the means of tying us back to God, but *spirituality* is our natural way of being in the world.

Life with God is a dynamic partnership, a love relationship, a joint venture in which the ordinary moments of our lives provide the opportunity for growth and grace. Religion does not take us out of the world but challenges us to fully engaged living in the world. Life with God can be an ongoing, intimate conversation, and in that intimacy with the Creator, we humans can wrestle and rest, seek and find, and work out our salvation with fear and trembling, just as Paul the apostle did.

Salvation, then, is not so much about escaping to heaven in the sweet by and by as it is about becoming whole and healthy in the here and now. Salvation is not so much an event at which you consent to start a relationship with God as it is a process, a joint venture in which God does God's part and life does its part, sometimes gently and sometimes violently. And we do our part.

"I'm spiritual," the woman announced to me, showing up for her first session of spiritual direction.[1] "I'm a spiritual person, but I'm not religious."

As a lifelong member of the religious establishment, I felt a flush of defensiveness rise up, but I liked this woman and I wanted things to go well in the first session.

"What do you mean?" I asked her, and she began to tell me about her life as a recovering alcoholic and how working the Twelve Steps had helped her develop a spirituality that kept her sane and sober.

"I never found that in church," she told me, "and I never found the honesty among people that I've found in AA at any church."

I cringed. I didn't want to hear what she was saying, and I didn't want what she said to be true.

In my lifetime, I've learned that my AA friend was right. You can be devoutly religious, keeping all the external forms of the faith, and never be changed from within. You can be religious and not spiritual.

You can memorize and quote the Bible from Genesis to Revelation, but never permit its transforming truths to penetrate your inner life.

You can perform all kinds of religious rites, cite creeds perfectly, and do good deeds, and never be touched or changed by the life-giving breath of the Spirit of God.

You can talk the talk of religion and never walk the walk of spirituality. You can float around in the clouds of intellectual ideas about God and never experience the fire of God's living Presence.

You can play the role of a religious person, and even that of a religious leader, but treat those close to you as objects to be manipulated and controlled, used and abused.

You can profess to be a religious person, but never play out what you profess in practical, everyday ways.

You can talk the God talk and never walk it.

On a hot June night in summer 2009, I sat in the Municipal Auditorium in San Antonio, Texas, eager to hear the distinguished writer and teacher Eugene Peterson speak at the first general session of an international Renovare conference. I've loved reading *The Message*, Dr. Peterson's rendition of the Bible, as well as many of his books.

The crowd was hushed as Dr. Peterson walked to the podium. Without fanfare or fireworks, he began to talk about "the Jesus way."

"I want to live the Jesus way," he declared, making his first point, and then he added two words. "Robustly human."

What a concept! Instead of escaping our God-given humanity or debasing it, instead of denying it or ignoring it, Dr. Peterson suggested that we are to live it robustly!

Instead of becoming artificial saints, detached from who we are created to be, we are to embrace and live as human beings, just as Jesus did.

In my life and in this book, in my teaching and in my writing, I am committed to the idea that spirituality is about our life with God at the most intimate level.

I am committed to the idea that our spiritual practices are intended to feed, nurture, support, and encourage the growth of our souls, but that those spiritual practices have practical implications for our everyday lives.

I am committed to the idea that salvation is about becoming whole, healthy, and well—and *robustly human*.

I am committed to the idea that becoming whole on this side of heaven, whatever and however and wherever heaven may be, is about the process of becoming who we are. I like the term *authenticity* about as much as any word in the English language, and I am committed to the idea of becoming authentic and to the process of *individuation*.

I am committed to the idea that spirituality is not about keeping the rules, but about living in a vital, dynamic love relationship with God, and I believe that God, at work in us through the mysterious ways of God, intends to heal us, transform us, liberate us, and empower us *in this life*.

I am committed to the idea that life with God is a joint venture. Today, we talk so much about spiritual formation and spiritual growth; I believe those processes take place in the everyday, ordinary, practical realities of life. I am what my friend calls a "pedestrian mystic." I believe God is at work in the marketplace and the laundry room, the board table and the dining table, the highways and the hedges of daily life, attempting to shape us, get our attention, comfort us, and confront us. I believe God wants our wholeness and is at work to partner with us in that venture; how we cooperate or how we don't cooperate makes a difference in how we live.

> *For most people in the world the question is not, is there life on the other side of death? It is, rather, is there life on this side of death? Until we Christians give evidence that there is life on this side of death, the world does not need to believe our dogmas and giant churches. It doesn't need our words of hell; it needs our promise of heaven.*
>
> —RICHARD ROHR

I have come to understand faith not as something I can get or have, but as the impulse of life itself, pushing us forward into life, compelling us to seek and ask and knock, insisting that we grow and change and stretch our minds and hearts. Faith is the impulse within me that has often felt like restlessness and sometimes pain, pushing me to seek relief, yes, but also answers and solutions and . . . God.

Faith is the impulse that has drawn me toward the Mystery of God; faith has demanded that I move outside and beyond doctrine and dogma to experience the reality of the Living God. Faith is the energy within me that has refused to let me sit in any kind of flowery bed of ease. Instead, faith has pushed me out onto the razor's edge of risk; faith has inspired and motivated and demanded that I leave home and go on a journey into the unknown.

This book, then, is not a how-to manual. It is about living the actual life you have been given as though all of life is sacred. It is about partnering with God in the everyday, ordinary *stuff* of life.

This joint venture is about engaging fully with your own one wild and precious life in such a way that you come to know yourself and God more intimately.

NOTE

1. Spiritual direction is the process of discerning together with a person (called a directee) where the Holy Spirit is directing that person. In an earlier book, *Shared Splendor*, I describe the role of a spiritual director as "standing in God's stead in loving that person." The director encourages that person toward wholeness and authenticity, listening for the voice of the person's True Self, supporting and validating it.

Chapter 2

THE CALLING TO THE SACRED JOURNEY

The first time I heard Keith Miller speak was when I was a freshman at Baylor University. The author of the widely popular book Taste of New Wine was there to speak at chapel in Waco Hall. As I remember it, he was part of what used to be called "Religious Focus Week," but new to the campus, I had little interest in participating in the special events and workshops of the week. As Keith started to speak, I was absorbed either in reading the Baylor Lariat or a letter from my boyfriend.

However, there was something about this speaker that was different from most of the speakers who came to speak at chapel, a twice-weekly required attendance for two years for all Baylor students. He wasn't preaching to us. He used practical, down-to-earth language, and he was speaking directly from his own life experience. I was to learn later that his style was called "confessional," and I was fascinated by it. Little did I know that hearing Keith Miller would start my spiritual journey down the road I've been on from that week until now. All I had heard up until that point were testimonies about how people had "gotten saved," but I hadn't heard much about how they had lived out the complexities of daily life between that moment of conversion and the day they would die and go to heaven.

My spiritual journey would be one of attempting to integrate faith with everyday life instead of separating religion from ordinary life. Keith would introduce me to the integration of psychology and spirituality and, most of all, the amazing, radical idea of being honest about issues of faith. For me, the mere prospect of coming out from behind the various masks of a preacher's kid that I had felt forced to wear was so liberating that even now, I tremble at how important that message of freedom was for me. To consider the idea and live into the reality of living out in the open without having to pretend to be something I wasn't or fake a piety that wasn't mine or act as if we didn't have normal, garden-variety problems like every other family was comparable to being set free from a silent, insidious slavery.

Looking back, I shake my head at my naiveté and innocence on that morning in Baylor chapel when Keith, with laser sharpness, beamed a particular question in the direction of a crowd of Baylor students, riveting the attention of every one of us who had been trying to read our Lariats, do our homework, or take a nap.

Leave your country, your people, and your father's household and go to a land that I will show you.

—GOD, TO ABRAHAM
(GENESIS 12:1)

"How many of you out there are sweating pregnancy right now," he began, pausing to get our attention, "or have girlfriends who are?"

As I remember it, the silence in response to his question was deafening.

What was he thinking to ask such a question? Was this for shock value? Had he lost his mind? Would he be invited back?

This was 1963, and such things were not talked about in Baylor chapel. While pregnancy issue was not my issue, I'd experienced what happened to friends in high school who were dealing with an out-of-wedlock pregnancy, a fact that no longer carries the stigma that it once did. Sitting there, I remembered how the church people talked about such a thing, so when Keith asked his question I was shocked. Then I wondered what on earth my mother would have thought about such an outrageous speaker, but finally, I was mesmerized, not only by Keith's message, but by the very idea that someone could be that honest in the context of a "Christian" conversation.

Such was the beckoning to me to go on the first spiritual quest of my young adult life, not because of Keith's reference to pregnancy, but because he invited us all into an adventure of the Christian life that integrated the principles Jesus taught with everyday life for ordinary people.

The incident sounds almost too strange to believe now, but the truth is that when I was a college freshman, this was a shocking statement for a speaker to make in Baylor chapel. What was so shocking was not so much that Keith introduced the idea of pregnancy in that crowd, but it was that kind of bold, raw honesty from a chapel speaker. Looking back, I have to smile at how far we've come in what shocks us, but maybe we haven't come so far when it comes to what Keith really did.

What Keith did was puncture any hypocrisy, duplicity, or denial about the realities of what was going on among us.

I attended every workshop Keith did while he was on campus because I was starved for a faith position that included that kind of honesty. His honesty about his own life was like oxygen for me. Listening to Keith's call to a more authentic life was like having someone take the shackles off my mind and my spirit, and in that experience of hearing Keith's journey, I was set on a path that has compelled and fulfilled me, challenged my status quo and my ego's need for comfort over and over, and moved me relentlessly toward the wholeness my soul craves.

I have learned since that tender time that while there may be one big hero's journey we are invited to take, there are many journeys within a lifetime. In a way, just getting up and going to work each day is a hero's journey!

Over these many years, I have learned from Keith, as well, that we all falter and fail, and while we are flawed, God meets us at the point of our need, our brokenness, and our failures with his radical love and uncommon mercy and grace. That I have been privileged to see God's redeeming love in the mentors, teachers, and guides I have had in my life makes me want to fall on my knees with gratitude.

> *We must be willing to let go of the life we planned so as to have the life that is waiting for us.*
>
> —JOSEPH CAMPBELL

I know this one thing for sure: living a religiosity that denies the humanity of each of us and slaps a patina of righteousness over ordinary daily life is suffocating and, I believe, an affront to the Creator who did, after all, pronounce creation to be "very good."

This first call to a spiritual journey was a call away from a worldview that separated religion from spirituality and a call toward the integration of my religious life with the rest of my everyday, ordinary life. Incidentally, this ordinary life acknowledged and included the vital issue of human sexuality!

The next time I heard Keith Miller speak was at a gathering at the Hyatt Regency Hotel in Houston, Texas. As participants in a conference titled "Meaning and Belonging: New Patterns for the Church," we were asked by Lyman Coleman to draw a time line of our lives, marking the most significant turning points.

As we talked about our turning points later in a small group, I realized how each significant experience contained within it a call to leave one place or one season of my life and journey into the next. Whether it was an experience I'd chosen or one imposed on me from an external event, whether it was an occasion of loss or gain, sadness or joy, defeat or victory, each event served as a catalyst for transformation.

Each experience required leaving home, either literally or figuratively. I was asked over and over to leave the place where I had become comfortable and complacent and set out into unknown and uncharted territories. Each experience provided tests and trials, pitfalls and dangers, and each time I was required to learn as I went.

The biblical record is replete with the journey motif. Abraham was asked by Yahweh to "go to a land that I will show you," just as the other great heroes and heroines of the Bible were asked to follow God's guidance into grand adventures that would change their lives and the lives of those they influenced (Gen 12:1). Job was asked to venture into the depths of suffering, though his journey took place on an ash heap at the edge of town and on the ragged edges of shame and agony. Mary received the life-altering call to give birth to Jesus, sending her out on a journey she could never have imagined when she first said, perhaps naively, "Be it done to me according to your will" (Luke 1:38). Mary Magdalene was called on a radical adventure when she was told to go and tell the disciples that Jesus was alive and would meet them in Galilee. By empowering Mary Magdalene, Jesus set her on her own heroine's journey.

The hero's journey is a story found in all cultures, and the process of spiritual growth contains the same elements of the hero's journey. There is the call to the journey and a departure, an initiation in which you are given one challenge after another, and then there is a return home with the challenge to give back to your world the gifts of wisdom you have gained from having made your journey.

Throughout the life cycle, we are beckoned, seduced, pushed, pulled, and sometimes thrown out of what has become too comfortable and directed into another stage of growth. How we respond determines whether it is a hero's journey or just a trip. Praying the prayer of surrender, the Third Step of Alcoholics Anonymous, and choosing to turn your will and your life over to the care of God as you understand God is a dangerous and daunting thing to do. We must do it with care.

"Buckle your seatbelt," I was told by the Jungian analyst who would accompany me on the arduous, tedious, and laborious process of depth analysis.[1] "I don't romanticize spiritual journeys."

Neither do I.

As a spiritual director, I have journeyed with many people into the unknown territories of spiritual formation. Always, I stand apart from the sacred journey of another human being with a sense of deep respect and awe. You never know where a person's journey will take that person. I have learned that when I choose to enter into another person's journey, I also set out on a journey of my own, for spiritual direction or depth analysis is indeed a joint venture.

The Lord is with you. . . . Do not be afraid. . . . You have found favor with God.

—THE ANGEL GABRIEL TO MARY (LUKE 1:28, 30)

The intricate, sacred dance of spiritual direction and the call to the journey often start with an issue that confronts you in the outer world or a question that agitates you from within your own psyche. Setting out on a spiritual journey often begins with a problem, dissatisfaction, or confusion.

"I have this problem." "Something has happened." "Can you help me?" The joint venture of spiritual direction often begins with words like these.

Each time I sit with a person who has asked me to be a companion on this journey, I breathe a prayer to the real Spiritual Director, and I listen deeply to discern where that Director is moving in the person's life. In what direction does the person's True Self need to go? What are the roadblocks? Where is the pain? What are the possibilities calling the person forward into growth?

Always I'm asking myself, "And what is my part in this soul venture?"

Trained at the Spiritual Direction Institute in their three-year program for spiritual directors, I know I need to listen, not only to the narrative of the person sitting before me, but for what speaks between the sentences in the pauses, the sighs, the tears, and the laughter. I must listen to the mental traffic in my own head, pay attention to physical responses I have to the person or her story, and stay aware of my own projections so that I don't flip my material onto the other person, contaminating her story with elements of my own.

Most of all, I attempt to listen to the still, small voice of the One who made this person, for we are in a dance, the three of us, and I want God to lead it. It's a dance, a shared pilgrimage into the outposts of the soul's longings, but it is also a joint venture. Spiritual growth takes place as God does God's part, the person does his or her own inner and outer work, and family, friends, helpers, situations, crises, inner turmoil, and outer trauma do their part to shape and form faith and to bring forth the authentic person.

"I tend to be depressed." I hear these words often from those I counsel, and I have learned that while there are many causes and kinds of depression, my job is to be present to the suffering of the soul. Highly respectful of the many different causes of depression, I am always attentive and cautious to discern what is not within my area of expertise. Some depressions are too complicated for the work of spiritual direction, but sometimes depression can be a call to wake up to one's own life— to the roadblocks and barriers that inhibit the person from living his purpose or experiencing the presence of the Living God.

"Your depression is your agenda, then," I told someone, once I knew the person's depression was within the sphere of soul suffering. "It will be your teacher. Let it speak to you and show you what you need to know."

> *If you can see your path laid out in front of you step by step, you know it's not your path. Your own path you make with every step you take. That's why it's your path.*
>
> —JOSEPH CAMPBELL

Earlier in my own journey, I had faced the reality that my own fear was going to set my agenda, pointing me toward a journey I didn't really want to take.

Early in my process, I was told, "Whatever you fear the most, that is where you most need to go." I didn't want to hear that. However, I have learned that the place of pain is the place where God wants to bring about healing.

It does seem that while some people face greater, bigger, and more devastating sorrows (and how does one compare sorrows and horrors?), none of us get out of this life without suffering. Everyone faces something hard. Everyone has his own burden. "Life is wounding," says James Hollis, Jungian analyst, author, and my teacher. "We all get wounded."

We all have a shadow, the part of ourselves that we don't want others to see and can't bear to look at. Shadow material is what we have either repressed or suppressed, denied or avoided, often for a long time.

Sooner or later, if you live long enough, life is going to happen to you, and when it does, there is always an invitation to wake up! No matter how long you avoid facing your own shadow, it doesn't go away. Instead, it stays out of sight, building energy and growing in force, often leaking out in projections, slips of the tongue, physical symptoms, relational difficulties, or career snafus. What is buried alive stays alive.

Indeed, our wounds, our fears, and the barriers in relationships or in our life's work are our agendas. Whatever inhibits the full expression of the person's unique purpose in life offers the questions, the tasks, and the challenges the person must address. The process is difficult, but it is better than attempting to ignore, deny, or avoid a problem.

There is good news about the wake-up call. Life also hands us an invitation to mine for the gold that is buried beneath the surface of our consciousness, for within every human being there is something unique and rare—the true and authentic Self, the *imago Dei* that is inscribed within every person.

Mining the gold in the unconscious, working through the pain, naming the problem, and dealing with it are all part of the process of salvation. They are all part of becoming whole.

In recent years, "spiritual formation" has become the buzzword in some churches, and in some instances, churches have hired a minister of spiritual formation instead of a minister of Christian education. How the work of spiritual formation unfolds depends on the experience, education, and perspective of the minister whose job it is to oversee the program of spiritual formation within that particular church. Spirituality has been "in" for the last two decades, and sometimes it is difficult to discern what is meant when a person uses the term "spiritual."

What is spiritual formation? And why do I use the term "practical spirituality"? What's the difference between being spiritual and being religious?

Sometimes I'm told, "I don't want to think this hard," and "You're too serious; you need to lighten up." But for those who yearn for more and long to go beneath the surface to the depths of life, making a spiritual journey is unavoidable.

Why bother with spiritual growth? Isn't it easier just to go to church or go to the lake and take life easy? Why don't we leave well enough alone?

We can, when things are well enough.

Does everybody need to go on a spiritual journey?

In a series of lectures at the Jung Center in Houston, Texas, analyst Pittman McGehee was asked a question about whether or not all persons are intended to go on a hero's journey or a spiritual quest. "All are called," Pittman responded. "Few choose."

For clarity and understanding in the context of this book, it's important to define some terms.

I define *spirituality* as our natural way of being. We are innately spiritual beings in that we have a spirit, a force that animates us, and we are made in the image of God. I believe that we cannot *not* be spiritual beings and that a great deal of our suffering as humans occurs when, either by ignorance or neglect, we starve the spiritual part of ourselves or when we try to "feed" our souls with objects, pastimes, persons, or substances. "It is interesting," Pittman also says, "that the word 'spirits' is another word used for alcoholic beverages." We do have a tendency to believe that we can purchase, ingest, or drink something that will fill the holes in our souls or "in-spirit" us.

Spirituality is the part of us that is connected with the Source of life I call God. Spirituality is about waking up, and then waking up some more— to God, to our own lives and the purpose of our lives, and to the other people in our lives.

Augustine has said it well: "Thou hast made us for Thyself, O Lord, and our hearts are restless until we find our rest in Thee."

The word *religion* means "to tie back together," and so I have come to understand that our religion is the means we have to find the rest Augustine describes. In the context of this book, religion has to do with our outward acts—rites, rituals, spiritual disciplines—that attempt to tie us back to God and to our own souls.

Spiritual formation is about how our inner lives, our spirits and souls, are formed (or de-formed or reformed), and that process takes place in a variety of ways. Some models include the one set out by Ignatius in his *Spiritual Exercises* or the one of spiritual disciplines described by Richard Foster in his classic

> *I will lead the blind by ways they have not known, along unfamiliar paths I will guide them;*
> *I will turn the darkness into light before them and make the rough places smooth.*
> *These are the things I will do; I will not forsake them.*
>
> —ISAIAH 42:16

Celebration of Discipline and lived out in his work.[2] A recovery program such as the Twelve Steps of Alcoholics Anonymous is an example of a process of spiritual formation. For me, depth analysis has been a profound, life-changing experience in spiritual formation.

In the realm of spiritual formation, the guide or teacher plays a vital role in who one becomes and how one's spirit is formed, just as the résumé of a chef indicates the person or persons who trained (or formed) his or her approach to cooking. An artist often expresses the influence of the teacher who taught (formed) his or her approach to the visual expression of beauty. Children wear the T-shirts of their favorite athletes, and those athletes influence the children's ideas of what it means to play a particular sport. They go to sports camps to be formed as athletes according to a certain coach's philosophy, method, or technique. In the same way, our thinking is inspired and shaped by the teachers we follow, and our souls and spirits are formed by the guides we choose.

Spiritual growth refers to a deliberate and intentional process along the path of the life cycle. In my work, that process indicates an integration of psychology and spirituality. Spiritual growth is about consciously attending to our lives with God or improving our contact with God and with our own souls. It is about engaging with life in such a way that we become fully who we are intended to be.

In the first chapter, I made the point that salvation is more than staying out of hell and getting into heaven. If indeed that is all that salvation is, then spiritual growth is not an issue. However, since we are designed to grow and develop, there has to be something more.

This book is about the process of growing and maturing, of coming home to your authentic Self. It is about the joint venture of becoming whole, individuating, and being saved from the things that would destroy the authentic Self. It is about being saved for the purpose you were intended to fulfill when you were created.

There is a paradox in this joint venture, and it is that each of us must make the journey that is ours to make. No one can make the journey for you or tell you how to make it. No one can force you to take the journey, and the truth is that some people aren't really interested in the journey or in your journey. Furthermore, people often take journeys that I don't understand or know about. The point is for each of us to do what is right for our lives and allow the Spirit of God to move freely. God is infinitely creative and resourceful, adapting to meet the needs of others in ways I may not be able to fathom.

On this highly personal and solitary journey, however, we need people who will help us. We need companions on the trail, and we need those who can be there as supporters who realize that we are all in this life together, and in a way, we all have to walk the lonesome valley of our own lives. We have to do the work ourselves, and we need others to work with us.

"I alone must become myself," Pittman McGehee declares in his lectures on individuation, "and I cannot become myself alone."

Such is the joint venture of life. It is filled with irony and paradox, anxiety and unease, but every time one human being does something to become more fully who God intended him to be, everyone else benefits. Every time one individual becomes more free, more authentic, and more loving, the world is a better place.

> *Religion points to that area of human experience where in one way or another man comes upon mystery as a summons to pilgrimage.*
>
> —FREDERICK BUECHNER

Each of us is born in a specific time and place, stamped with the image of God and carrying a unique set of strengths and abilities, talents and gifts.

Along the way, each of us gets a burden, a wound, a problem, a rock in the shoe.

Each of us also has a gift, a calling, a purpose for our lives.

Each of us is a steward of the authentic Self we are—our gifts and our wounds.

Along the way, others affect and influence life's venture.

Always, God is at work in all things, attempting to bring about good.

We do not make this joint venture only for ourselves, however. We are not blessed just to enjoy our blessings, but to be a blessing. We are not saved just for our own benefit, but to serve our fellow human beings. We don't become enlightened for ourselves alone, but to spread light where we are.

At the end of 2009, *Time* magazine's cover announced that the previous ten years were "The Decade from Hell," and a long article detailed a series of catastrophes ranging from wars and tsunamis to corporate greed leading to the collapse of major companies to political scandals and economic recession. Personally, people experience their own tragedies in a world in which the old institutions that used to give structure, stability, and predictability are no longer providing such security.

At a recent conference at Truett Seminary on the Baylor University campus, Old Testament scholar Walter Brueggemann described the "cultural narrative" in which we live and have been formed as one in which commercialism, military dominance, independence, competition, and materialism are the prevailing values, and then he asked us to consider where that pre-

> *Follow me.*
>
> —JESUS OF NAZARETH

vailing cultural narrative take us. "It is a wounding narrative," he suggested, and then he proposed the counter-narrative, the biblical narrative based on the covenant relationship with God in which God is an active and creative agent of love.

In *Fra Lippo Lippi*, the poet Robert Browning wrote, "God uses us to help each other, lending our minds out." I would add that we also lend our hearts and our hands, our very presence, to each other, and in those exchanges we are changed.

"I'm going to Alcoholics Anonymous. I'm going to a therapist. I'm taking classes in family systems and psychology," a man told me recently after recounting how he had lost his family and his job. Not once, however, did he say, "I'm finding what I need in my church."

James Hollis, Jungian analyst and author, has said that the prevailing "-isms" of our culture are narcissism, hedonism, and materialism, and that not only are our religious institutions not addressing those sicknesses of the soul, but in many cases they are colluding with them. He says the word "psyche" is the word for soul and the term "psychopathology" is about the suffering of the soul.

"I have to go outside my church for help with my problems," I have heard people say, and it makes me weep to face that terrible reality. We are seduced by programs that promise to "grow our churches" when we need processes that will heal our souls, nourish our inner lives, and make us whole and healthy human beings.

What burns within my heart, and what I want for others, is the call I heard from Keith Miller when I was a college freshman: the call to honesty and wholeness through the integration of our everyday, ordinary lives with our religious lives, and the call to intentional, conscious, and radical psychological/spiritual wellness.

When you begin reading Mary Oliver's poem, "The Summer Day," she makes you think you're just observing a grasshopper with her on a lazy summer day. Then, suddenly, she zaps you with the question at the end, stunning you and making you pause to consider the challenge of personal responsibility. "Tell me," she asks, "what is it you plan to do with your one wild and precious life?"

This book is about participating in the joint venture of setting that one wild and precious life free, a venture in which God does God's part, we do our part, and life does its part.

It is an invitation to spiritual growth, which is initiated by the Spirit of God who is the spiritual director. Our task is threefold: (1) to listen and discern where God is at work in our lives now and where and how God has been at work in our history; (2) to observe and read the story of our lives and come to a new understanding about where we are and how we got here; and (3) to "pray with" our lives, to see them through the eyes of God, and to discern the direction God is leading us now.

The basic premises of this book are these:

1. We are not alone. God exists for each of us and in each of us, and we have available to us the same power from God and intimacy with God that Jesus had.

2. God is always up to something. God is at work in all things, attempting to bring about good for those who love him and, I believe, for all people.

3. God works through circumstances, events, and persons to accomplish his intention.[3]

4. The events of our lives become the raw material, the clay, that God can use to mold us. Our relationships, both the difficult ones and the easy ones, become material that God uses to mature us.

5. The joint venture is about facing the things that bind us from within and discovering the unique calling and gifts we have been given. It is about finding the places where we are separated from God, from our own true nature, and from each other in order to find our way *home*, that place where we can live from the inside out, from the True Self in authenticity and integrity.

"Life is raw material," says Cathy Better. "We are artisans. We can sculpt our existence into something beautiful, or debase it into ugliness. It's in our hands."

NOTES

1. Depth analysis is the process in which I would be attending to my dreams, paying attention to my inward motivations, and learning to listen for the voice of the True Self. In biblical terms, I would be listening for the "still, small voice" of God who speaks within the "inner chamber" of any life.

2. Richard J. Foster, *Celebration of Discipline: The Path to Spiritual Growth* (San Francisco: Harper and Row, 1978).

3. I use masculine pronouns for God not because I believe that God is a male, any more than I believe that God is female. I use them because it is easier to comply with traditional language in this book than it is to go back and forth or try to use both masculine and feminine pronouns.

Chapter 3

WHO IS GOD TO YOU?

When I was a child, it would have been impossible for me to have differentiated *at an emotional level* between God and my mother and father, so great was their influence in me. When I could distinguish between my earthly deities and the real God, I pictured God as a male, of course, sitting on his throne in heaven, which was up there, far away.

And God was always watching me to judge what I was doing.

I am not a child anymore, and on this balmy April morning I sit in my upstairs study and look out at the big oak tree whose tender, new-birthed leaves will soon cover my yard with a merciful shade. I just made a tour of the yard with Jose, the humble saint who tends it.

Plant by plant, he knelt before each of the winter-ravaged remains almost as a supplicant, and with his tender, rough hands he scratched away at the old stems and bark to see if any life was underneath. "Do you think it will come back?" I would ask of each plant, and if he found no life in the plant, Jose would shake his head, but he wouldn't look at me.

My back yard, one of those "thin places" that holds such mystery and respite for me, has never been through a winter like this past one.

Near my deck, Jose knelt before my favorite plant, a gorgeous bougainvillea. I held my breath as he moved down toward the root and scratched the outside of the plant.

"Oh, yes," Jose assured me, nodding. "This one, we'll bring it back."

The first person plural pronoun got my attention. Jose and I are partnering with the Life-giver in a joint venture of renewal and rebirth, but it's going to take some time and lots of care, and a good deal of replanting.

Watching Jose make his way around my yard, I basked in the coming of spring, the return of bud and blossom and the glory of Easter. Like a gentle nudging, the Spanish rendition of John 1:1 beats in my heart: "*El Verbo se hizo hombre.*" God, the Verb, became man.

God as Verb?

God as the animating, life-giving, redemptive force in all of creation, moving here and there, like the wind? My heart lifts from the doldrums of winter at the thought of God as Verb!

What about my old idea of God as a fixed person, a glorified man sitting on a throne in the heavenlies, just waiting to catch me doing something my mother wouldn't like? What about that God? Or, to be more accurate, what about that *image* of God?

Indeed, the Spanish version of John 1:1 states, "*En el principeo era el Verbo, y el Verbo era con Dios, y el Verbo era Dios.*" In the beginning was the *Verb*, and the *Verb* was with God, and the *Verb* was God.

God as Verb? That certainly isn't the concept I had when I was growing up, but from the first time I read the title of a book by Marilee Zdenek and Marge Champion—*God Is a Verb!*—I resonated with the image of God who cannot be contained in doctrine, temples made by human hands, or any small idea or dry definition I have about the Creator of the cosmos. As Rick Davis asked, "Can you get God to hold still?"

Really? God as noun? We humans, holding God still?

It's not going to happen. God as *el Verbo* makes a lot more sense to me.

When speaking at an event within a church, I can really shake things up in a hurry if I begin by asking the participants to tell me who God is.

"He is our Father," someone will say, and then sometimes someone will turn around and counter with, "What about our Mother?" That usually makes at least half the crowd nervous.

At a book signing for my book on gender, *Joining Forces: Balancing Masculine and Feminine*, a man told me how much he liked my book, except for what he called the chapter on "that female God."

"Do you mean *the feminine side of God?*" I asked, smiling.

"Well, yes," he said. And then he pumped his arms and said, "I like for my God to be macho."

"God is the Supreme Being," someone will say. "The Creator," another will add, and by that time I can usually predict that a gentle soul will add sweetly, "He's my Savior."

This is neither the time nor the place for me to expound on whether God is male or female or neither, or to challenge the sentimentalism that sometimes weaves its way into the discussion. I don't take this as an opportunity to talk about whether or not God is "mine," my own personal possession, and I don't see it as my place to try to define God.

Starting out, I emphasize three things: First, those of us who speak *about* God must be careful not to presume or imply that we are speaking *for* God. Second, I would not believe in a God I could define. Third, I am acutely aware that in talking about God, the best any of us can do is talk about our ideas of God, for God is so infinitely vast and mysterious that no one could ever capture who God is in words.

> *In the beginning was the Verb,*
> *and the Verb was with God,*
> *and the Verb was God.*
>
> —JOHN 1:1

In 1992, my family and I moved from San Angelo to Houston, leaving the wide-open spaces of West Texas for the frenetic world of the city. Before we had unpacked our boxes, I called the Cenacle Retreat Center to explore the possibility of entering their Spiritual Direction Institute, to be trained as a spiritual director.

I entered that three-year program in 1993, and I was the first Baptist in the program. It was a pivotal turning point for me, and one of the things that made it so was our director, Sister Mary Dennison, who also became my spiritual director.

"Who is God to you?" Sister Mary Dennison would ask, both in class and in my personal times of spiritual direction with her. "And who are you to God?" Over the years, those questions have brought me back from interior far countries and re-anchored me in what is most vital. Later, when I experienced the 19th Annotation of the Spiritual Exercises with Sr. Mary, those questions took me deeper into my own journey, and sometimes I didn't like the answers I'd carried unconsciously.

"The most important concept you carry around in your head is your concept of God." I've said this in countless settings with hundreds of retreatants and small group, workshop, and Bible study participants. It's my starting point for talking about the process of spiritual growth.

This time, the setting was Hereford, Texas, where I lectured on the concepts in this book at a gathering of members of the Fellowship of Believers.

Set in the Texas panhandle just before you get to New Mexico, Hereford is known as "the Beef Capital of the World." Though I've lived most of my adult life in the cities of Texas—Dallas, Forth Worth, and Houston—I have lived enough of my life in West Texas to know that just because I'm saying what I think about God doesn't necessarily mean people will buy it, and I like that about people.

I love it when people think for themselves and push back with challenging questions. I like it when people think deeply and question thoroughly the things that matter most. I like the challenge of earning the right to be heard. I ask the students in the classes I teach to question what I teach and to test it in daily life. I know, and I want others to know, that just because I talk a lot about God doesn't mean I speak for God. I make a point to suggest to my listeners that if someone comes along with too much certainty about his or her own opinions about God, they should run!

Andre Gide said, "Believe those who are seeking truth. Doubt those who find it." I resonate with that.

On this pleasant October night in Hereford, I continued my introduction to the idea of the importance of the God-concept by explaining that whenever I said the word "God," every one of them had a different idea of God come to mind. I suggested as well that each person responded with a different feeling to the name of God, so loaded is that name with unconscious baggage.

Looking across the congregation of the church my husband has pastored for nineteen years, I marvel at the different understandings we have of God, understandings that come out in business and planning meetings, casual and structured conversations. How amazing it is that we do as well as we do, living in community together with such widely divergent images of God.

For most of my life, I assumed that when someone said "God," we were all thinking about the same Being. At one time in my life, I assumed that my idea of who God was was in fact the right idea and even the only idea, and now I am embarrassed to realize how unconscious and narrow-minded I was. Now I know that the best any of us can do is talk about our God-image, and that all of the ideas we have about God are neither big enough to be all that God is or untainted by our own projections.

Sadly, human history is littered and blood-stained with wars and conflicts over who has the "right" idea about God and whose God is superior, a reality that is antithetical to the God who is described in the Scriptures as Love. Because I have chosen to follow the way of Christ, I believe Jesus is the best picture of God that has ever been, but even with the accounts of Jesus' life in the Gospels, we cannot know all there is to know about the Mysterious One. *That we cannot know or define or capture God in a doctrine, a theology, a concept or an idea is part of what makes God God!*

There in Hereford, as the sun set and the cool evening breeze began to blow, I talked about how our God-image is formed when we are infants, perhaps even in the womb, and that it forms based on our experience with our earliest caregivers and authority figures who are our first "gods." Until we become conscious of how we think about God, most of us don't even know that we have a God-concept that is different from God, and so we operate at an emotional level with a God-concept that is immature, inadequate, limited, and limiting.

We may have an unconscious Sunday school image of God and be able to spout Bible verses about who God is based on what we think we should believe and say. At another level, an emotional and unconscious level, another image of God is pumping away, affecting our lives in ways we don't know until we begin to unpack our beliefs and reflect on them.

Some of us hold a concept of God that is helpful, and some of us live every day with an image of God that is harmful and hurtful. Some imagine God as the County Sheriff, just waiting for them to do something wrong. Some image God as Kindly Old Grandfather, Cruel Taskmaster, Jolly Santa Claus, Rejecting or Devouring Mother, Absent Landlord, Sugar Daddy, or Judge and Jury. Some of us project our experiences with parents or teachers onto God, and some of us believe God is either an irrelevant idea for weak people, an irrational projection of sick people, a concept to study, or a theory to refute.

Everyone has "a god" and a god-image. I have heard it said by Jungian lecturers that Carl Jung said it did not worry him whether or not people would have a god or a religion, but which one they would choose!

Growing up as a preacher's kid, it took hard work and consciousness for me to differentiate the man behind the pulpit from God. Even though my dad would never have had me confuse him with God, he was in a position of power and authority, speaking for God, and that affected me at an emotional level. My mother's attitude toward me and toward God also affected my emotional experience of God, and while I did not rationally and consciously decide on who I thought God was, my parents' presence in my daily life shaped my earliest concept of God.

When I was a child, we visited a particular church sanctuary in which the top of the dome had "the eye of God," the symbol intended to communicate God's ever-watching, protective presence. For me, however, it was a reminder of the song I learned in children's choir:

Oh, be careful, little feet, where you go.
Be careful little feet where you go.
The Father up above is looking down below,
So be careful, little feet where you go.

The song had several verses, cautioning us to watch what our hands did, our mouths said, and even what our eyes saw, for crying out loud, and the effect on me was powerful. From that time on, I knew there was nowhere I could go that the watchful, stern, disapproving eye of God was not on me and that there was nothing I could do that would go unseen, unreported, or unpunished. Perhaps there were times when that image of God was reinforced by actual experiences with various figures who represented the rejecting, negative mother and punishing, punitive father, but mostly it kept me anxious about others' disapproval and rejection of me. (Obviously, a negative image of God can be one of a rejecting, negative father or a punishing, punitive mother. It can also include an image of a controlling, manipulative mother or father.)

Later, as I developed a life-altering contemplative practice and consciously nurtured the idea of the Presence of God as helpful, supportive, loving, encouraging and nurturing—all feminine images—I began to be freed from my fear of the watchful Eye of God.

Occasionally, but rarely now, that childhood image kicks in and I feel watched by a god who is out to get me. More and more, though, that god has died in my inner landscape, and the Real God of love has become stronger.

Looking into the faces of the new acquaintances in Hereford who had welcomed me warmly into the sacred space of their church on a Friday night, I wanted to explain this life-changing truth in a way that would expand and enlarge their lives. I wanted to connect with them at a heart-and-soul level, but I also wanted to engage with their minds and imaginations. I wanted to earn their trust and represent God well.

Bidden or not bidden, God is present.

—ERASMUS

I take that task seriously. I approach talking about God with reverence and hesitation. In a world in which there is a profusion of God talk, religion and our most sacred words have left the synagogues, churches, and mosques and been emblazoned on billboards, T-shirts, and bumper stickers. At times I shudder when I remember the commandment, "Do not take God's name in vain," and almost yearn for the Jewish refusal to speak the name of God, for it is so holy.

At a recent workshop sponsored by the Foundation for Contemporary Theology, Marcus Borg talked about his newest book, *Speaking Christian: Why Christian Words Have Lost Their Meaning and Power—And How They Can Be Restored* (HarperOne, 2011), in which he proposes reclaiming, redeeming, and liberating sacred words such as "salvation," "justice," "redemption," and "compassion" from the culture that has distorted the meaning of the words and domesticated Christianity. As a lifelong participant in a mainstream denomination, I am often shocked and even horrified at the ways in which what is now being called "cultural Christianity" has mongrelized and minimized words that hold great meaning for me.

The burning intention to speak with integrity and reverence about holy things fuels my putting these words on paper, and my intention in writing this chapter and when I address this subject "Who is God to you?" is threefold. First, by asking the question, "Who is God to you?" it is possible to illustrate the different "versions" of God human beings carry, and the reason this exercise shakes people up is that most of us, especially if we worship together in a community of faith, assume that when someone says "God," everyone knows what that means.

"How could she believe that?" someone will inevitably ask about me. "I've been in church with her my whole life, but I didn't know she believed that!"

"I've learned a lot from hearing peoples' ideas about God," a pastor or teacher will say to me. "No wonder we have trouble making decisions together; our competing ideas of God are getting in the way of moving forward!"

The idea that all of us in a particular church or within the same denomination have the same image of God simply isn't true, for the images of God people carry around in their heads are widely divergent and are based on factors and forces that are, for most people, unconscious! So it is that when people start listening to each other's concepts of God, perhaps verbalized for the first time in a group, it's a little disorienting!

(If you want to be even more disturbed, listen to the political rhetoric today and ask this question of the people who are shouting most loudly: "What is his/her concept of God?" and "What does that person believe about God that is making him/her act in this way?")

At a gathering of fellow Baptists in Charlotte, North Carolina, this summer, Bill Underwood, president of Mercer University in Macon, Georgia, began his speech by stating, "We say we want a Christian nation." Then he asked the disturbing, provocative question, "But whose definition of Christian do we want?"

When I ask the question, "Where did you get your image of God?" most people, especially church people, will answer quickly, "At church!"

The second reason I ask the question "Who is God to you?" is to illustrate that there is a wide gap between our Sunday school concepts of God, which come from our heads, and our on-the-ground, real-life understanding of who God is. That second set of ideas about who God is and how God behaves toward us is formed at an emotional level and at an unconscious level, and that is the image of God that runs the show.

The third reason I begin with the question about a person's image of God is that it sets me up to state the foundational principles of the joint venture with God: *A person's God-concept is the most important concept he has. The second most important concept a person carries is his/her self-concept. Those two concepts are interwoven, each of them affecting the other, and from those concepts a person will choose actions and behaviors, make choices, and create a life that is consistent with those two core beliefs.*

The beginning point in understanding one's spiritual development is in understanding one's concept of God, and yet we wonder how we can possibly talk about or even understand that which cannot be defined. Perhaps we work so hard to contain God in a doctrinal system, by means of systematic theology, in an image that is fixed and constant because we are rendered speechless before that which is limitless, numinous, ineffable, mysterious.

What if someone tried to introduce you, a mere human being? Would that introduction start with one of the roles you play? Would that really define you?

What if someone, in trying to identify you to someone else, said, "Oh, you know her. She's the one in the Hummer in the carpool line"?

Not only would that one statement diminish you, but it would also be laden with the person's interpretation of what kind of person drives a Hummer. The assumptions made about you might have absolutely nothing to do with who you really are. Besides, the Hummer might be borrowed from a friend because your own old Ford is in the shop!

Often I am introduced by someone as "my Bible study teacher," and while I love to teach the Bible, that is only one part of my life. I'm proud to be Martus's wife and Michelle's, Julie's, and Amy's mother, but that is only part of my life. I am more than any of my roles, and *if you take all of them away from me, the essence of who I am, the True Self, is still there.*

What if someone identified you only by a mistake you made, a failure, a character defect? You know how that goes: She's the one who got pregnant in high school. He's the one who failed third grade. She is a drunk. I often say that I am grateful I do not live now around people who knew me in eighth grade.

What if someone is identified by his or her most heroic deed? Does that leave any room for failure? Surely the tragedy we saw unfolding in the life of golfer Tiger Woods illustrates the complexity of human beings. We ask how this disciplined, dignified, world-class athlete could have gotten himself in such a mess. We have known the champion, indeed, but we didn't know about the other forces that were playing out in his life. Apparently, neither did he.

How do our labels about each other constrict our real knowing of each other? How do our attachments to our roles and our images keep us stuck in one-sidedness? If knowing each other is such a challenge, how much more difficult it is to say that we really know God!

When we make a statement about who God is, we also have to ask, "What am I leaving out?" If we dare to explain or define God or make pronouncements about what God is doing, we are compelled to ask about the Holy One, "And what else is there to say about this God?" If we presume to issue edicts and proclamations in the name of God, we might need to run for cover when we hear the thunder roll.

I am convinced that if we added up all our definitions of God since time began, we still could not cover the majesty and scope and height and depth and breadth of the One whose being emanates throughout creation, giving life to the world he loves.

No single story in the Bible tells everything there is to know about God, and so we need to read and ponder the whole Bible in order to get a full picture of the biblical record of God. The Hebrew people would not even say God's name because it was so holy, and they had many names for God. Indeed, Jesus called him Father, and yet the biblical revelation demands that we see the fuller picture of who God is: creator, sustainer, provider, protector, redeemer. Then there is Jesus, who appears as the best picture of God we have, showing us God as physician, shepherd, teacher, helper, savior, and lord. Jesus identified himself as light, living water, the bread of life, the resurrection, the way, and life itself!

We continue to try to name and tame God. We cling to our favorite images of him so that we won't be afraid, but also so that we can somehow have power over the Almighty and make him do our bidding. Who isn't afraid of the Almighty? Who doesn't tremble before the power of the unseen force behind all things?

Carl Jung suggested that man invented religion to protect himself from God. We love to put God in a box and make him conform to our ideas of who he is, but by doing that we make God way too small and limit his power.

You are the healing
the loving
the touching
You are the laughing
You are the dancing

Jesus, Verb of God
You are the moving—
move in me.

—MARILEE ZDENEK,
GOD IS A VERB

One day, confronted by an experience that defied any definition of God I had held in the past and pushed beyond every comfort zone, I wrote the following words:

I'm O.K. with the Force
as long as that knee-buckling,
ego-threatening, heart-stopping
energy is
contained within the safe
and predictable boundaries of a
Noun. You know, a ritual, a rite, a
symbol I can move and dust, myself.
I like the Force as long as it is a theory
or an idea, a doctrine or a rule.
When God is a noun, a fixed object
I can safeguard in my head and
think about . . . I can handle it.
The Force in a box,
a sure certainty or a clearcut
idea, is far less disturbing to
my poor ego who demands
that I stay in my place, do
what I'm supposed to do and
keep on marching in place.

Nouns. Yes, I can manage nouns.
Theories I can handle. Ideas I
can analyze and debate and then put
them back on the shelf
I want my theology
systematic.
It's when the Force, that
    Verb-whose-name-is-God
    breaks out and asks me to
    accept his wild and winsome ways—
when the Numinous escapes and
asserts verbness against my defenses,
demanding to be honored and
embraced—and when the Daimon
invites me to dance to a new and different
dance . . . and Love asks everything of me for
God's sake . . . I freeze
in the fire of God,
for I do not know if it will consume me or
refine me . . . Oh, God I want
what You want for me,
even when I'm scared of just
what it is You want for me and
where it is You want me to go with You.

On that day when I turned my will and my life over to God, God must have thought I meant it, for nothing in my life has been the same since. With every venture I make into new terrain or territory, I discover and experience aspects of the Numinous One I'd not imagined. Often I learn something heart-stopping in the most ordinary and mundane moments, and I love it when a surprising and sometimes delightful truth comes to me at the hands of the Trickster God, the playful side of God who seems to show up out of the blue. I feel as if I'm on a journey in which God is constantly saying to me, "Look! Listen! There's something more I want you to know about me!"

There is a chocolate shop near my neighborhood that I'd passed many times since it opened several years ago. I'd always been intrigued by the old-world charm of the shop's door and windows, but had also known that if I ever crossed the threshold into the shop, I might wind up in the window with chocolate slathered all over me like the man in the movie *Chocolat*.

On a cold, dreary January day, I needed a birthday gift for two special men in my life, but I'd just been to see an oral surgeon and was not in the best of moods. I pushed myself to get the gifts, however, and it occurred to me that perhaps the chocolate shop might have what I wanted and might even mail the gifts for me.

So it was that I ventured into Chocolat du Monde for the first time and was met by eighteen feet of chocolates, artfully arranged in beautiful cases.

Overwhelmed by the dazzling array of choices, I began looking for something I recognized. Pleasant and friendly, the owner, David Heiland, offered to help me, and we began a discussion about whether my friends would prefer dark or milk or white chocolate.

"I don't like dark chocolate," I informed him, as if it mattered what I liked.

Nonplussed by my pronouncement, he said, "When people tell me that, I tell them that they probably haven't ever had good dark chocolate."

"Hmm," I responded, absorbed in my dental concerns.

"Would you like to try a sample?" he asked, and I declined. I think I even made a face like someone who'd been offered bad medicine. I knew I was being close-minded and a bit rude, but at the moment I just wanted to complete my errand, go home, and suck my thumb.

"Try it," he said gently, and I saw his hand extending a small piece of dark chocolate across the gleaming counter.

I felt as if I were being offered the proverbial apple. I knew in my heart that this was a turning point in my life with chocolate, and I would never be the same.

I said something childish like, "I'll try it, but I know I won't like it," as I took the morsel into my hand.

I nibbled a small bite of the dark chocolate and, well, I almost swooned.

"It's good, isn't it?" he asked, smiling, and I had to admit he was right. I'd never had good dark chocolate. In one bite, I became a convert and spokesperson for my dark chocolate, my new favorite shop, and my new best friend. After all, it's a proven fact that dark chocolate is good for you!

I left Chocolat du Monde feeling warmed and encouraged, something I hadn't expected. Since it was near Valentine's Day, it wasn't hard to integrate that experience into thoughts about loving and being loved as I sat to write my column for the San Angelo *Standard-Times*.

Reflecting on conversations I'd had with people over whether or not they would ever try or trust or dare to open their hearts to the possibility of love again, I decided how few people have experienced authentic, true love. Between humans, love often gets tainted with codependency and control, power and manipulation, withholding and stipulations. We confuse our needs with love, and we think people-pleasing is love, but it is not.

Maybe love, authentic love, is like dark chocolate. Maybe people don't trust it because they've never had the real, healthy, nourishing love that isn't contaminated with the additives of power, stinginess, selfishness, and pettiness. Perhaps people who can't love were abandoned or treated cruelly by the same person who said "I love you" to them.

And maybe people don't trust God because what they have seen and heard about God from God's representatives has been corrupted by misinformation, ignorance, and sometimes wrong or harmful intent. Perhaps God gets a bad rap from people who use religion to control and manipulate others for their own purposes by guilt and shame, fear tactics, and power trips.

Maybe we all need to reflect more deeply on our concepts of God and let the old gods (the hurtful and wounding god concepts) die so that the Real God who loves us can be born in us again.

For in him we live and move and have our being.

—ACTS 17:28

So much of a person's concept of God is confused with denominational baggage, institutional trappings, and what we've been taught or have caught from others. It would be wonderful if everything that is talked and taught about God were life-giving and true, but the reality is that we who represent God are flawed and frail, imperfect, and often bewitched by our limited and limiting images of God.

We can't buy love, and we can't buy a new god concept, but we can become conscious of what we think about God and whether those thoughts and felt experiences are wounding or empowering. The way forward in life may be to become intentional and thoughtful about God and about love, adjusting our God concept until it serves us instead of making us a slave to it.

Authentic love is like good dark chocolate. It does cost more and you may have to develop a taste for it, but it satisfies the palate and is good for your heart. And once you eat the good stuff, you won't want the junk anymore.

An authentic love relationship with God is also like good dark chocolate, but infinitely more. It will nurture and nourish you, heal and transform, liberate and empower you, and it will for sure cost you. It will cost you plenty and give you much more in return, and sometimes you'll discover that when you wake up, what you yearned for was with you all along.

It may take a lifetime to learn how to love God and receive God's love, but maybe learning how to love is our assignment on this plane. Loving God and loving others and loving one's own wild and precious life is a venture worthy of our best efforts of a lifetime.

In that same event sponsored by the Foundation for Contemporary Theology, Marcus Borg spoke in his unique and eloquent way about the life of Jesus. At one point during the weekend lecture series, a woman began with a statement I often hear—"Yes, I hear your call for love"—and then she moved into the question, "but what do we do about all the evil out there?"

(I've noticed that when people ask this question, it's always about the evil that is *out there*, in *those people*. Rarely does someone say, "What about my character defect? What about the evil in me, the Judas in me, the betraying Peter in me?")

Ever humble and generous in spirit, Marcus Borg responded by acknowledging that within the Scriptures, both the Old and New Testaments, there is the punitive, angry God and the loving, compassionate God. He explained that we must start forming and holding our God-image in the person of Jesus.

"At some point, though," he said gently, "we all have to choose which God is going to be our dominant image. If we try to choose both, the punitive image will prevail."

Later, Marcus Borg came back to emphasize the vital importance of the God-image we carry. "It is so important which God we choose," he said, "because we will reflect the image of God we carry. We will become like the image of God that prevails."

And so we are led to the next important question: *Who am I to God?*

Chapter 4

WHO ARE YOU TO GOD?

When she was pregnant with her first child, a son named Lucas, my daughter Amy introduced me to a traditional African fable that describes how every child comes into this world knowing his or her own song or special purpose in life. As recounted by Dennis, Sheila, and Matthew Linn in the children's book *What Is My Song?*, a pregnant mother goes away by herself to listen to her heart until she hears the special song of the child within her. Once she hears that song, she returns to her village to teach it to the child's father, who joins the mother in singing that song, inviting the child to come to them.

As the mother's pregnancy develops, she sings the song over and over, teaching it to the people in the village, so that the first thing the infant hears at birth is the women of the village, gathered around the mother when she is giving birth, singing that child's song. As the child grows and develops, the villagers continue to sing his song to him, helping him learn who he is and what his purpose is in life. When he forgets it, they sing it to him to remind him. "The most important thing," the child says, "is that my song never leaves me even if I forget it for a while."

At the end, the narrator says, "And when I leave this world and go back to God, they will gather around my deathbed and sing my song to me for the last time."

At the beginning of the biblical narrative, the writer declares that the Creator made human beings in his own image. Every one of us bears the imprint of God, and that imprint is expressed uniquely through each person in his or her individual song.

The "song," as it is called in the African fable, seems bound neither by time nor space, but lives forever. I understand this part of the human being to be the soul. When studying the works of Carl Jung, I learned that he called it the Self. The book of Genesis seems to indicate that the sacred reality is the *imago Dei*, the image of God stamped within human beings.

This simple African story charms and inspires me. It challenges me, taking me back to a moment in my early adulthood when I was introduced to the concept of the song within. I first heard about "the True Self" in the language of depth analysis. As a young adult, I'd agreed to attend one session, and only one, of a Yokefellow Spiritual Growth Group. Small groups of all kinds were popular at the time, and I was fascinated by them, but only from a distance. I thought small groups were for other people who "needed" that kind of thing.

> *So God created them in his own image, in the image of God he created him; male and female he created them.*
>
> —GENESIS 1:27

Looking back, it seems appropriate that I was pregnant at the time with my first child. I have sometimes described the process of spiritual growth in terms of birth and rebirth, and of course within my faith tradition the term "born again" has been used, misused, and misunderstood. Having come to a deeper understanding of the process of rebirth, I realize why Nicodemus could not fathom what Jesus was asking of him during his nighttime visit with "the good Rabbi" (see John 3:1-21).

At times I have felt as if I were the one being born, the midwife, and the laboring mother giving birth all at the same time. Always, the process of rebirth is like that of our first birth. It is painful, laborious, messy, and fraught with the possibility of danger. When I agreed to attend this first small group, I was saying yes to being reborn.

"I'll go with you one time," I told my husband, "but I won't talk. I will listen, but I won't talk." To his credit, Martus did not resist my resistance.

I had a bit of defensiveness about *being known* at the time, but I would never have admitted to anyone that I had a deep fear that if anyone knew me as I really was, they would not like me. I'm not sure I had ever admitted that fear of being known to myself; maybe it wasn't even a conscious thought at the time, but more of a low-grade infection of my soul.

Consciously, I had no idea about the pervasive fear of rejection that existed at some level of my unconsciousness along with a deep longing to be known, accepted as I was, and loved for who I was. I was unconscious of the ways I hid my True Self from others, and I didn't know that my fears of being known or rejected were universal fears. Everyone I've ever known has them; the difference is in degree and in awareness of them. Mine were controlling every decision I made, but I didn't know it.

William Shakespeare said, "The worst prison is the one you don't know you're in." Joseph Campbell said, "The cave you fear to enter holds the treasure that you seek." I was to discover that both wise men were telling the truth.

Gathered in that living room on the first night's session with people who were essentially strangers to me, I listened as the leader introduced a concept that was deceptively simple but profoundly true and life changing. In the initial group session, we learned about the True Self, the part of us that is authentically real.

The concepts of these particular Yokefellow Spiritual Growth Groups were based on work by a man named Cecil Osborne, the director of the Burlingame Counseling Center in Burlingame, California. He had built on the ideas of Paul Tournier, a Swiss psychiatrist who had studied with Carl Jung, and the work of Elton Trueblood.

At the beginning of the session, our leader read the Scripture that formed the basic foundational idea of the group process. I'm sure I'd heard and read the words of Jesus in Matthew 11:29 many times in my life, but on that night, it was as if I heard them for the first time. They resonated with something that seemed to be at the core of myself.

Come to me, all you who are weary and heavy-laden, and I will give you rest.

At that point in my life, how could I already identify with being weary and heavy-laden? What was so heavy? Why could I already understand being laden with the demands and expectations of life? I was only twenty-six years old; how could I already be tired enough to understand that Scripture? Was it that something in me knew how burdened I was, trying to live in conformity to external standards, being a people pleaser, and adapting to what others wanted and needed?

Take my yoke upon you and learn of me, for my yoke is easy and my burden is light.

It was strange language for a contemporary young woman. I had no experience with yokes or oxen. What rang true to me in that Scripture, given the archaic language? I wonder if Eugene Peterson's version of the verse in *The Message* would have resonated even more deeply (Colorado Springs: NavPress Publishing Group, 2002):

Are you tired? Worn out? Burned out on religion?
Come to me. Get away with me and you'll recover your life.
I'll show you how to take a real rest.
Walk with me and work with me—watch how I do it.
Learn the unforced rhythms of grace.
I won't lay anything heavy or ill-fitting on you.
Keep company with me and you'll learn how to live freely and lightly.

The journey we were beginning as a group would be a journey that we would take together. Each of us, "yoked with Christ," would also be joined with each other, helping each other to see ourselves as we were and as we could become. At that first group session, we got the idea that the spiritual life is a joint venture in which we are intended to help each other become whole and healthy.

At some level, I resonated with the idea of being yoked with Christ, though I had no idea what it meant. As much as I feared being known by other human beings, it made sense to me that we could be yoked together, joined together, in a process of transformation.

In the spiritual growth process and later, in practicing Centering Prayer, and in a lengthy and laborious process of depth analysis, I was to learn first-hand the wonder of the joint venture. Two things are true: (1) To be reborn, I must take the solitary and sometimes lonely journey of self-awareness and individuation, working out my salvation with fear and trembling. (2) And I need other people to journey with me.

As young as I was when I participated in that first spiritual growth group, I could relate to being weary and heavy-laden, but I did not know why. Over time, I learned how trying to be someone you aren't can wear you out, numb your mind, and wound your soul. I had stuck my neck in the yoke of other peoples' expectations, and my neck was chafed and sore from trying to conform and adapt to the outer world. I was stuck, as well, with ideas, misconceptions, and misunderstandings about God and about myself that were binding my soul and retarding my spiritual growth.

"If you aren't yourself, who are you going to be?" This question deceives us with its simplicity. It's not that easy to be who you are!

In the initial session of that group, I began to understand the difference between the ego or the false self, the self we present to others, and the True Self, the authentic and original Self. The ego is called a false self not because it is a lie but because it is formed to adapt to the outer world. The outer self is composed of the personas we display in public, the roles we play, the images we project, and the masks we wear to cover what we don't want others to see.

It is important in this formulation to understand that the ego is necessary, for it is the organ of consciousness that we need as we move around in the world, taking care of our daily lives. Having an ego is essential in ordering our world; egocentricity is what gets us in trouble.

However, it is the True Self, the *imago Dei*, the soul that is at the core of each human being, and the Yokefellow Groups were intended to unbind the Self. The process began with awareness. Again, spirituality is about waking up and then waking up some more.

From the first presentation of this concept, I knew that this idea of the True Self was profound truth. What I did not know at the time was that the pursuit of the freedom of the Self within me would form the core of my personal journey and become the central, organizing principle of my teaching and writing.

Countless times and in a myriad of venues, I have taught the idea of the True Self, and there is always instant resonance, regardless of the age of the people in the group. Something deep within us,

> *I believe that what Genesis suggests is that this original self, with the print of God's thumb still upon it, is the most essential part of who we are and is buried deep in all of us as a source of wisdom and strength and healing which we can draw upon or, with our terrible freedom, not draw upon as we choose.*
>
> —FREDERICK BUECHNER

it seems, understands that there is more to us than meets the eye. There is a common understanding about how we conform and adapt to please and placate the outer world, often leaving the urgings of the True Self behind.

The True Self is the essence of the person. The Self (with a capital S) is the part of the person that bears the stamp of God. It is designed by God and is at the center of our being. Obviously, as Dr. James Hollis says in his lectures, if you cut someone open to find the Self, you won't find it, but it is there as the central operating system of every human being. If you perform surgery on a human being, you won't find the soul or the *imago Dei*, but it is there, operating from the depths of the person.

The True Self is the song the African child is taught. It carries what Jungian analyst and writer James Hillman calls "the Soul's Code," and it is about both who we are and what we are to do in life.[1] I have likened the True Self to an internal GPS. It is "the kingdom within" that Jesus taught, and his counsel was to seek it first, but it sometimes takes a long time to learn what that means.

When I am teaching this concept, whether in a spiritual direction session or at a workshop or retreat, I draw a circle on the board to represent the True Self. Around that circle I draw a larger circle so that my drawing looks like a fried egg. The outer circle represents the adapted self. It is the persona we wear in public in order to be appropriate and to carry out our daily responsibilities. It is the image we want to project to others. The adapted self includes the roles we play throughout our lives, with behavior that is appropriate to the roles, and it can also be the masks we wear to keep others from knowing who we really are. Some call it "the small self."

"The greater the distance between the True Self and the adapted self, the greater the discomfort, suffering, and pain," I say, and I can almost feel the resonance with the other person or persons. "The more we stifle the impulses of the Self, God-within, the more we suffer." Often, I see someone in the group wipe away a tear.

Typically, at this point I talk about the things we do to alleviate that suffering or assuage our discomfort. We numb ourselves in a variety of ways with substances—food, alcohol, drugs. We distract ourselves from the pain of inauthenticity by watching television, shopping, working too much, or being codependent and people pleasing. We medicate ourselves in countless ways, not because we are bad but because we haven't yet learned how to listen to that still, small Voice from within.

Sitting on a bench on a cloudy spring day in England, I savored the present moment, but I was also lost in memories of other times. I was on the grounds where William Wordsworth once lived, soaking up the beauty of Dove Cottage while I recalled Ann Miller's English class at Baylor University and, further back in my memory, the day I recited Wordsworth's poem about daffodils to my father. It was a *kairos* moment for me—a moment that transcended time and space. The moment was filled with the delight of former days, youthful memories, and present-moment pleasures.

I bought a book of Wordsworth's poems in the bookstore at Dove Cottage, and for the rest of the trip, I pondered the words from the poem "Intimations of Immortality from Recollections of Childhood" that had

intrigued me for decades. With my understanding of the Self, I kept return-
ing to these words for the rest of the trip: "Trailing clouds of glory do we
come / From God, who is our home." Is "home" the True Self, I wondered?
I think it is.

Where do you start your theology? Or have you ever thought about
that?

What difference does it make if you start your theology with a firm conviction that we are made in the image of God or with a firm conviction of
our "original sin"? What are the practical, everyday ramifications of which
choice we make?

Have you heard that we are born in sin and have a black stain in us?
Does your theology start with that black stain, the story of the "fall" in
Genesis 3? If it does, where does that belief system take you?

On the other hand, what if you begin your theology with Genesis 1 and
what Matthew Fox has described in his book *Original Blessing,* "the original
blessing"? Does it make any difference if you begin where the Bible begins—
with God—and then move to creation when God created male and female
in his very image and then pronounced his creation *good*?

Where does this theology that begins with God's blessing on the people
he created take you?

When I speak about what it means to be made in the image of God, I
begin by saying that when we accept that we are made in the image of God,
it changes the way we act in the world, the way we feel about ourselves, and
the choices we make moment by moment. "When you believe that you are
made in the very image of God, you will never allow anyone to mistreat you
or abuse you," I say, regardless of my audience, and the room always
becomes silent.

"And here is the other side of that," I continue. "When you look into
the eyes of another person and know that that person, too, was created in the
image of God—and carries the spark of divinity in her—you cannot abuse
or mistreat her."

To accept that you are made in the image of God, to embrace that reality, is life changing. I don't know the scope of what it means that we are
made in the image of God, of course, but here is a starting point: *To be made
in the image of God means we are created with the capacity to communicate
with others.*

The entire Bible is the story of God's speaking to a particular people. It is God's nature to communicate with us, and we have been created with the capacity to speak to each other and to hear each other. (I've heard it said that since we have one mouth and two ears, we should consider listening twice as much as we talk. That's not bad counsel!) We have been given the capacity to talk with each other, and through the mystery we call prayer, we have the possibility of talking with God and receiving guidance, impressions, and sometimes direct revelation from the Creator.

"I'm not very good at communicating," I've often heard, and I always counter with, "But you can learn how to do that." In today's world, with access to infinite resources of training in communication skills and conflict resolution, there is no excuse for not being able to communicate.

In her residency training, my daughter Julie learned that if a doctor will take ten minutes to hear the patient's concerns and to communicate clearly with that patient, patient satisfaction improves significantly and the incidence of lawsuits drops. To hear another human being, to hear what that person is saying, and to care about what he is not saying or cannot articulate is a gift of inestimable value. When we communicate well, we reflect the image of God in us.

For you created my inmost being; you knit me together in my mother's womb. I praise you because I am fearfully and wonderfully made; your works are wonderful.

—PSALM 139:13-14

How many marriages could have been saved if the partners could have heard each other? How many parent/child relationships could be eased if each would take the time to listen to the feelings and longings of the other? What if we who exist in the Body of Christ made the effort and paid the price to hear what our brothers and sisters are saying?

To be made in the image of God means we have been created with the capacity to be creative. Obviously, humans cannot create from nothing as God can, but God has invested in us the ability to be co-creators with him, fashioning all kinds of works with our minds and hands. Creativity is not limited to the literary, visual, or performing arts, but includes balancing financial ledgers, planning a trip, repairing a car, and teaching a roomful of children how to read. My friend Delores Flood is trained as a CPA; she is also a master at creating meaningful and enjoyable trips.

Some of us are left-brain creative and some of us are right-brain creative, and some have learned to move back and forth between logical, sequential, and rational thinking and circular, diffused, and nonrational thinking. We create our days, either consciously or unconsciously, and sometimes we humans create masterpieces, but we all have the capacity to be creative.

If you say you aren't creative, you will cap the wellspring of energy that is in you; if you agree to your creativity, you will say "yes" to what some have called "an unlimited Swiss bank account."

To be made in the image of God means we have been created with the capacity to love and be loved. One of the first memory verses little children learn in Sunday school is the one in which God identifies himself as love: God is love (1 John 4:8). Love is God's nature, and we are created for love. That love is God's nature indicates that we, too, have this nature within us.

Some people have been wounded deeply and are afraid to love or be loved, but the capacity for love is still there. Some have become cynical, and others simply don't know how to express love or to receive it, but that doesn't mean the ways, the language, and the behavior of loving God and loving others isn't inscribed deeply within their being.

When Jesus summed up all of the law and the prophets, he spoke this Greatest Commandment: "Love the Lord your God with all your heart and with all your soul and with all your mind and with all your strength . . . , and love your neighbor as yourself" (Mark 12:30-31). Then he said, "There is no commandment greater than this."

Perhaps one of our most urgent and important assignments on this earth is to learn how to love each other. If that is so, then our homes and our houses of worship are meant to be laboratories of learning how to love more fully. The importance of being able to love and of loving others is so great that I have wondered if the test for us when we face God might be, "How well did you love?"

I take these words of Jesus as seriously as almost any in the Gospels: "Let me give you a new command: Love one another. In the same way I loved you, you love one another. This is how everyone will recognize that you are my disciples—when they see the love you have for each other" (John 13:34-35). Note that Jesus' words are spoken as a command.

To be made in the image of God means we have been granted the gift and the burden of choice. One of the guiding Scriptures of my life is

Deuteronomy 30:19: "I have set before you today life and death, blessing and curse; therefore, *choose life.*"

In a thousand different ways throughout a day, we shape and form our lives by the choices—conscious and unconscious—we make. Debates have raged over whether we have free will, and sometimes when something from the deep waters of my unconscious rises up to sabotage a healthy decision I've made or makes me say things I wouldn't say if I were in "my right mind," I wonder just how free my will is. However, when I pay attention to myself throughout the day, I am astounded at the number of choices I face.

As a college student, I was profoundly affected by Viktor Frankl's book, *Man's Search for Meaning*, in which he describes the different ways in which people imprisoned in concentration camps during World War II responded to their conditions. In the end, he says, our last freedom is our freedom to choose how we will respond to our circumstances, and that cannot be taken away from us.

There are countless things over which we have no control, but we are not helpless victims. God has dignified us with the gift of choosing and deciding. We have been given minds with which to assess facts and factors, differentiate among them, and then make decisions. Ultimately, we all bow to the sovereignty of God, but in our daily lives we have the gift of choice. How we choose, moment by moment, affects our behavior, our moods, our future, and other people. It is no wonder, given the power of choice, that people are afraid of it, stay dependent, and want others to make their decisions for them and tell them what to think, but God's nature within us compels us to step up to the plate of our lives and assume the responsibility of the freedom to choose.

How do we lose touch with the image of God within? What happens to Wordsworth's "clouds of glory"? How do we forget the soul and attach ourselves so firmly to the outer world?

The answer, it seems, is fairly simple. It's all about survival.

When a child is born, he or she is completely dependent on adults to provide the basic needs of survival, and so early and unconsciously, a baby asks, "Who's in charge here?" and "What do I have to do to get them to take care of me?"

The process of adapting to the outer world, conforming to others' expectations, and tuning in to the demands and needs of "the big people" starts early. Because the child's needs are so great, he begins early to "read" the outer world to learn how to get his needs met.

As tiny infants, we begin to conform and adapt to the outer world in order to receive the care we need. Some of us even learn how to shut down our needs and "take care of" our mothers or fathers; I've heard it said that some infants learn how to do that even before birth. (See Alice Miller's landmark book, *The Drama of the Gifted Child*, to explore this phenomenon further.)

The reality is that for the first half of life, the ego is charged with the tasks of adapting to the outer world, and that is appropriate. Sometime on life's journey, however, there has to be a turning inward, a process that will be explored in later chapters.

Through the years in my ongoing journey, the idea of the True Self has been a constant and guiding force, the "still small Voice" within, and it has shown up in various places and through a wide variety of people.

At the Church of the Savior in Washington, DC, I found the books of Elizabeth O'Connor, and her treatment of the "inner landscape" of the unconscious fit perfectly with what I'd learned in the spiritual growth groups. Drawing from the work of Carl Jung, she had written what was to become an important book for me, *Our Many Selves*. Instantly, I understood what she was talking about when she referred to the tormented man in the Bible from whom Jesus cast out many demons. "What is your name?" Jesus asked him, and he replied, "Legion" (Mark 5:1-20). That there are many "people" in the unconscious world instantly made sense to me.

It was also at the Church of the Savior that I bought my first copies of Richard Foster's *Celebration of Discipline* and John Sanford's *The Kingdom Within*, books that have been pivotal for my life. Foster's book introduced me to the various kinds of spiritual disciplines as a "celebration," differentiating between those disciplines of the inward journey, such as prayer, meditation, solitude, and silence, and the discplines of the outward journey, such as corporate worship, ministries, acts of service. John Sanford's book transformed my thinking about Jesus' statement to the disciples about the inner kingdom and, in fact, my whole way of relating to the Living Christ.

After years of practicing meditation and even writing books about it, I went to the Benedictine Monastery in Snowmass, Colorado, to learn how to do Centering Prayer under the guidance of Thomas Keating. Each day as we sat in the living room of the retreat center, I was amazed as I listened to Keating's teaching about what Centering Prayer does in the inner kingdom of a person. Once again, the idea of the True Self and what he called the false self (the adapted self) was part of my journey and my process.

"When you practice Centering Prayer," Keating said, "you are giving the Divine Therapist your consent to work deep within the unconscious and to heal the emotional programming of a lifetime." My experience with Centering Prayer is that it releases the True Self from bondage, much like the onlookers unwrapped Lazarus from his death wrappings (John 11:1-44).

When I began attending classes at the C. G. Jung Center in Houston and through the long, laborious, tedious, miraculous process of depth analysis, all that I had been doing in my adult journey began coming together in healing, transformative, liberating, and empowering ways. My spirituality stands on what I call a four-legged stool. Because of my early childhood training and experience, Bible study and teaching form the first leg. I have worked the Twelve Steps of Alcoholics Anonymous not for alcoholism but for codependency for most of my adult life, and in working the eleventh step (seeking through prayer and meditation to improve our conscious contact with God, seeking to know and follow his will), I developed a lifelong practice of meditation that is as essential to the health of my whole being as air is to my lungs. This is the third leg. Finally, the teachings and work of Carl Jung are the fourth leg of this stool.

"What we are doing is not self-absorption or narcissism," Dr. James Hollis has explained many times in his lectures at the Jung Center. "Instead, self-reflection, self-understanding, analysis, individuation are some of the kindest gifts you can give your family and, actually, the world."

It seems strange and counter to our culture that following the guidance of early sages could be an act of kindness to the world. "Know yourself," said Socrates. "To thine own Self be true," said Shakespeare. The Apostle Paul said, "Do not think too highly of yourself, but come to a sober estimate of yourself."

Coming to a sober estimate of yourself—knowing your inner motivations, tendencies, and strengths—keeps you from projecting onto others what is really inside you. With self-awareness, you are less likely to act out or take out what is in you on other people, and so it is an act of maturity and responsibility to know yourself.

You've gotta make your own kind of music,
Sing your own special song.
Make your own kind of music
Even if nobody else sings along.

—"SING," WRITTEN AND SUNG BY BARBRA STREISAND

Beginning a spiritual growth process, whether it is recovery from an addiction, depth analysis, or any other process of self-understanding, is a little like the experience Abram had when God came to him and said, "I want you to go on a journey *to a land that I will show you*" (Gen 12:1). Imagine it! There was no itinerary, no motel reservations, and no known destination—only an invitation to leave what was familiar and go with this unseen God into unknown territory and unknowable experiences.

Abram did what God asked him to do. The journey was difficult and fraught with danger. In the process, however, he was transformed and given a new name, Abraham.

We—you, the reader, and I—are on a journey together now. And we are not alone. The One who invited us on the journey goes with us.

On a tour of San Francisco for our thirtieth anniversary, my husband I rode the ferry across the bay to the grim, grey prison known as Alcatraz. Touring the corridors and viewing the cells, the dining hall, and the confining bars, we grew quiet. Finally, blessedly, we walked out of the prison and onto a wide span of concrete, fresh air, a clear blue sky, and the splendor of the water between Alcatraz and San Francisco

Most glorious of all was the profusion of wildflowers triumphantly pushing up through the hard, cold concrete.

I caught my breath, and tears burned my eyes as I remembered that within every prisoner who had spent time in this place, there was still the True Self, the image of God, somewhere deep below the hardened surfaces of the smaller self.

I snapped a photograph of those flowers and kept it above my desk for many years as a reminder of the force of the True Self, the Self that has to push through ego defenses, the habits of a lifetime, hardened resentments, and gripping fears to bloom.

In every one of us lies that True Self whose purpose is the growth, development, transformation, and expression of the human being made in the image of God. That one wild and precious life within each of us sometimes gets to flourish. Sometimes it is buried, but it is always there, wanting to live.

"The Self is ruthless in accomplishing its purposes," Jim Hollis often reminds those of us who attend his lectures, "and every triumph of the Self is experienced as a defeat by the ego."

How is it, then, that we can cooperate more fully with the forces that want to flourish? How can we help God help us thrive? How can we make sure the song that is in each of us gets to be sung?

This prayer, written by Thomas Merton in *Thoughts on Solitude* and given to me by Howard Hovde, my dear friend and the former director of Laity Lodge, has sustained me through many parts of my journey.

My Lord God, I have no idea where I am going.
I do not see the road ahead of me.
I cannot know for certain where it will end.
Nor do I really know myself, and the fact that I think that I am following your will
does not mean that I am actually doing so.
But I believe that the desire to please you does in fact please you.
And I hope that I have that desire in all that I am doing.
I hope that I will never do anything apart from that desire.
And I know that if I do this you will lead me by the right road
though I may know nothing about it.
Therefore I will trust you always though I may seem to be lost
and in the shadow of death.
I will not fear, for you are ever with me,
and you will never leave me to face my perils alone.

NOTE

1. James Hillman, *The Soul's Code: In Search of Character and Calling* (New York: Grand Central Publishing) 1997.

Chapter 5

THE MAKING OF ORDINARY SAINTS

What if a child could be blessed from the time she is born to be the person she was created to be?

What if the goal of parenting and childhood education were to discover, evoke, support and encourage the True Self inscribed within each child?

What would happen if a child were encouraged from the beginning, even as he was taught the necessary structures for living within a civilized society, to be who he was born to be instead of living out the desires or the agenda, unconscious or conscious, of a parent?

One of the most disturbing things Carl Jung said was that "the greatest burden of the child is the unlived life of the parent." Having to carry either the agenda, the mistakes, or the shame of a parent can stunt the purpose and growth of a child and, in some cases, even murder the soul of that child.

My husband tells me the original meaning of Proverbs 22:6, "Train up a child in the way he should go, and when he is old he will not turn from it," indicates that this is the biblical model for parenting. A child is supposed to be raised to become the person God designed her to be instead of having the culture's or the parent's way imposed on her from the outside. According to this proverb, it is the parent's job to prepare a child for the life he is intended to live instead of the life someone else designs.

Sitting with our three young daughters in the morning service at Southland Baptist Church, I listened intently as my husband preached a sermon, probably on a day when we had baby dedication. He unpacked the original meaning of the Scripture and then charged our church with the task of assisting God in helping children become who they were intended to be.

I remember looking down the row at Michelle, Julie, and Amy and wondering what was in them that needed to be evoked and blessed. What, I wondered, was I doing that supported their growth, and what was I doing that stunted their unfolding process?

My daughters must have been listening as well, because in their own parenting, they have shown sensitivity to the uniqueness of each child. Others who heard my husband's sermon that day have told me that one idea changed their entire way of thinking and being in the world, and it changed their way of parenting.

Abraham Lincoln said, "My concern is not whether God is on our side; my greatest concern is to be on God's side, for God." I am confident that he spoke these words in relation to issues of

> *Train up a child in the way he should go, and when he is old he will not turn from it.*
>
> —PROVERBS 22:6

national concern, but they apply to our daily lives and to our parenting. What if we were on God's side in encouraging the soul's thriving in our children, our spouses, our friends, and even our enemies?

Growing up, the interpretation I heard of Proverbs 22:6 was limiting and limited. Indeed, I believed it was my job as a child and later as an adult to be who the Big People said I should be, conforming to the expectations of family, school, church, and peers.

As I began writing this chapter, I noticed a quote on my calendar of quotations: "Your whole idea about yourself is borrowed from those who have no idea of who they are themselves" (attributed to Osho, an Indian mystic and philosopher). Osho is right, but when a person becomes conscious and takes responsibility for his own life, the authentic Self emerges.

Like you, I have lived my life as a part of systems, organizations, and groups. In those systems, there are guidelines, rules and regulations, norms and mores to keep the system running and help people know what to do. However the rules were established in the beginning and however fair, unfair, appropriate or inappropriate they may still be, the people in the systems are expected to conform and adapt to the rules and regulations. Rules are necessary in a civil society.

There is always the possibility that the same rules that are intended to bring order and stability to the system may constrict and constrain, inhibit and oppress the individuality of those in the system. Sometimes rules and regulations cut off creativity and stifle imagination, and when the rules become more important than the people within the system, life begins to seep away from the system, and the light begins to go out of people's eyes.

I've certainly tried to conform to the systems I value—family, church, friendships, work, country. The religious world I have lived in is considered a conservative and narrow one, and I have spent my life doing what my spiritual director, Sister Mary Dennison, has called "defecting in place." It's not that I've gotten up in the morning and said to myself, "What can I do to disturb the peace today?" Instead, it's that I've wrestled with the system, its dysfunctions, and the places where it stifles and suffocates us.

One of my favorite cartoon characters is Dennis the Menace. From his chair in the corner, he protests, "I may be sitting down, but inside I'm standing up!"

Regardless of the restraints, rules, and regulations of my outer world, there has been a steady beat of freedom somewhere deep within me, and I now understand that drumbeat to be the voice of God who dwells in the kingdom that is within the heart and soul of every individual person.

Perhaps my rebellion has saved my life. Perhaps otherwise, the light would have gone out of my eyes. Perhaps the song that is uniquely mine to sing might have died unsung if I hadn't pushed against the system for my entire life. I dare say as well that I now believe the Spirit of the living God has voiced those protestations against anything that would silence the drumbeat or snuff out the Light within, though when I was young the protestations terrified me, so great was my need to please the people who were the keepers of the rules. Frankly, that steady drumbeat and the drummer have caused me lots of trouble.

In trying to break free of what, as Walt Whitman says in his preface to *Leaves of Grass*, "insults your own soul," I have yearned toward *authenticity*. The dictionary defines authenticity as "the quality of being genuine." I think being real has to mean you are living the life you were meant to live.

Carl Jung called the process of becoming authentic *individuation*, which is not to be confused with individualism. Individuation is the process of becoming who you were designed to be; in my framework, it is becoming who God intended you to be when you were made. Could that also be the process of "being saved"? I think so, though I'm sure that some people in my religious culture would argue with me.

We who grew up in my tradition were taught from childhood the memory verse, "Be perfect, as your father in heaven is perfect," and I suspected then and I know for sure now that the verse was intended to make us behave and threaten shame if we misbehaved (Matt 5:48). Again, my husband's teaching of the meaning of that verse from the original language, which translates "be on the way toward becoming whole," changed my perspective of it. That's greatly different from behaving myself, which typically involved a long list of things I could not do, as if salvation were proven or gained by not doing instead of by being.

Abraham Maslow coined the term "self-actualization" to describe the tendency inscribed within each of us to realize our potential, to express the giftedness and uniqueness that is within us. Thinkers like him who have dared to color outside the lines have much to offer the world of religion and spirituality.

Iraneus, a second-century theologian, said, "The glory of God is a man fully alive." (I'm sure that he intended to include women in his declaration, but had a momentary lapse!)

Standing in a small examining room with my daughter, I almost couldn't breathe. I was so excited about being present at one of her prenatal appointments when the doctor had ordered a sonogram. I wanted to cry when I saw the tiny arms and legs flailing, and we laughed when that small being sucked his thumb. Later, I felt awestruck in the aftermath of the experience, but I also felt that we were intruders into a holy, sacred place. Surely, my grandson Dylan must have been screaming, "Can't you give me a little privacy here? I'm not ready to be scrutinized!"

That we can peer into the womb of a woman and see her unformed child boggles my mind, and I wonder what my mother would say about it! She did not think highly of tampering with what belonged to the realm of Mother Nature. In the recent past, after all, people were murdered for daring to do an autopsy on a human body! We have moved far away from the mystery and sanctity of the human body, and all in the desire to know, to understand, and perhaps to have more control over what sometimes feels and seems and is out of our control.

Now, with the amazing technology available to us, doctors and parents can peer into the world of the unborn child to see if that fetus is developing in a healthy way. The physical development of a human being from pre-birth to death is fairly predictable, and in the first few months and years of a child's life, pediatricians look for particular behaviors and changes to indicate that an infant or child is developing in that predictable way.

There are particular markers, as well, for language and intellectual development. We talk with our children's teachers, who give us report cards of the academic progress of that child. Most parents are now more aware of the athletic, social, and emotional development of their children. Aware parents know that different children develop at different rates.

The reality is that all human beings have many things in common in our development, and each of us is also unique and unlike any other human being who has ever been born. That human beings develop spiritually as well as physically is a foundational principle of this book and of our joint venture with God.

James Fowler's work on the stages of faith development across the life span was my introduction to the idea that there is a process in the life of faith. Fowler, a developmental psychologist at Candler School of Theology, wrote what has become a classic book, *The Stages of Faith*, in which he proposed a staged development of faith across the life span of the individual. His work is closely related to the work of Jean Piaget, Erik Erikson, and Lawrence Kohlberg, who wrote about the psychological development of adults and children.

One of the most important people in my spiritual formation is Keith Hosey, Catholic priest and the former director of the John XXIII Retreat Center in Harford City, Indiana. Keith taught us in practical, earthy ways to pray with our lives, to pray with nature, and to place ourselves in the frame of mind and heart in which we could experience the presence of God in the ordinary, everyday moments of life. Speaking at a contemplative retreat at Laity Lodge, he used a time line to introduce the idea of how faith is formed. On that time line, Keith described the various stages of faith development by comparing them to water, earth, space, fire, and wind—all elements of the natural world.

I have used this time line with Keith's permission, though he does not remember presenting it. That he doesn't always makes us laugh. Of course, he was giving close to eighty retreats a year during those days, and so it is understandable that he might forget some of his material. I, however, have never forgotten it.

When I present this time line in a retreat or workshop setting, I ask people to reflect on their lives with open hearts and minds, with compassion and love. I also ask those who are parents not to sabotage their personal process of understanding their own lives by judging how well they parent and then sliding into parental guilt. Basically, the time line is intended to enlighten us and help us answer two questions: Who is God to me? Who am I to God?

Often, too, I use this time line in working with individuals in the sacred process of spiritual direction. The process helps a person step back from his life and gain a larger perspective of it. Often, there are breakthroughs of understanding as to why a particular event happened or what the meaning of a certain choice was. Always, I sense a growing respect for one's own life, as if the person begins to see her life through the compassionate eyes of grace.

Before introducing the time line, however, it is important to know these things:

- This is merely a pattern of how spiritual formation might take place according to the needs of an individual at the various stages of the life cycle.
- The time line is intended to show an ideal path of spiritual formation, but no one's life is ideal.
- The ages and stages of development are not fixed. People can get stuck in stages of development and be forced through external crises to skip an entire stage of development.
- The time line is intended to increase your understanding of your "one wild and precious life" so that you can then, with increased understanding, embrace and let go of the experiences that have wounded you, allow yourself to see your life with tenderness and compassion, and understand the patterns of thought and behavior that have led you to make your choices.

With these thoughts in mind, draw a line across a sheet of paper. On the left end of the time line, write the date of your birth. Then read through these stages and consider marking events that signal the turning points during each stage.

The first stage of faith development/spiritual formation is called the water stage, and it begins at birth. Some believe this process begins even before birth, when the child is held in the mother's womb in the amniotic waters. I believe intuitively that a fetus knows in utero whether she is wanted or not.

Imagine yourself standing at the edge of the ocean, letting the waves roll in and over your feet. In your mind's eye, see the water's clarity and transparency. Watch it carry any debris back out into the ocean.

Babies are like water. They are transparent and open, fluid and moving. When they feel something, they express it. When they are hungry or hurting, they cry; when they are happy, their whole bodies wiggle and squirm with joy.

Until they are about five or six years old, children absorb the moods and tone of the big people who care for them, just as water absorbs what it surrounds, and they are good barometers of the adults' states of feeling. They pick up tone of voice, note the roughness or gentleness of their caregivers, and observe everything around them. Again, my favorite cartoon character Dennis the Menace explained to Margaret, "I know everything that's going on; I just don't understand it."

During this time in a child's life, his image of God is formed. That image of God, the picture of God that the child will carry in his head for decades, is formed unconsciously and at an emotional level, and it is based on the child's earliest caregivers and authority figures. If the caregivers are present, attentive, and reasonably consistent, the child will have an easy time believing in a God who is trustworthy, loving, and present. If, on the other hand, the child is abandoned, abused, or neglected by his earliest caregivers or authority figures, those demi-gods that loom large in his daily life, he will come to view God in the same way.

> *What is necessary to change a person is to change his awareness of himself.*
>
> —EPICTETUS

During this stage of development, a child needs tenderness, gentleness, and consistent care. He needs to be delighted in; he needs the gaze of approval for who he is. A child needs to know that the people who brought him into the world are glad he made the trip.

"I'm glad you were born," I began telling my loved ones a few years ago. I am acutely aware that all children are not greeted with delight, and it has become important to me that the people I love know that their presence in my life brings me joy and pleasure.

During this season, children are almost natural believers in God, and it is easy for a child to believe in mystery. Prayers for children are simple, self-centered, and uncluttered: "Thank you for my puppy." "Bless my mommy."

I often tell the story about a little boy whose parents brought home a baby sister. The brother asked if he could be alone with the baby, and finally the parents conceded. They stepped outside the nursery, leaving the door slightly ajar so that they could make sure all went well within the nursery. They watched as the big brother moved his stool to the baby's bassinet, climbed up on the stool, and then leaned over into the bassinet. "Tell me, little sister, what heaven is like. I've almost forgotten."

Telling that story in Hereford, Texas, evoked the same responses I usually get no matter where I am. On that night, however, I received the surprise of another story of children's ease with the Mystery. A couple came up to me at break and said, "We have a story for you."

The man telling the story was dressed in a starched shirt and jeans. He had the telltale hat line of West Texas men from living his life in the sun. "I wasn't raised learning Bible stories," he began, "but when we had our boys, my wife told me I had to read them a Bible story every night."

He went on to tell me how one night he was reading a story about Moses, and he made the point that no one had ever seen God. "I've seen God, Daddy," his two-year-old argued, stopping this father mid-sentence.

"You have?" the father asked, eager to hear what the child had contrived. "When was that?"

"He kissed me," the child responded, knowingly, "right before he sent me to you."

Children understand the mysterious presence of the numinous. They have no problem believing in the reality of a God we cannot see but can know. Children know God in an innocent, trusting way—before adults program that belief out of them.

Speaking at an Episcopal Church in Houston this past winter, I told that story. At the break a woman came up to me and shared that when her sister's son was about three, he spontaneously said to her, "Mommy, remember when I was still up in heaven with God, I looked down to earth and chose you and Daddy as my parents?"

My own granddaughter Madeleine said to me when she was five, "Mia [her name for me], sometimes I see your mother." I turned, stunned, to look at her and she quickly said, "Not for real. In my imagination."

Not wanting to stifle either her imagination or the possibility of a mystical experience, I simply said, "Really?"

She sat still for a few moments as I continued doing whatever I was doing. Then she said, "She always tells me to tell you that she loves you."

When a child is born, the first question he begins asking, albeit unconsciously, is "Who is in charge here?" and then, "What do I have to do to get them to take care of me?" Thus, the ego quickly begins to form in order to help the child navigate life. The ego, the central organ of consciousness, is the accommodating, conforming part of us that begins to shift and shape itself around outer-world expectations in order to survive and as a defense against the universal fear of abandonment.

I hear people say, "He has an ego," and I say, "Of course. We all do." What is meant by that statement is actually, "He is egotistical."

In Jungian psychology, however, the ego is essential for getting around in the world, paying our bills, and getting things done; it is what we present to the world through persona, image, the roles we play, and the masks we wear. It is also sometimes expressed in our defense mechanisms. The ego is "who we think we are," but it is not all we are.

I've heard debates about when ego begins to form, and I'm guessing the time varies with the child, but I'm pretty sure that the moment a child learns to shut down what he's feeling or thinking in order to please, placate, manipulate, accommodate, divert, or conform to the needs or desires of the parent, the ego is birthed.

The ego's job is to maintain status quo. It loves predictability, familiarity, and homeostasis, and it does not like pain or suffering. The ego's attachment is to the outer world. While the work of the True Self is about being, the ego is about doing.

The next stage of faith development is called the earth stage.

The earth stage starts, in chronological order, at about age six, or when the child starts first grade. During this phase of development, the child thinks in concrete terms. Children are either/or, good/bad thinkers. This is called the earth stage, according to Keith Hosey, because it is a time in a child's life when he needs to run and play outside, connected by bare feet to the earth. It is a time when a child needs to get grounded. Whereas the water stage is a fluid and open stage, the earth stage brings a need for rules, routine, and ritual in the child's development.

During this period, a child learns the rules of being civilized, or at least you hope she does so that she can fit in, achieve and accomplish appropriate goals with her peers, her teachers, and the world she inhabits. At this point, a child begins to be graded on performance, on what she does, and so the issue of competition enters her world.

In the earth stage, a child begins learning the difference between right and wrong, and so God is Judge and Jury. The child attempts to bring order into his world, and prayers are often memorized. During this time, a child needs to learn the fundamentals of various areas—music, sports, religion— and much of what he learns at this stage of development is by rote, by memory. Who does not remember prayers, memory verses, and poems you learned during this time of development when the brain was most open to memory work? Often, adults in crisis or at the death of a parent will tell me that the Scriptures, songs, or prayers learned in childhood come back to them, as if springing from an ancient wellspring to comfort or sustain them through a difficult time.

When I began taking piano lessons, I learned the scales and arpeggios and was given finger exercises to strengthen my agility and flexibility.

Learning the basics of playing the piano made it possible, later on, to begin to play actual melodies and songs and to improvise.

My husband, Martus, was an all-state basketball player when he was in high school in Springdale, Arkansas. He tells about how the team would win a championship one night, and the next morning the coach would have them running laps and practicing basic drills over and over. "I want you to know the fundamentals so well that when you are in the game and the pressure's on, you will know what to do instinctively," the coach told them.

When moving from West Texas to Houston, I was charmed by the tall oak trees in the city, and one day, as I was walking in our neighborhood, I spotted a tree house. I saw what I thought had to be the rules of the tree house posted on the tree, and so I went to the fence, stood on my tiptoes, and read the "rools" for the club: "No gurls" and "No spitting."

Once the rules were in place, the boys could have their club.

Children are open to learning and need to learn the fundamentals of a faith tradition during this time, and such fundamentals provide the child with the structure, security, and stability that comes from being grounded. What is challenging is giving enough of the rules (the roots) to help the child form a good foundation in faith, but not so much that he gets root rot in too tight a container. There is, after all, an enormous difference between knowing the fundamentals of something and being a fundamentalist.

Many children of the 1960s and 1970s grew up in a time when freedom from rules was considered a healthy break from the real or perceived rigidity of previous decades. Often, people who do not get the initial grounding they need spend their entire lives looking for security from external authorities. Sometimes, they become unable to conform to any outer authority, including bosses, superiors, or supervisors.

Fundamentalism in all religions is flourishing worldwide, possibly as a reaction to the overpermissiveness of the 1960s and 1970s and the rapidly changing world in which we live. Because every part of life that we thought was predictable is in turmoil, including our families, the prominence of fundamentalism and feel-goodism in religion is flourishing as a natural compensation. Fundamentalism gives a feeling of certainty and security; feel-good, entertainment religion offers escape but does not provide a means for transformation.

For those of us who got too much of the rules, the danger is in spending our lives rebelling against the rules. When my husband and I started a new church in San Angelo, Texas, in 1978, we began with others who had also had too much of the rules and not enough of the joy in religious life. When others who had not had our strict upbringing came into our church, they were drawn at first to the freedom and warmth, but then they got scared. Finding a balance between too much and not enough is always a challenge, and the challenge begins again every morning.

The name Keith gave to the season of faith development that begins at puberty (whenever that is) and ends when a person becomes an adult is the space age. Things get interesting in the turbulent time known as adolescence.

During this season of faith development, adolescents become "spacey," thinking their own lofty thoughts, dreaming their own dreams of how life will be for them when they leave their parents' home, and focusing intensely on their own lives. Adolescents want to be in their rooms with the doors closed, in their own space, and they are drawn to friends and peers of their own choosing.

For the adolescent, God often becomes an idea to ponder or a theory to debate, and prayer is self-centered. As the child builds energy to make the separation from the parents and leave home, it is natural for him to be self-absorbed and self-centered. We hope he grows out of this adolescent self-concern, but in adolescence it's appropriate.

It is part of the job of adolescents to begin questioning and challenging what they have been taught, and it is not uncommon for children to come back from freshman year in college announcing that they no longer believe in God. When my husband was in campus ministry, it was a regular occurrence for a freshman or sophomore to come into his office and announce, either with fear, guilt, or defiance, that she no longer believed in God.

"Tell me about that God you don't believe in," my husband always said, opening the door for an adult-to-adult conversation about the God-image the student carried. "I probably don't believe in that God, either," he would say, acknowledging that the God-image we formed in childhood is likely inadequate

> *We are accountable for the life we have lived; we are accountable for the life we have not lived.*
>
> —JAMES HOLLIS

for the challenges of adolescence and the rigors of college life. Besides, forming one's own faith is part of the necessary separation from parents.

"By the time your kid is fourteen, you've done your job," Keith Hosey said, and there was a shocked silence in the Great Hall at Laity Lodge. I sucked in my breath; my girls were still young and impressionable, and I wanted to believe I was going to continue to have influence on them. Whenever I repeat Keith's wisdom, I always hear protests.

Keith explained that what most parents in America do is counter to the needs of the child. In infancy and childhood, parents are typically permissive and give latitude at a time when a child needs the security of consistency, routine, and healthy boundaries and limits. When the child approaches puberty, the parents get scared and begin clamping down when the child's developmental need is for freedom. "We get it backwards in our country," he said.

This is when parents often go into orbit because we remember how we were and what we did when we were adolescents. We want to believe we have control over our children, and our need for this control kicks into high gear when our children are about to leave home. The truth is that what haunts every parent is the "twenty-second" rule. You know what it is: you make a decision that, in twenty seconds, changes your life forever.

When our oldest daughter, Michelle, was going into John Glenn Junior High School in San Angelo, my husband asked our friend Gary Sanderford, a favorite science teacher at that school, if things were as bad as we'd heard among the students.

Gary's wisdom formed much of our attitude for the coming nine years that we would have a student in the school. "There's everything in that school that scares the parents, Martus," Gary said. "Drugs. Alcohol. Sex. Mostly, we have good kids who stay out of trouble and do their work, but the real problem is that the parents get scared and project fear onto their kids, and it's like the kids feel obligated to act it out!"

The next phase of faith development is called the fire stage, which begins whenever a person assumes responsibility for his own life.

"When are you an adult?" James Hollis asked one night in a class at the Jung Center in Houston, and various people offered a variety of answers. Is it when you leave your parents' house and set up your own residence, get your first full-time job, or get married? Are you an adult when you can buy beer or vote? What about people who are still on their parents' payroll up into their thirties because of extended educational processes or because they simply *are*? Are you really an adult if you're still supported by your parents?

In today's world, adolescence is sometimes extended into the thirties, which makes this transitional stage last a long time.

For the purpose of this time line, let's posit the idea that you are an adult when you begin your career, take your first full-time job, or set up your own home, whether you are married or single. The fire stage is the period of life when you have the torch to your back and the fire in your belly; you are setting the world on fire, building your resume and your reputation, and raising a family. It is a time of intense energy that is directed outward in achievement, accomplishment, and acquisition. During this season, you are involved in making it in your world, whatever that means, and establishing yourself in a career and in your community.

"During this stage of life," I remember Keith's saying, "God goes on vacation."

It's not that God goes away, but you are so busy that your prayers are likely to be of the "Are you running with me, Jesus?" variety. In this time, the sign of "success" is an overbooked calendar and a rushed life. Even if you are involved in a church, you could be over-involved and overzealous in church activities, so that what you are doing is still directed to the outer world. It is still about the ego, making change in the outer world one way or another, or being directed by events, motivations, people, and stimuli from outside yourself.

People always get nervous when they hear about the fire stage. We hate to admit the truth of that time. The more resources an individual has— either financial, educational, social, familial, or personal, whether earned or inherited—the less a person needs to rely on God. The better you are able to take care of your own life, the less you need God, even if you are a religious person and an active member of a church.

My husband and I were a part of starting that new church when we were in our mid-thirties, and most of the people with us were also young and full of energy and drive. Of course, the church took off and soared because collectively our members brought enormous energy, talents, and gifts to the process. We also brought a strong sense of purpose and calling to the formation of the church, and we believed God was blessing us. On the other hand, we were moving forward and ahead, and while we did pray and ask for God to guide us and show us the way, the truth is that we had push and force that came from our own power and youthful enthusiasm. Being a part of that initiative for fourteen years was a grand and glorious experience, and I would do it again in a heartbeat, but this time I'd use a different set of strengths and a different source of power.

The one thing we know for sure about life is that nothing stays the same forever. Change is the one sure constant. At some time, there comes a turning point.

I am convinced that all of life is sacred and that choosing to reflect deeply on your history gives value and meaning to it. Reading your life, coming to an understanding of what shaped and formed you, is a sacred process. Looking with eyes of love and compassion at the events that helped you or harmed you can help you see how God has been at work.

What is man that you are mindful of him, the son of man that you care for him? You made him a little lower than the heavenly beings and crowned him with glory and honor.

—PSALM 8:4-5

When I was younger, I found Romans 8:28 to be troubling when it was read in the older translations. Even as a young girl, I'd seen enough tragedy and sorrow to doubt that "All things work together for good for those who love God and are called according to his purpose," and I heard my father talk about how inappropriate it was for people, albeit well-meaning, to use that Scripture as a bromide for suffering individuals.

Much better, I think, is the Scripture as it is rendered in the newer, more accurate translations. Putting the primary mover in creation as the subject changes everything: "God is at work in all things, attempting to bring about good." Now *that* makes sense. God, the Verb, is present, active, alive, and working for good in all things and even in our suffering.

In using this time line for three decades, I have learned these things:

• Upon reflection and with time, an open mind, and an open heart, I can begin to see that God has truly been at work in my life. Over time, I've become convinced that God has been and is at work for good, and it is my job to discern what God is doing and to cooperate with that goodness.
• You can use this time line to look at your relationship to various parts of yourself, and in doing that, you can gain insight and understanding about your whole life.
• You can use this time line to mark the big turning points in your life, looking for what led to those turning points, what stage of development you

were in at the time, and how that turning point (usually a crisis) affected your faith development or precipitated a crisis of faith.

- It is helpful to ask these questions about each stage of faith development:
  - Who was there for me? Whom could I count on, and who let me down?
  - Who was the face of God, the hands and feet and heart of Christ, to me?
  - Who hurt me? What did I decide in that experience about myself, others, and God?
  - Did I make decisions that helped me or hurt me?
- At any given time, you can be at one stage of development in one area of your life and in another stage of development in another area of your life.
- What part of your history needs to be revisited in order to help you move forward?
- What stage did you skip altogether? Where are you stuck in a stage of development?

To make this time line even more interesting, look around on Sunday morning when you are gathered for worship, and think about how every person there has his or her own journey. Sometimes, those who look like adults may still be in a previous stage of development. Imagine what it is like trying to plan educational processes for this group, each with his or her own image of God and in one stage of development or another. What about making decisions together? If you are part of a particular denomination, in what stage of faith development is your denomination? Wherever there is a conflict over doctrine, could it be a conflict of one stage of faith with another stage?

Look around you the next time you stand in a line at the bank or the grocery store, or perhaps even the voting line, and wonder about the image of God each person carries. Think about whether the person's image of God is a wounding image or a healing one, and wonder about the stage of faith development in which that person might be.

Carl Jung said he didn't worry if people had a god or not, but that which god a person chose was of concern. What God do you serve?

How big is your God?

Is your God big enough for the challenges you face?

And how does your self-image reflect your God-image?

Chapter 6

HITTING THE WALL

It was one of those pristine summer mornings in the Frio Canyon when I first heard Keith Hosey compare the stages of life to the elements of the universe. Satisfied by the good food, restored by the hours of silence, and enchanted by the gifts of nature—the canyon wren trilling the scale outside, the cool waters of the Frio River, the solid rock formations of the canyon wall—I'd settled in for the morning's lecture in the Great Hall.

I was young enough to still hang on to the unconscious belief that if I did the right things, life would be good to me. Tucked away at a contemplative retreat in the beautiful setting of Laity Lodge, I got the idea that if I could turn my will and my life over to the care of God thoroughly and sincerely and often *enough*, I would experience life in all its abundance. If I could make better choices, work harder at knowing myself, be more loving, and *have enough faith*, I could finally solve the issues that troubled me and be able to transcend my faults and failings.

I had also seen and experienced enough tragedy and suffering in my lifetime to know that, indeed, the rain falls on the just and the unjust.

In his presentation on the stages of faith, Keith Hosey said that at some time around mid-life, somethings happens that has the potential of moving us into what he called the best stage of life, the *wind stage*.

When I first heard that stage of life described, I was eager for it, but then as I listened intently to Keith's description of the transition from the fire stage to the wind stage, I realized that there was no guarantee that the transition would be smooth or easy.

The spiritual journey is not a linear, clear path from beginning to end, but more a circular and sometimes circuitous path. The children of Israel wandered around in the desert for forty years before finally making it from bondage to the promised land. On the journey, we circle back to the same issues. We take a step forward and two steps back, and along the way we don't discard our histories. We carry them with us.

"I thought I'd taken care of this issue," I've lamented when faced with a nagging character flaw, a repetitive self-sabotaging pattern, an old problem that won't go away no matter how many approaches I take to solving it or obliterating it from my life.

The child I was is still with me, and given the right stimulus in the outer world, she can come roaring back from the basement of my consciousness, either needing attention of one kind or another or making me act like a two-year-old. At other times, the free child in me helps me live in the present moment, and sometimes she helps me play. The adolescent I was is still a part of me as well, and sometimes she keeps me young and open to life, and sometimes she gets moody or rebellious. The adolescent helps me remember my dreams and stand up to the oppressive critical judge or heavy-handed parent who tries to keep me bound.

In the middle of the journey of our life I came to myself in a dark wood where the straight way was lost.

—DANTE ALIGHIERI

"The great thing about getting older," Madeleine L'Engle said one day at a Writer's Retreat at Laity Lodge, "is that you don't lose all the other ages you've been."

I'll never forget the session in which Keith Hosey described what happens around midlife, describing it as "the big boom." As he talked, I knew I was chronologically at the right place for a midlife transition. I had all the symptoms, and having a name for what was happening to me was comforting, just as it is comforting to go to the doctor and finally get a diagnosis for vague, nonspecific, troubling symptoms that won't respond to the home remedies that have worked in the past.

What Keith told us is true. At some point in the adult journey, something happens to set us on a new path. While it is true that events—crises, tragedies, unusual opportunities—happen to individuals in childhood and adolescence that can either deepen or stymie spiritual growth, during midlife something happens that forces a change and a reorientation toward life. The course from birth to death is smoother for some than for others, but ultimately life happens to everyone who survives to midlife.

THE AWAKENING

If only every one of us could be ushered into the next phase of life with something as easy and pleasant as an awakening to life in a new way. Indeed, it is possible to hear a lecture, a sermon, or a song and suddenly realize that your vision is clear and you see the world in a new way. How wonderful it is to find a teacher who inspires you so much that you will follow him or her to the ends of the earth to learn what you can from that one person.

Jesus drew people to him in such a way that they left their old ways of life to follow him into the unknown. Indeed, the call of Jesus to the disciples and his involvement with the significant women in the Gospel narrative—the woman at the well, Mary Magdalene, Mary and Martha, and the others, named and unnamed, who attended him and traveled with him—must have been an awakening for them, a call that fired their imaginations in such a way that they were compelled to venture forth toward a new way of being in the world.

We also wake up when we begin to see ourselves or our lives in a new way, and any number of factors can prompt that onset of new sight or insight into the way things work. One of the things Jesus did was open peoples' eyes to who they were or who they could be. Healed of various forms of illness, individuals were given new chances and new roles. Waking up in a new world in which you feel different can be an exhilarating and sometimes frightening experience.

Couldn't it be said that Jesus' invitation to his followers then and to us now was and is the same call of God to Abraham? "Leave that which has become familiar and go to a land that I will show you" is a universal call, and it is the call of the midlife journey. Usually, the invitation does not come in a fancy envelope, written in beautiful calligraphy, but in the form of something that makes life uncomfortable or makes us uncomfortable in our lives.

THE HUNGER

For some, the midlife transition begins when, after spending a couple of decades building the perfect life—achieving, acquiring, and accomplishing the goals you'd set out to reach—you wake up one morning with a strange yearning. An old song sung by Peggy Lee describes this hunger with the mournful line, "Is this all there is?"

Accompanied often by a sense of guilt because you have so many blessings, you may try to talk yourself out of your dissatisfaction. Other people may try to shame you out of it if you share your feelings with them by asking, "Isn't this what you wanted? Why can't you be satisfied? Look at all you have! You should be grateful."

It is trite but common to hear a man at midlife talk about having spent his adult years relentlessly climbing the ladder of success only to discover that the ladder was leaned against the wrong wall or a wall that was going nowhere. Women who have invested their early adult years primarily in caring for their husbands and children often wake up to the reality that they have left their own lives behind. Woody Allen defines codependency as the state of being in which, if you're dying, someone else's life passes before your eyes!

In his book *What Matters Most: Living a More Considered Life*, Jungian analyst James Hollis writes poignantly about how we often live lives too small for our souls. However, he says the True Self or psyche will eventually come calling, demanding to be heard and expressed. Often that hunger shows up as depression, a sense of futility or despair.

THE THORN IN THE FLESH

The apostle Paul talked about his thorn in the flesh, and through the years various theories have been proposed as to what the problem that wouldn't go away actually was. As I have heard those theories through the years, I've often thought about the issue of projection; perhaps those who are sure about Paul's stubborn problem are projecting their own stubborn problem onto him.

Regardless of what Paul's thorn in the flesh was, it seems that there are things in every life that won't go away, and often at midlife they often come calling in such a way that we can't deny or ignore them any longer. They belong to us.

A thorn in the flesh can be a character defect, an addiction, or a physical condition that you have been able to avoid or ignore during your youth, but that suddenly becomes a major issue. At some point, you either have to call it what it is or become its victim. An incident in childhood, a mistake you made in adolescence, a troublesome relationship that you cannot avoid or end qualify as thorns in the flesh. Sometimes, too, there is a person in your life who affects and sometimes controls your life in such a way that your life quality is compromised.

On the contemplative retreat when I was first introduced to the time line of spiritual formation, Keith Hosey spoke at length about how a child is welcomed into the world . . . or not. He talked about how an infant knows before she is born if she is wanted. I listened intently, remembering how much I had wanted each of my three daughters and how from the moment each was born, she was exactly who I wanted her to be.

At another level, Keith's words about one's birth touched something tender in me, something I didn't want to know or feel. I felt that if I allowed whatever it was into my conscious mind, it might be too painful, so I kept focusing on how much I delighted in the birth of each of my daughters and how glad I was that each of them was so *wanted*.

Two days into the retreat, I chose to skip the morning session and go to the jogging track to get in my run before the fierce Texas heat became unbearable. As I began to run in that shaded area above the river, I started to cry, but I wasn't sure why. Soon, I was sobbing, and when I finished my run I walked away from the track, toward the river, and found a good sitting rock. Something vague, unconscious to me, and deeply painful was boiling just below the surface of my conscious mind.

Suddenly, unbidden, these words came to me: "On the day you were born, the angels danced!" I don't know if I'd seen those words on a greeting card or if they simply came to me, but with them came a new torrent of tears. Keith had told us that we might tap into a wellspring of tears, and he had said, "Remember, tears are the body's way of praying."

At the moment, I couldn't allow myself to articulate what was happening within some deep place in my soul, but I knew it was significant. Years later I would hear Thomas Keating describe how deep, Centering Prayer gave the Divine Therapist permission to go into our buried emotional knots and begin to heal the emotional programming of a lifetime. When he said that, my mind traveled quickly back to that moment, and I knew it was the moment when the Divine Therapist began working from within to heal a wound of a lifetime.

As I began to feel quiet and still again, I had a flashback that is inexplicable if you think in logical, sequential terms, but if you understand *kairos* time, it makes sense.[1] In that moment, I felt as if I could remember myself as a newborn in the nursery of the hospital where I was born, and I had the sense that God had come to get me and had never let me go. In the amazing way of being in *kairos* time, I was actually sitting on a rock overlooking the Frio River at Laity Lodge, but in another dimension I was aware of being in the newborn nursery in Sweetwater, Texas, already learning how to adapt and conform to the world as it was for me.

The Divine Therapist, I have learned, is not bound by time or space.

THE JOB EXPERIENCE

"Does everyone hit the wall at midlife?" I'm always asked, usually by someone who is still in the fire stage and is likely hoping to be good enough, smart enough, or spiritual enough to avoid what Keith called "the big boom."

We all hope to avoid the sudden crisis that changes your life in one phone call or one moment when you made one choice instead of another choice.

I've written about the Job experience in my book *Sitting Strong: Wrestling with the Ornery God* (Smyth & Helwys, 2006), and in it I've defined a "Job experience" as a life-altering event. From that point on, you date your life as "before" or "after" the event. The sudden blitz may come in the form of a bad health report, the death of a spouse or a child, a financial collapse, a personal or family scandal, a crippling illness or a debilitating accident, a divorce, or a call from the police department about your child.

Other Job experiences come when a long-term problem, illness, or issue that has been gathering force for some time suddenly becomes a crisis. A Job experience with a uniquely bitter and painful component is one in which you have caused suffering or loss for another person.

A Job experience is different from a problem you can solve, an irritation or an annoyance. You know it is a Job experience because no matter what resources you have at your disposal, you aren't rich enough, smart enough, pretty enough, well-connected enough, religious enough, or anything enough to fix it. You know it is a Job experience when you are thrown on the ash heap, like Job, and you will either learn how to carry the suffering in a transformative way, or you will buckle under the pain and agony of it.

FOLLOWING YOUR CALLING/BEARING YOUR BURDEN

Over the years, I have expanded my understanding of a particular expression of the midlife crisis: "following your calling" or "bearing your burden." For a while, I interpreted this expression as "using your gifts to alleviate the suffering of others," and I still believe in that sacred calling.

When my husband and I started the church in San Angelo, we were heavily influenced by the teachings of Gordon Cosby and Elizabeth O'Connor at the Church of the Savior in Washington, DC. Back from his duties as a chaplain in World War II, Cosby formed a new kind of church that emphasized the importance of balance between the inward and outward journeys of faith. This church required that each member be part of a small group of accountability, identify his or her own calling, and then express that calling in ministry. Martus and I attended a four-day retreat at Wellspring, the retreat center for the Church of the Savior. While there, I experienced a twenty-four-hour period of silence, and through that experience I found my spiritual home in contemplative prayer, a discovery that shaped the rest of my life and led me down paths for which I think I had always hungered.

The next year, we returned for an eight-day workshop. In a group process that lasted several days and concluded with a lengthy session with Gordon Cosby teaching us about call and gifts, I did something that radically altered my understanding of myself and my place in the world. Because of my upbringing and other factors, I'd wanted only to be a wife and mother, and even as I write these words today, I am struck by how strange they seem in modern times. Nevertheless, that was what I wanted, and I had a good start on that goal.

However, Gordon asked each of us to write and then state our personal call within the small group in which we had spent the day. Hesitantly and timidly, I wrote out this call: "I believe I am called to reconcile people to God and people to each other through writing and teaching."

Fear not . . .
When you pass through the waters,
I will be with you;
and when you pass through the rivers,
they will not sweep over you.
When you walk through the fire,
you will not be burned
the flames will not set you ablaze . . .
Do not be afraid . . . for I am with you.

—ISAIAH 43:1A, 2-3, 5A

Looking back, it makes me sad to realize how it scared me to state that call aloud. Who did I think I was to make such a bold claim about my life? What would "they" think upon hearing such a big assertion? I told myself that once we left the retreat center, I could forget about my calling and would likely never see the group participants again.

Without hesitation, every person in the group instantly affirmed my statement of my calling. Stunned, I went home with a new sense of who I was and what I was to do in the world.

Following my calling has changed my life. I've had to stand up to my original programming, to the role expectations of my world, and to my inner demons and complexes in order to be and become what God had in mind when he—or she—made me.

In recent years, however, I have added another dimension to this particular crisis in the life of an adult, and that is the challenge of becoming authentically who you are, of individuation, of becoming saved and whole and healthy. Indeed, we are to bear the cross of our own uniqueness, and we are to become conscious. It is our moral responsibility.

I am struck by the fact that from the cross Jesus prayed for those who had crucified him, "Forgive them, for *they do not know what they are doing*" (Luke 23:34). Could it be true that *unconsciousness, not knowing what you are doing*, is an affront to God, a moral violation, a sin?

As adults, we are responsible for our gifts and for our character defects. We are responsible for how we handle our misfortunes and for what we do with failures. We are stewards of our talents and our opportunities, and we are stewards of the blessings we do not earn and for those for which we pay dearly. Fortunately, God is merciful, compassionate, and full of kindness, and I believe God gives us many chances to start anew.

I'm reminded of the fact that following one's calling and living the authentic life or the hero's journey can be fraught with frequent and unexpected blocks in the road and less than generous responses on the part of those who love you most. In an early draft of *The Lord of the Rings*, J. R. R. Tolkien had Gildor the Elf say, "If you go looking for Adventure, you will usually find as much of it as you can manage. And it often happens that when you think it is ahead, it comes on you unexpectedly from behind."

As far as I'm concerned, there's not much cuter than a one-year-old trying to learn to walk and talk, and no matter how many times I see a yearling make that journey from all fours to standing on two feet, I'm thrilled. What is it, I wonder, that makes a child suddenly decide to *stand up*? What gives the child the impetus and the courage to take the first step and keep taking steps, no matter how many times he falls? What pushes a child to get up over and over, even after a bad tumble, and keep practicing putting one tiny little foot in front of another until soon she is walking and then running and climbing and, someday, dancing?

Dylan Thomas's image of "the force that through the green fuse drives the flower" is the same life force coursing through a child that makes him yearn to be mobile and that somehow sends the signal that it is time to walk.[2] It is the same force that begins stirring in an adolescent, telling her it is time to grow up and move on and out into her life. We are driven from within by both known and hidden forces to progress, to grow, to stretch ourselves, and to learn how to walk and run and dance, symbolically, over and over.

Yet it seems that when we hit the wall of the midlife transition, we either freeze in terror before the largeness of the task before us or we regress into an earlier stage of life, as if we feel a need to pick up crumbs we left along the way. We think we need them to find our way through the deep, dark forest of the unknown. I don't know that I have ever seen someone confronted by drastic change who jumps up and down, shouting, "Oh, good! I'm going to get to grow some more!"

What I have observed is that some people, confronted by life's midlife challenges, often regress to the fire stage and simply work harder and longer, as if doing more of the same thing will result in a different outcome. Analyst Pittman McGehee says, "That which keeps you alive in the first half of life can keep you from living in the second half of life."

"God helps those who helps themselves" is often the mantra of those who regress to the fire stage. In the effort to help herself, the person tends toward self-reliance and independence, both good qualities, which prevent her from stepping up to the plate of her life, calling issues what they are, and then pushing through them to the other side and the next stage of faith development.

Some people go backwards in time to the space stage of their teenage years and try to retrieve something they left behind in adolescence, sometimes deciding that a different spouse, a change of geography or career, a new sports car, or a facelift can help them feel young and alive again. "We must *seize the moment*," they say, justifying a lapse into adolescent behavior. "I want to be happy." "You don't understand; I've got to be free!"

Indeed, living in the moment is a hallmark of conscious people, and freedom is one of the gifts we are given in life. It is, however, freedom and not license. The truth is that real freedom carries a corresponding burden of responsibility.

Interestingly, regression to the earth stage can be positive in that it is natural to want to "get organized" after facing a crisis and feeling disoriented, destabilized, or confused. Often I hear people talk about "getting their life together," and in Christian circles people who are in chaos sometimes begin to focus on the laws of the Bible as compensation for a loss of control over their lives.

Getting more rigid and rule-bound, adopting the tenets of fundamentalism, and becoming legalistic (generally wanting other people to straighten up and follow the rules even more than you require them of yourself!) are compensations for the chaos in one's life. They are a way to avoid the challenges of a world in which either/or, right/wrong, good/bad designations of childhood thinking are not adequate for the complexities of adult life.

There are those who regress all the way back to a childish state (the water stage), becoming dependent, passive, and helpless, drowning in the stormy waters of what has happened to them. While I have benefited greatly from much of the work that comes under the category of "inner child healing," I also resist the tendency to encourage irresponsibility and childishness. "I've got to take care of myself" is a good mantra unless taking care of oneself is a synonym for childish narcissism and self-centeredness.

Who doesn't want to escape pain and suffering? Who wouldn't like to avoid the terrors of daily life, not to mention the crises along the way, by submerging oneself into the ecstasy of "worship" or a religion or a religious leader that promises you relief from your problems in exchange for blessings and privilege?

In the Montessori school where five of my grandchildren have been enrolled, a child is transitioned from one class to the next according to his readiness for more advanced learning and complicated tasks. When my granddaughter Madeleine was crawling, she would go to the glass door that separates the baby room from the toddler room and bang on the door until they let her in. She could hardly wait to transition to the next level of development.

However, there were days in that transitional period when she would go back to the baby room, lie on a mat, and suck her thumb. Finally, though, she made her transition to the big room and never went back.

> *The rain, it falleth everywhere,*
> *in the just and the unjust fellow . . .*
> *but more, it seems, on the just,*
> *for the unjust have the just's*
> *umbrella.*
>
> —QUOTED BY MADELEINE L'ENGLE

There is a life force within us that pushes us forward, and yet there is another force that resists the forward movement. We want to grow, but we want to stay safe and comfortable. We want to step into the largeness of our lives, but we also resist getting out of our cozy comfort zone. We want out of our problems, but often not enough to take the required risks because it is hard to grow up.

Our movement through the stages of faith development is never a clear, straight line forward with no pauses, regressions, or stalls along the way. In fact, I'm told regression is a necessary part of the progression, and knowing that, I find that I can be far more patient with others and myself along the rocky path of faith.

At birth, the infant screams in protest at being thrust or taken from the warm womb in which everything is done for him and he is safe and comfortable in the amniotic waters, close to the heartbeat of his mother. Who wouldn't protest leaving that first home and being assaulted by bright lights, noise, cold air, and fabric? Of course babies cry, I've told my daughters as they have tried to soothe an infant's wailings. Perhaps they are mourning the loss of the womb.

Who wouldn't always, at some level, long to return to the maternal home? So it is that in the human journey and what Pittman McGehee calls "a birth we did not request and a grave we cannot escape," we must say good-bye over and over again, and we say it so that we can say hello to the next stage of development.

The system executive for chaplain services for the Memorial Hermann Hospital System in Houston, my friend Tim Van Duivendyk, has attended thousands of deaths, standing by families as they made agonizing choices and said good-bye to their loved ones, and then counseling those family members through the difficult months of learning to live in a world without their loved one.

Grief, Tim writes in his book *The Unwanted Gift of Grief,* is the process we are given to help us make the transition from the way things used to be to the way things are. It is the way we let go of our loved ones or, as it applies to our life's journey, the seasons of life that are over.

When I describe the grief process as it pertains to the life cycle, I don't write the stages of the grief process in a neat list. Instead, I use circles to describe the processes of denial, anger, bargaining, depression, and acceptance. It seems to me that when we are in the process of letting go, we cycle around and back and forth in each one.

We stay especially in denial as long as we can, and yet one of the things I want to avoid most is denial, for I have reaped a bitter harvest on more than one occasion when I have refused to see things as they are or to accept what I know. Frederick Buechner says, "She was right that reality can be harsh and that you shut your eyes to it only at your own peril because if you do not face up to the enemy in all his dark power then the enemy will come up from behind some dark day and destroy you while you are facing the other direction."

We go into shock at sudden, difficult news. We avoid calling things by their real names, and we sometimes filter out information because knowing what we know is too hard. Some people can stay in denial for a lifetime, it seems, and in doing so they avoid stepping up to the challenge of their lives. However, it is possible to move out of that numbed-out, shut-down, half-alive state and cycle over into anger.

In the anger stage of grief, we lash out. We blame someone for what has happened, pointing the finger at another and attacking the ones we believe are at fault. Some anger is clearly identified as anger; other anger is sometimes wrapped and sugarcoated in platitudes and religious bromides, but it is anger nevertheless. Just because we don't want to face it doesn't mean it goes away.

I am drawn to the angry psalms when I am in this state of mind and this stage of grief, for it is comforting to know that the psalmist laid out his feelings before God. Unfiltered, unedited, raw, and sometimes violent, the angry psalms help give language to our agony and show us that God can handle it when we vent our anguish to him.[3]

In a healthy grieving process, we move into the bargaining stage of grief, trying to find yet another diagnosis, one more treatment, a different doctor, or *the reason* this thing has happened. During the bargaining stage, we try desperately to understand what is happening to us, and so we read another book, attend another workshop, or seek some other approach as a defense against the pain.

I have said that for every problem I have encountered in my life, there is a shelf of books in my bookshelf about that problem. Learning everything I can about whatever hurts me or challenges my safety, security, or ease is a coping mechanism for me. It is my way of bargaining with reality. If I can understand it, I can stand it.

After so many efforts to try one more thing that just might be *the answer*, there comes a time when we cycle into depression. Whereas anger is turned outward toward others, depression is anger turned inward on oneself.

For many years I participated in organized efforts to "save my denomination" from the political powers that were in competition within it, powers over which I had no control whatsoever. However, because something that had been meaningful in my life and in my family's life was at stake, I wanted to "help." I'm not sure when I came to the point of accepting that what we had was lost and that what had been was over, but prior to my acceptance of it, I grieved deeply and felt a deep sadness that was like depression.

People grieve in many ways. Some work through the process more quickly than others. Some get stuck at various points along the way, cycling around in what seems to their loved one forever in one of the stages. It is my experience that people can move back and forth among the various stages of grief, but once the move is made to acceptance, the cycling ends.

Acceptance, however, is not resignation. It is not giving up and giving in. It is not an act of weakness or a sign of defeat. Instead, it is an act of strength and courage; perhaps it is the "green fuse that drives the flower," pushing through the layers of the grieving heart to ignite enough of a spark of hope to allow the person to say, "This is what it is. I surrender to it. I will not fight it any longer, but neither will I be defeated by it."

Personally, I rely on the Serenity Prayer of Alcoholics Anonymous, and I have taken the first three steps of the Twelve Steps more times than I can count. "I cannot do anything about this," I have prayed, with my own variation of the first step. "I believe that you can," I continue, and then I offer my own version of "Thy will be done": "I'm going to let you." The short version is, "I can't. You can. I'm going to let you."

Yielding to reality must be accompanied by a sense that you are also yielding to the Power who is greater than you. When I turn my will over to the care of God as I understand God, I am surrendering what is most precious to me to the One who made me and who is present and active in me, for me, and with me.

Acceptance is a radical act of faith. It is an affirmation of life, a yelp of freedom, and a cry of hope. Acceptance is the "Yes!" to the abundant life, the fully engaged life that includes everything.

The moment of acceptance is a transformative moment. *Something* has to happen to make you willing to walk up to the wall you've hit instead of regressing back into an earlier stage of development. Something's got to make you muster the will power to push through the wall and into what Keith Hosey said is the best stage of life, the stage he called the *wind stage*.

From the time we are born, we develop ego strength. To accommodate ourselves to the environment of our parents and then our schoolteachers, our peers, and our bosses and supervisors, we form personas that help us fit in where we are. We develop an image we want to project, depending on the situation. We fulfill roles and put on masks to hide our real feelings, and along the way we develop defense mechanisms to protect ourselves. It's not a federal crime to do this, Jim Hollis often says, but it is the way humans work.

From the time we are born, as well, the primary engagement is from the ego self to the outer world. When the heat gets hot enough and we finally come to the place of surrender, it is necessary to become vulnerable, transparent, and dependent on the Power greater than ourselves—and sometimes on other people. We must open our minds and our hearts to new information and a new way of being in the world. We must absorb what has happened and learn to carry it in ourselves. *Doesn't that sound like the water stage of development?*

How it must have startled the disciples who wanted to secure a place of greatness in the kingdom of heaven—a kingdom they still imaged as a place of privilege, position, and power—when Jesus called a child over to him and said, "Unless you become like a child, you will not enter the kingdom of heaven" (Matt 18:2-3).

According to Jesus, we must become child*like*, but not child*ish* in order to experience the wholeness, health, and abundance of salvation. It is humbling to become childlike, and most adults don't volunteer to be humbled. For some of us, the process is so difficult that it is called *egocide*.

To move into the next stage of life, the wind stage, the ego's way of being in the world up to this point has to die. There has to be a conscious, willful, intentional choice to live another way. When the ego surrenders, it is like a new birth, and the new order changes our orientation in the world. From this pivotal moment, the primary connection is from the True Self to the ego, and the individual begins living from the inside out instead of from the outside in. The inner voice of God, speaking through the unique and authentic Self, begins to be the primary motivating force, and the ego has to take the subordinate role.

NOTES

1. *Kairos* time, which is not measured by minutes and hours, weeks and months, is a moment in time when something unusual happens, when events come together in an unusual way. It may be a moment in time when you can, through the power of memory, re-experience something that happened long ago as if it were happening in the present moment. The bliblical term "fullness of time" is *kairos* time. I'll describe this more fully in chapter 12.

2. Dylan Thomas, "The force that through the green fuse drives the flower," *Collected Poems of Dylan Thomas* (New York: New Directions Publishing, 2003).

3. For a much more detailed exploration of the psalms, see Jeanie Miley, *Ancient Psalms for Contemporary Pilgrims* (Macon: Smyth & Helwys, 2003).

Chapter 7

THE GREAT CONSENTS

When I was a child, my father stood at the front of the sanctuary after the morning service while the choir and congregation sang the invitation hymn. One of them, sung by Cynthia Clawson in the movie *Trip to Bountiful*, begins, "Softly and tenderly Jesus is calling . . . come home." Looking back on the countless invitations I witnessed, I know my dad saw his role as that of welcoming people from wherever they had been wandering to the "home" of eternal life. "Give me your hand," he would plea, "and give Christ your heart."

Jesus himself defines eternal life in John 17:3 as knowing God, and that "knowing" is not merely intellectual assent or the knowledge of facts, but the knowledge that is the fruit of intimacy with God. Eternal life, then, is as much about quality of life as it is length of life.

I know now that that invitation really is about going home—home to God who dwells within, and home to oneself.

Two experiences from Jesus' life reveal the struggle that even he had consenting to his path. Both incidents reveal the struggle to surrender to the calling of the True Self.

In the first account, recorded in Matthew 4:1-11 and in both Mark and Luke in what has been called "the temptations of Jesus," Jesus stands up to the temptations to draw people to him by wielding earthly power, entertaining them with spectacular acts, and or meeting their physical needs. If he had succumbed to any one of these temptations or tactics, he could have drawn a crowd and wielded earthly, ego-driven power over them, but he chose the harder way. Jesus chose to act in peoples' lives in a way that would heal them and transform them, liberate and empower them to be and become all they could be.

The Body of Christ on earth today, the church, must wrestle with those temptations over and over, generation after generation.

As I read about Jesus' agony in the garden before his crucifixion, I am always moved that his vulnerability is made available to us. As the human Jesus at that time, surely his heart was broken that he had seemingly failed to teach the disciples all they needed to know to carry on his transformative work. Surely he felt the agony of the betrayal of those he had loved and called into his work. The poignant plea to his disciples, "Can't you stay awake?" reveals a depth of loneliness and aloneness that resonates in deep places in me.

I resonate with the interpretation of the crucifixion and resurrection that states that the human Jesus had to die in order for the Risen Christ to be born. One of the Scriptures that fascinates me most is the assertion by the writer of the book of Hebrews that "We do not have a high priest who is unable to sympathize with our weaknesses, but we have one who has been tempted in every way, just as we are . . ." (4:15).

In contemplating the life of Jesus for a lifetime, I have decided these things: *The way of Jesus, and thus the way home, is the way of surrendering the ego and allowing the True Self/Christ within to lead, guide, and direct us. The way Jesus shows us in this surrender is the way of truth—telling the truth, living the truth, being authentic—and it is the way of life.*

I have heard Jim Hollis state countless times in his lectures at the C. G. Jung Center in Houston that "every triumph of the Self is experienced as a defeat by the ego," and "the True Self is ruthless in accomplishing its purpose."

Can it possibly be true as well that what is true for us was also true for Jesus?

Indeed, Jesus fulfilled ultimately and completely the purpose for which he was sent, and in the moment of his anguish in the garden of Gethsemane and as he was crucified as a criminal, it appeared that his mission was a failure. Thankfully, the resurrection reveals that the powers of oppression are not the ultimate power or the final word.

I was introduced to the Twelve Steps of Alcoholics Anonymous by my first true friend, Elaine Rohr, when I was only twenty-six. Having grown up in a minister's family, I had been taught that even one drop of an alcoholic beverage would destroy our brain cells. I was also taught that dancing might lead to terrible consequences.

Elaine brought those steps to my house one day, but I had to promise her that I would never tell anyone that I had even seen them and that I would not mention that she had gotten them at Al-Anon, for at that time anonymity was much more of an issue in recovering circles than it is today, when anyone can find the Twelve Steps easily on the Internet or in hundreds of books.

As soon as I read those Twelve Steps, I knew they were for me. I knew they were biblical, which was important to me, and I knew I needed to work the steps, as Elaine was doing in Al-Anon. At first, however, Elaine wasn't even going to let me copy them.

"You're not an alcoholic," she said, "and your spouse isn't an alcoholic, and so you can't have this! Besides, what if someone found out that I had given them to you? I've got to protect the anonymity of the people I've met in Al-Anon!"

Finally, Elaine let me copy the steps, and I began to work through them. Each day after I put my newborn daughter down for her nap, I read one of the steps and journaled about it. I couldn't yet name what was hurting in the place deep within me, but in that first step where you say you are powerless over alcohol, I substituted fear or whatever else presented itself to me at the time as a symptom. I worked alone, except for the processes in the Yokefellow Spiritual Growth group. Of course, I did not confess to them my secret involvement with the Twelve Steps!

One cannot consent to creep when one has the impulse to soar.

—HELEN KELLER

Because of my childhood training, it was easy for me to take the second step and come to believe that a Power greater than myself could restore me to sanity. In spite of the legalism or rigidity of my particular religious group, I also got a healthy helping of the love and compassion of God, God's forgiveness, and a sense that God was active and alive in the world and in our lives. I also had my flashback to the hospital nursery when I was on the jogging trail of Laity Lodge, an experience that occurred years after I was introduced to the Twelve Steps. Although my earliest concept of God was that of a watchful, critical parent who waited for me to mess up, that concept had evolved and grown to include a loving, supportive parent who wanted to help me.

At that time, I was reading books by Paul Tournier and Keith Miller, and they referred back to the teaching and work of Carl Jung.[1] I also learned that Jung had a part in developing the Twelve Steps, working with Bill Wilson (known as Bill W.) in the creation of Alcoholics Anonymous. In an amazing synchronicity, what I needed was coming to me to point my way on "the way." Step by step, I was doing what I could to cooperate with what I believed to be the Divine Therapist, though I did not yet know either what caused me so much pain or what it meant to have one's own Divine Therapist, working on my behalf.

I've heard Jim Hollis say that in his training to be a Jungian analyst, he was taught that you didn't dare strip away a person's defenses; instead, you must tread gently and respectfully. "You never know what is underneath those defenses," Jim said in class one night, "or if the person has the ego strength to survive without them."

Over the next many years, I believe the Divine Therapist was leading me forward, providing the experiences, the processes, and the resources in people, learning opportunities, and books to build my ego strength so that I could at some point face the deep feeling of rejection for who I am and my fear of abandonment. These feelings were so great and pervasive that I learned early to do what was necessary to placate and please "the authorities" in my outer world so that I would never have to be rejected for who I was or abandoned because of who I was again.

My parents loved me, and it would have hurt them terribly to know that I carried such an intense fear of rejection and abandonment. It was never their intent to hurt me, and I know that. I do not blame them for my feelings or put on them what is not their fault.

Nevertheless, by the constellation of various forces in my early, formative years and by events in my early adolescence, I developed the ability to shut down my needs and desires in order to take care of others'. I developed the gift of people pleasing and placating to survive. I could shut down what I thought and felt in order to present the "right" impressions to the outer world, and I learned to live with disapproval from those who were authority figures in my life.

Once during high school, I suddenly burst into tears during a piano lesson because I could not perform as my teacher was insisting that I should be able to do. "Why, Jeanie," she said, "you always seem so happy. Whatever could be wrong?"

Indeed, I *seemed* happy, but that was a persona and mask I'd learned to wear with perfection so I couldn't bother anyone with the turmoil that lay below the surface.

The unvarnished truth is this: an original wounding, an early and profound rejection and abandonment, set me up for a lifetime of codependency and inauthenticity. When I first saw the book *When Pleasing You Is Killing*

Me, I held my breath.[2] Someone else apparently understood, and when I heard the word "codependency," describing how it develops in a child and what it is like for an adult, I felt as if the floor beneath me was trembling.

My earliest childhood decision was "I am not okay as I am," and that decision, made unconsciously, set up all the choices I would make for decades. That one wounding experience was my most primitive and primal and deep wound, and the most unconscious to me for more than four decades. Indeed, as the song declares, "the first cut is the deepest."

Over a lifetime, however, I developed a variety of ways of covering up that wound, which I will describe in the next chapter, but in the mysterious ways of the Divine Therapist, healing and help was set in motion on the day when my friend Elaine brought me the Twelve Steps.

The eleventh step states that "we sought through prayer and meditation to improve our conscious contact with God, seeking only to know his will and to carry it out," and just as fervently as I had worked the first ten steps, I began practicing meditation, which would turn my world upside down and lead me to that pivotal experience on the jogging track at Laity Lodge when I remembered my time in the newborn nursery. As I've mentioned, that experience was one of many over the next several years that helped me recover from my original wounding and learn to live with it in a new way.

Indeed, I was to learn that salvation is both event and process. What I did not know is that the process is a hero's journey and that it will last for a lifetime.

At a conference sponsored by the C. G. Jung Center in Houston and the Honors College at the University of Houston, Connie Zweig, author of the book *Romancing the Shadow*, described her practice of meditation in the 1970s. She talked about how she and her friends used meditation as a way to deal with stress, but the more they meditated, the worse their stress became. Finally, she said, they realized what was happening: they were tapping into what Thomas Keating calls "the emotional programming of a lifetime." As they connected with the depths of their souls, their unconscious, their inner world through the practice of meditation, disturbing emotions and memories rose to the surface, demanding attention.

I was relieved to hear this from someone else, for that is what I had experienced over long years of practicing contemplative prayer. From my earliest experience of "entering the quiet" or "practicing the presence of Christ," I had known that the practice was "home" for me. I was drawn to interior prayer as a deer is drawn to find water. For me, it was essential to my daily life, but I could not understand why I also experienced deep upheavals of emotion.

When I took the third step of the Twelve Steps and "made a decision to turn my will and my life over to the care of God as I understood him," God apparently took me seriously. From that time until this day, I've been on a journey of reconstruction, restoration, renewal, and rebirth. When I chose to begin life as a contemplative and to practice the presence of God in daily life, that too set me on a path of adventure.

Sometimes the wounds of a lifetime are healed instantaneously, I suppose, but more likely they are healed in a process, and in that process you have to say no to some things and yes to others. You have to learn to stay "Stop!" to the inner and outer voices that would sabotage your process, and on some days the outer voices scream the loudest, while on others the inner voices work to defeat, discourage, and dismay you.

Carl Jung said perseverance in the process is the key to overcoming what limits, wounds, and defeats us.

I have persevered, working out my salvation and trying to find relief or healing for a wound in the soul that I could not fully name. The wound was like a bum knee or a bad back, acting up when I least needed the pain of it. It was like a ton of bricks I carried around on my back, and no matter how many ways I tried to lay that burden down, I would pick it up again.

One bright April morning at least a decade after my experience on the jogging track of Laity Lodge, I found myself in the analytic room of an Episcopal priest who was also a Jungian analyst, and it was in that long, laborious and tedious process of depth analysis that I was able to recognize that my ego was attached to being unwanted, rejected, and abandoned and that my part in my various dramas was

> *Whether you turn to the right or to the left, your ears will hear a voice behind you saying, "This is the way; walk in it."*
>
> —ISAIAH 30:21

playing the roles that fit my inner programming. Little by little, I began to change my mind. Over a long, slow process, I began to work out my salvation—my wholeness and health, my emotional sobriety—and there was fear and trembling.

Then there came a day when I knew I had come home to myself, that the wound of a lifetime, though now a scar, was healed. In the mysterious ways of a joint venture, the Divine Therapist had led me to a place, a process, and a person so that I could finally say the truth about what was hurting me and not be judged, imagine a new way of being in the world, and learn how to be a good, nurturing, caring, and affirming mother to my own wild and precious life.

Quoting Carl Jung, Pittman McGehee lectures about the two centers of consciousness, the ego and the Self, describing how one of those centers will be superordinate and the other subordinate.

Upon hitting the wall of midlife, when nothing that has worked for you is still working, you have the choice to surrender your old ways and your ego position, to open your mind and heart to being guided from within by the still, small Voice of God who dwells within, to be carried by the wind of the Holy Spirit, the Spirit of life and love and, I think, laughter.

Over the years, several paths led me to the work of Thomas Keating, and on a spring day in May 1998 I walked into the retreat house associated with the Benedictine Monastery in Snowmass, Colorado, for the first time. I'd participated in numerous contemplative retreats at Laity Lodge and had even written books on the contemplative life. I had used Scripture as "seeds of contemplation" and had written books helping seekers like myself to enter into the Gospel stories as a way of integrating the truths within them into their inner lives. For years I had researched and practiced various methods to help me, and the people I taught, to go deeper in awareness and in the practice of the presence of Christ. I had taken the words of John 15 to heart and had worked diligently to abide in Christ.

As a requirement for this eleven-day retreat, I had taken a workshop that introduced me to the practice of Centering Prayer. Somehow I knew this practice would be life changing; the simplicity of it belies the profundity and power of the practice.

In that first retreat, we were introduced to Keating's work through videos that we watched between hour-long "sits" in the meditation hall, a large room with windows that open to Mt. Sopris and the big blue Colorado sky. As we walked into the retreat house, I felt the usual butterflies of anxiety and anticipation. I both wanted to be there and was afraid of what it would be like to participate in such an extended time of silence. I was so taken with the experience that I have returned four times and have been trained to be a facilitator. Always, when I teach a workshop, I begin by saying that I should put a CAUTION sign on the door with a warning: "This practice will change your life."

In introducing the concept of the "sacred word," the word we use to begin the recommended twenty-minute sits, Keating stressed the fact that the sacred word is not magical or invested with special powers. You don't use it, he said, like a flyswatter to swat at nagging thoughts that invariably come up while you attempt to be still and quiet.

Instead, the power of the sacred word a person chooses is in the intention that person has. The sacred word expresses one's *consent to the presence and action of God.*

In other words, when I repeat my sacred word in Centering Prayer, I am saying these things: *I consent to Your presence with me, and I consent to Your action within me.* In the language of this book, the sacred word declares to God, "I am willing to collaborate with you and do my part in this sacred journey we are on together, and I ask you to lead the way."

God doesn't need our permission to be God or to act as God does, but there is something powerful and transformative when you give God permission to go to work within your inner life, for you and through you.

Keating's God-concept is that God is alive and active in creation and in our own lives, both in the inward, secret places and in the outer world. Fr. Keating believes that by the practice of Centering Prayer, we can access the presence and action of God, opening our minds and hearts to that reality and participating with God in the working out of our own salvation.

Later I heard Fr. Keating talk about the "four consents" we have the opportunity to make.

We are called to consent to be who we are created to be.

"Well, of course we are," a friend said to me, "but why do you have to go off to a retreat center and navel-gaze to learn that?"

Stunned, I was instantly put in a momentary crisis. Would I be authentic in that moment and remain true to my personal quest and integrity, or would I regress to people-pleasing and discount or shrug away something sacred to me simply because someone else ridiculed or rejected it.

Consenting to be who we are against the forces to which we have conformed and adapted for a lifetime is no small thing, and yet consenting to be who we are is a sacred and moral responsibility. We are, therefore, invited to consent to these things:

• to be the gender we are;
• to be the age we are;
• to be the personality temperament we are; and
• to use the gifts, talents, abilities, and natural strengths we have.

Most of all, we are invited to consent to living as one who is created in the image of God, stamped with God's likeness.

"She is so at home with herself," a friend told me about another friend. I happened to know the price that friend had paid to make it home. Indeed, those who continue to wander around, prompted and prodded by external cues, are living a kind of homeless existence.

We are called to do what we were sent here to do.

I believe there is purpose in the life of every human being, and while I cannot speak for God, I believe it is God's desire and will for every person to discover that calling and purpose and to live it to the fullest.

Hearing Keith Hosey describe the process of "the vision quest" of Native American Indians, I wondered why we ever abandoned that process in which a young person would have a desert experience in order to discover his purpose in life. What a sacred thing it is to know why you were sent here and what you are to do while you are here.

I grew up in a family in which one's calling was more sacred than anything. I learned at home that you ignored your calling at your own peril, a principle that is at the heart of what I've learned from the teachings of Carl Jung. In my religious world, when God called you to something, you were supposed to follow, but in my growing-up years, there were also two limiting beliefs about calling. In the first place, a calling had to do with going into religious work, and of course, being a preacher was near the top of that hierarchical model. Being a missionary was even loftier than being called to preach. Frankly, as a young girl I was terrified that I would be called to be a missionary, which would mean I would never marry and have children and I would have to go to deepest Africa.

What a narrow and limiting understanding of the sacred calling!

The second limiting belief was that the calling was for the men in my particular group. That idea seems so strange now that I can hardly believe what I'm writing, and yet I know that was reality. It was my job as a woman to support my husband in his career and to be the caregiver for the children. Whatever gifts or talents I had were to be subjugated and used for the welfare of my children, and if I thought my calling was from God, I could use my talents to teach a Sunday school class, play the piano, or work in vacation Bible school. I quake to think that those limitations are still imposed upon young women today.

It wasn't that my parents were trying to limit me or stunt my development. In fact, my father used to tell me I could do anything I wanted to do, which wasn't actually true. He did, however, want me to have a home and a family, and I wanted that, too, and so it was easy for me to fall in line with what my parents suggested and do what would give me "good insurance" in case something happened to this husband I was supposed to find and marry before I left college.

It wasn't until a warm summer day at Wellspring under the guidance of Gordon Cosby that I hesitantly stated what I thought might be my calling. As Gordon had related the story of Moses, he had illustrated how everything in Moses' life had prepared him to do what God asked him to do. Later, reflecting on my life, I began to see that God had been at work in me as well, preparing me to do what I was sent here to do. I saw that my natural way of being in the world as an intuitive, introverted, and feeling person was exactly what I needed to be to fulfill my purpose. My heart for relationships, my love of life and people, were part of the raw material God packed in my trunk to help me not only enjoy life but also do what I am supposed to do.

If we could free ourselves from the temptation to make faith a mindless assent to a dusty pawn-shop of doctrinal beliefs, we would discover with alarm that the essence of biblical faith lies in trusting God.

—BRENDAN MANNING

When I was trained to facilitate a workshop on self-management, the workshop creator told members of the Junior League of San Angelo, "One of the major causes of depression in people, and especially in women, is that they do not have a sense of their own purpose in life and are not using their gifts in a way that fulfills their purpose."

When little children are bored and unchallenged, they get into trouble or whine. When older people no longer feel useful or relevant, they often become depressed or grumpy. Every human being needs to be doing what he or she was sent here to do. Frederick Buechner spoke to the truth of this consent: "The kind of work God usually calls you to is the kind of work that you need most to do and that the world most needs to have done. . . . The place God calls you is the place where your deep gladness and the world's deep hunger meet."

Fortunate and blessed is the person who knows what he was intended to do and then has the courage to do it.

We must consent to our limitations.

Positive-thinking gurus, feel-good preachers, and plastic surgeons have something in common. They all hold out the idea that if you think enough good thoughts or believe in yourself enough or lift up what has fallen enough, you can stay young forever, have everything you've ever dreamed of having, and live your best life. Who doesn't want that?

Yet every human being lives within the constraint of limitations. Knowing what those are at least gives you a chance to work with them.

All of us are limited by age and opportunity. Earlier, I was too young to do some things, and now I am too old to do others! In his bestselling book *Outliers*, Malcolm Gladwell tells amazing stories of how being in the right place at the right time contributes to success.[3] He also shows that sometimes no matter how hard we try, the times are against us.

We are limited by intelligence, education, physical strength, stamina, or handicaps. We are limited by gender, either the physical reality of gender or the prejudices against either males or females. We are limited by finances, in some ways by having too much money and in many ways by not having enough. We are limited by the gifts and talents we don't have. Our prejudices and our biases limit us, and we are constrained and constricted by the spoken and unspoken norms and rules of our particular tribes.

I love the idea of human freedom, and I speak often about how we have been given free will, but I'm also acutely aware that there are forces beneath the surface of our conscious minds—Carl Jung called them complexes—that keep us bound in old patterns, habits, and beliefs that sabotage our healthy choices, inhibit our freedom to make changes, and prevent us from taking the risks we need to take to transcend our limitations. Old patterns die hard, and our earliest programming is the most powerful.

We must consent to the natural and inevitable transitions in our lives.

We make our first transition from the womb kicking and screaming. My children's pediatrician Dwain Dodson told me it is good for an infant to struggle some to get her lungs and heart moving and beating so that she can make it outside the womb, untethered to her life support system, the mother. Of course, the delicate balance between enough stress and too much can make an enormous difference in the child's life.

Transitions from one phase of life to another are inevitable, and along the way we have what author Judith Viorst called "necessary losses."[4] We understand the natural transitions from infancy to childhood, from childhood to adolescence, and from adolescence to adulthood. Only in recent years has attention been focused on the many stages of adulthood, each requiring a process of letting go of things we would love to have forever as well as the things we are eager to shed.

We can resist our transitions. We can cling too long to the past, either wallowing in how awful it was or romanticizing how perfect it was, and miss the present moment with its opportunities and challenges, gifts and blessings. We can resist by refusing to choose or be proactive. It is sometimes difficult, after all, to sift and sort through all our options, and sometimes we are confronted with moments when we don't want either option and other moments when we have too many desirable options. Maturity demands that we stand up to our lives and make choices, saying no to what would limit us and yes to what will enlarge us.

In a tender moment in a spiritual direction session one day, Chris Harris, a friend and directee, shared a quote that had been important to her: "The best *no* is rooted in a very deep *yes.*"

How true it is that when we say yes to our own lives, yes to being who we are created to be, consent to do what we were sent here to do, and consent to our transitions and limitations, saying no becomes easier. When we know what matters to us, and when we are truly committed to living our own wild and precious lives, it is easier to say no to what does not serve our purpose, limits our growth and expansion, or shuts down our minds and hearts. Saying *no* to a life others design for us, refusing to be boxed in by another's label, and staying awake and aware enough to say no to what keeps us from moving forward on the journey is part of making it through our transitions.

I've heard Thomas Keating tell about Bernie, one of the monks in the monastery at Snowmass who knew who he was and what his purpose was. Bernie worked in the monastery kitchen, and at one point he pushed through restrictions and restraints and began providing occasional ice cream for the monks. That seems like such a simple act, but given the times and the constraints, it was huge for Bernie to give that gift. Fr. Keating described Bernie as someone who had made his important consents, and when he died, he died quickly and easily.

Bernie consented to being who he was made to be. He consented to doing what he was sent here to do. He consented to his limitations and to the natural transitions of his life. At the end of every silent retreat at the monastery in Snowmass, there is an ice cream party to honor Bernie and to affirm and celebrate the sacred act of consenting to the presence and action of God in our joint venture with him.

I have set before you today life and death, blessing and curse; therefore, choose life.

—DEUTERONOMY 30:19

Having attended many deaths in the monastery, Keating made the comment that it is often true that people who have made the necessary consents are able to make the final transition into the next life more easily. I have talked to hospice nurses about this, and they concur. Consenting to life's transitions along the way must make it easier to make the final consent to the next plane of reality.

Consider Mary, the mother of Jesus, and what she must have experienced in her lifetime after he died. Remember how she said yes to the angel's invitation to participate in a grand project.

In any of life's big experiences and on any hero's journey, you have no idea what you are getting into when you begin the journey. I have learned along the way that in living the abundant life, you don't only get the blessings and the holy highs, but the full spectrum of life. Like Mary, none of us have any idea where we are going when we are invited into the spiritual journey. I'm confident we have a choice, just as I am pretty sure Mary could have said, "No, thank you; I'll pass on this one." Yet, in saying yes, we enter into a sacred process. Thinking about how Mary, the mother of Jesus, agreed to go along with the invitation of God, delivered through an angel, I wrote this poem to read at a Christmas Eve service at our church.

Mary's Yes
She told the angel "Yes!"
It was not a demure, hesitant—"maybe,"
but a gladsome "Yes!"
No downcast eyes.
No martyr's sighing.
No clenched fists against her fate.
No tentative, whispered
"Well, if you say so . . . ."
but a strong-hearted, bold "Amen"
to a radical, outrageous proposal—
a bold and wild "Let it be!"
that keeps on ringing out across the centuries, cascading
in love into this very
moment.

And so she offered
her womb
and her reputation
to a glorious illegitimacy.
      She said "Yes! to the creative
      act of God . . . .
. . . and to the humiliation
of her disgrace.
      She said "Yes!" to being favored
      among women . . . .

. . . and "Yes!" to the disbelief
and scorn of the doubting.
      She said "Yes!" to letting God
      use her . . .
. . . and "Yes!" to uncertainty and
to the unknown.
      She said "Yes!" to birthing a
      man-child . . . .
. . . and "Yes!" to running and
hiding, protecting with
her own life what God had
entrusted to her.
      She said "Yes!" to loving and
      tending her son . . . .
. . . and "Yes!" to the
responsibility of bringing
to maturity
that which she had
been given.
      Mary said "Yes!" to being full of grace
      in a world that valued reason and
      logic.
      She said "Yes!" to giving up
      control of how and when and
      where . . . and "Yes!" to the One
      whose name is Love.

      She said "Yes!" to the Mystery.

      She said "Yes!" to
      Bethlehem and the hosannas . . . .

and "Yes!" to Calvary.

> She said "Yes!" to it all . . . .
> the joy . . . and the sorrow . . . .
> the privilege . . . and the pain . . . .
> the honor . . . . and the horror.

Mary said "Yes!"

And I?
What would I have said?
I wonder.
> And I?
> What do I say now?

NOTES

1. Paul Tournier, *The Adventures of Living* (New York: Harpercollins, 1979); *The Meaning of Persons* (Cutchogue NY: Buccaneer Books, 1999); *Guilt and Grace* (New York: Harpercollins, 1982); Keith Miller, *The Taste of New Wine* (Waco TX: Words Books, 1966); *The Becomers* (New York: Bantam Books, 1977); *A Hunger for Healing* (New York: HarperOne, 1992); *Habitation of Dragons* (New York: Pillar Books, 1976).

2. Les Carter, *When Pleasing You Is Killing Me* (Nashville: B&H Pub., 2007).

3. Malcolm Gladwell, *Outliers* (New York: Little Brown & Co., 2008).

4. Judith Viorst, *Necessary Losses* (New York: Simon & Schuster, 1986).

Chapter 8

FIG LEAVES, MASKS, AND OTHER COVER-UPS

In the movie *Get Low* (dir. Aaron Schneider, 2010), Robert Duvall plays the role of backwoods hermit Felix Bush who has lived for forty years with suspicions and rumors swirling around him about an unidentified, horrible deed in his past. Whatever he did was bad enough that he built himself a jail, he said, and locked himself in it, depriving himself of family and friends, love and fulfillment, a wife and children. Coming to the end of his life, he craves forgiveness and redemption. Before he dies, he wants to come clean and set the rumors to rest.

A psychological principle that seems to prevail is that guilt will either be punished or forgiven. Either you ask for and accept forgiveness, or you find a way to punish yourself.

What's a person to do, given our tendency to do the things we don't want to do and be unable to do the things we want to do?

Looking back over my life of sins and sinning, I realize that for the most part, my earliest experience of myself as a sinner was formed around the idea of not pleasing someone who had authority in my life. As a child, I didn't murder, steal, commit adultery, or read the comics on Sunday, and so early on I could cloak myself in a coat of many colors of righteousness—of the self-righteousness variety. Needing to appear righteous, I learned many tricks for putting on a mask, pretending to please and placate, and hiding my True Self. Given what is acceptable in today's culture, the things that got me in trouble are laughable today, but what happened to me was not funny. I learned early to hide what I felt in order to survive.

Given a distorted view of sin, I had no healthy way to identify or deal with authentic sin. I could have become either a plastic saint, giving off the appearance of being holier than thou (depending on who I needed to impress) or rebellious and self-destructive, flailing away at the bondage of needing to please and placate others. I danced around the edges of those adaptations enough to know that they would kill me—if not my body, then my soul. Thankfully, I found help for dealing with my sin in the Yokefellow Spiritual Growth groups, the Twelve Steps of Alcoholics Anonymous, and depth analysis.

When I was researching and writing my book *The Spiritual Art of Creative Silence*, I discovered the work of Daniel Goleman and his book *The Art of Meditation*, and so I was especially interested in hearing him speak on his bestselling book, *Emotional Intelligence*, at an event at River Oaks Baptist School in Houston.

In his lecture and in his book, Goleman described studies in which children with relatively similar intelligence, family support, opportunity, and nutrition were shown to achieve at different levels. One of the primary factors in that difference was what Goldberg calls "emotional intelligence." Apparently, being able to recognize and feel what you are feeling and handle your emotions in an appropriate way helps you get through life better.

I was especially interested in Goleman's research because the inner work within the Yokefellow Spiritual Growth groups centered on working with the emotions that fuel self-sabotaging and self-destructive behavior. From Goleman I learned that what I had interpreted as a spiritual obligation—working creatively with one's emotions—had been researched and found to be helpful in the way children perform in school, both academically and socially.

> *O would some power the gift to give us to see ourselves as others see us.*
>
> —ROBERT BURNS

The rules in a dysfunctional family, according to many writers who have written about and worked with families in recovery from addictions and codependency, are "Don't talk, don't trust, don't feel." Those rules, lived out by the adults and inherited by the children, separate persons from their instinctual and natural selves, from God and from each other.

Learning to feel what you feel, see what you see, know what you know, and trust yourself and your inner knowing restores you to yourself and to others. And blocking those afflictive emotions separates us from ourselves, from God, and from other people. So it is that we come to the issue of what separates us from each other and ourselves. Why do we feel alienated from God? Why do we sit in our family gatherings or at church and feel so lonely we could die? Why do we feel that no one sees us or fear that we will be rejected if we are known for who we truly are? *Could it start with some of the teachings we've heard about sin and what it is?*

The problem with the teaching that we are born in and with original sin and that we have a terrible black stain within us has many dimensions. I do not believe that belief or doctrine has made us better people, and I have been on a long quest to find a better way to deal with my character defects and tendencies to choose what will hurt and harm me and others rather than what will help.

Part of the problem with this teaching is that it leads little children to grow up thinking there is something intrinsically wrong with them. Pounded with that teaching long enough, a child has to grow numb in one way or another. Told that she is a sinner from the time she is young, a child often lives with the fear of getting caught, with the burden of guilt and shame, and with a pervasive feeling of inadequacy. Sometimes the child acts out what she believes about herself.

I cannot accept that it is good for a young child to be told repeatedly about his "sin nature" when he is in the early stages of spiritual, intellectual, and emotional development and when his self-image is being formed. It cannot be good for a child to hear that his very nature is sinful. Whatever a child believes, especially if he hears and learns it from the adults who are the authorities for him, and especially if it is communicated in religious language, is going to shape how the child behaves and what choices he makes. How he acts over time will form his habits and ultimately his character.

I remind the reader that it makes a difference if you start your theology with creation and the original blessing or if you start it with the fall of Adam and Eve.

"I am afraid I am going to commit the unpardonable sin," I've heard from countless people. There is confusion about what that unpardonable sin is, depending on the denomination in which you grew up or the parent you had, but the vague, uneasy feeling that you might commit the one act that will throw you into the fires of hell leaves you with a permanent case of spiritual heartburn.

On the other hand, some react in the opposite way, as if there is an imp within them that says, "Aw, come on, you know you're not *that* bad." These individuals are set up to push the limits, defy authorities, and play "catch me if you can," often leading others on a wild goose chase across the norms and rules of culture, enjoying the "bad child" image.

Others buy into the idea that if their eternal salvation is secured either by a decision to join a church or by a baptism, then they can live any way they please between now and the time they arrive at the guaranteed heaven. Still others choose to work hard to be good enough to qualify for admission to heaven, keeping the law, doing good deeds, and wearing themselves out for Jesus. If, God forbid, they ever slip and commit a sin, they either work hard to hide it, or they work hard to do penance, hoping against hope that their image won't be tainted by what was obviously a one-time slip-up.

Then there are those whose personal faults and failings are so split from their awareness that they don't recognize their flaws but project them onto others. I've learned to pay close attention to television evangelists and politicians in recent years; often the things they rail against are the things they are doing.

In the Yokefellow Spiritual Growth groups, I began moving out of the darkness and into the light about the issue of sin. What I learned in those group sessions has provided a framework for my personal journey for my entire adult life. Later, as well, it was life changing to take a fourth step with my sponsor, Sandra Hulse, in which I "made a searching and fearless moral inventory of my life."

I'm not sure how fearless I was in that process of naming the exact nature of the wrongs I had committed against myself and others. I can remember being fearful of what I would find when I began excavating my hidden life and bringing the darkness of it into the light, but I knew the fear had to be natural, and I was convinced it was necessary.

"How do you understand the world 'moral'?" Sandra asked me as I began the fourth step, and of course I answered from a child's understanding because I had no other reference point.

"I've come to understand 'moral' as having to do with wholeness," Sandra said, guiding me gently through the process, "and that means we are going to take an inventory of all that is in you, including your strengths, your gifts, and your talents."

I liked that idea. Somehow I could breathe more easily when she said that. Deep below the surface, I think I must have anticipated an exercise in self-flagellation and self-condemnation. Instead, the purpose of the inventory is to set the person free from all that has her bound and to set her free for a new way of being in the world!

Sandra's approach to the fourth step fit with what I had learned in Yokefellow, which had begun with a redefining of sin. Sin, I learned is what separates you from God, others, and yourself. As an archery term, it is also defined as "missing the mark." In the formulation of this book, then, sin is whatever keeps you separate and apart from the Source of life, God, who dwells within you. It keeps you from being and becoming who you are intended to be and doing what you are intended to do.

In the Yokefellow formulation, there is a differentiation between the little "s" sins and the big "S" Sins. The big "S" Sins are the cause of the little "s" sins, the behavior. The Sins, then, are feelings and attitudes that separate us from God, ourselves, and others. The sins we commit, the behaviors we enact that hurt others and ourselves, are the result of the Sin in us. The sins are symptoms of our brokenness.

In our Yokefellow groups, as well, we were introduced to the power of the unconscious mind, a concept that immediately resonated with me. Later Thomas Keating drew an iceberg as he taught, cutting off the top of it as representative of the conscious mind, which is estimated to be about 5 to 10 percent. The rest of that iceberg, 90 to 95 percent, is unconscious to us.

Think about it! Most of us operate our lives, make our choices, run our businesses, and carry out our family life with 5 to 10 percent consciousness! Scarier still, we vote with that level of awareness! The unconscious mind, then, holds much power. It is where many of our emotions are buried and many of our decisions are made unconsciously.

"What were you *thinking*?" Jay Leno asked Hugh Grant on national television after he had been arrested with a hooker, and Grant responded, "I don't know." Obviously, he wasn't thinking, but he was choosing out of unconscious forces that motivated him below his level of consciousness.

Before I get too self-righteous, however, and declare that I could never do what Hugh Grant did, I have to remind myself of times when I have done self-sabotaging things, said hurtful words, and acted in ways that I can hardly stand to remember, often declaring, "I just wasn't myself today." It's then that I have to ask, "Well, who were you?"

Given the right circumstances or the right factors that come together in a perfect storm, any one of us could do what any other one of us is capable of doing. There is a Judas in us, and there is a Hitler in us, and, most distressing of all to admit, whatever it is out there in someone else that we hate most is either in us, though plunged down into the basement of denial, or we fear it might be.

When Jesus said, "Do not judge others, for as you judge you will be judged," he was speaking of the terrible truth of projection (Matt 7:1-2). We most clearly see in others what we do not like in ourselves. To become conscious of one's faults requires an act of courage and responsibility.

In Yokefellow language, and in the book we used in our group, *Prayer Can Change Your Life,* sins are called *demons*, and there are four primary ones: (1) guilt/shame, (2) hate/anger, (3) feelings of inferiority, and (4) fear.[1] These demons are the fire; our behavior is the smoke, and most people flail away at the smoke. What needs to be faced, named, and owned is the root cause, the fire of the problem.

I thought it was outrageous when our leader proposed that we could address our problems by identifying the demon that fueled a particular harmful behavior. At the time, I discounted what he said because I thought my problem was what someone else was doing, and if only he or she would stop, my life would be fine.

One of the most remarkable things I have ever learned was that I am 100 percent responsible for my state of being in any and all situations. If I want to change a situation, I go to work on myself and not others. If I want peace of mind, I make the conscious decision to stop blaming someone else for what is wrong and work on my part of the problem.

> *Do not think of yourself more highly than you ought to think, but rather think of yourself with a sober judgment.*
>
> —ROMANS 12:3B

These are the demons, one by one:

Guilt is the terrible feeling you have when you have done something wrong. From Paul Tournier, however, I learned that there is true guilt, the valid guilt you feel when you have done something to injure another person, when you have committed an immoral or harmful deed, or when you have taken something from another person that rightfully belongs to him or inflicted suffering on another human being in any number of ways.

There are many ways to wound another human being, and it seems that humans are infinitely creative in finding those ways and alarmingly able to inflict violence and oppression on other people made in the image of God. To feel guilt about hurting another human being is appropriate.

However, to feel guilty about what you have not done or what is not injurious to another, to fret about minor infractions or mistakes, or to live in a state of guilt is to live in what Tournier calls *false guilt.*

Guilt, I learned, will either be punished or forgiven. When you don't allow yourself to be forgiven, you will find a way to punish yourself, often by repeating the same self-destructive behavior again.

I have heard Thomas Keating say that if you are still feeling guilty after confession, you are confessing to the wrong God and that "God as you understand him" may need to be revised in your mind and heart.

Shame is the terrible feeling about who you are. It is the feeling of not measuring up, of not being enough, of being intrinsically flawed. Shame is a universal feeling experienced by people in all cultures but about different things. It can be inherited from your family of origin, passed down seemingly through the nonverbal and verbal cues that say, "You are flawed." You may find that you need to hide behind some cover so people won't find out how flawed you are.

Shame and guilt, unfortunately, are often perpetuated by religious systems in order to control and manipulate people.

Hate and anger are the feelings directed toward those who have hurt you or those you believe want to take something from you. Those feelings are sometimes expressed in rage, jealousy, or resentment. Sometimes they leak out in words or acts of passive aggression.

It is appropriate to be angry at violence and injustice. It is appropriate to feel hate toward those who hurt others. However, a lifestyle—or would it be a deathstyle?—of hate, a habit of anger as a way of being in the world, is injurious to your health and to that of others.

As a young girl growing up in my culture, I learned that "ladies" didn't get mad. More accurately, I learned that real ladies didn't show their anger. I have heard more than one woman say, "I have never been angry in my life." Women have permission to get depressed but not angry. Today, even savvy teenagers know depression can sometimes be anger turned inward.

Hate and anger are natural feelings that arise in all of us at times. Knowing when to express your anger and in what ways and in the appropriate proportions is a key challenge of a mature person. Owning what you feel is a gateway into freedom.

Inferiority, another demon, is natural to all of us, though we may be unconscious of it.

None of us are capable, competent, or proficient at everything. All of us have areas in which we don't know enough or can't do certain things. In addition, we all are caught in the enormity of life, and, though we don't like to admit it, hindered by our vulnerability, our smallness, and our helplessness before the forces of nature, the actions of others, and the seemingly random occurrences of life. Ultimately, all of us bow to inevitabilities over which we have no control.

Some of us work hard to overcompensate for gaps in education, experience, intelligence, or financial resources. Others, frozen by feelings of inferiority, become incapable of taking charge of their own lives, being proactive, or learning necessary skills.

However, created in the image of God, we have a choice over many more parts of our lives than we acknowledge, and we have capabilities, strengths, and resources to live our lives. Thus, to be driven or paralyzed by the enormity of life or by feelings of inferiority, to be controlled by insufficiencies, inadequacies, or crippling focus on what we don't have or can't do separates us from the power we do have. Feelings of inferiority show up in a variety of behaviors, and they will keep us separate from our life's purpose and from other people.

Holding on to an attitude of inferiority is basically saying, "I'm a mistake," and "I'm not good enough (or, simply, enough)," and that attitude will lead us to places we don't want to go.

My sisters were fourteen and eighteen years old when I was born. For the most part, I was around adults for the first few years of my life, and simply because I was so much younger and smaller than the big people in my world, I started out feeling small and inferior. I was also painfully shy. Sometimes I could perform well when I needed to. I learned to be friendly when it was appropriate, but a deep feeling of inferiority controlled me.

As a young adult, I read somewhere that shyness was a sign of self-centeredness and self-consciousness, and I was horrified. I began to work on reaching out beyond myself to overcome that shyness, to take an interest in others, and to learn skills that would get me through agonizing social situations. During those years, I kept a magnet on our refrigerator with this quote by Eleanor Roosevelt: "No one can make you feel inferior without your consent."

It took years for me to overcome the tendency to roll myself into a ball of inferiority, and sometimes I still do that. For the most part, though, shyness doesn't control me any longer.

Everyone experiences *fear*, and it could be said that fear is at the root of the other four demons. Over and over Jesus said, "Fear not," so apparently he recognized the pervasive tendency human beings have to be afraid, anxious, and worried.

It is natural to be afraid of a snake or a hurricane. It is appropriate to fear someone who is pointing a gun at you. It is not, however, healthy or helpful to live in a state of fear so that your life is controlled by a focus on the bad things that may happen.

My mother had many anxieties and worries, but she did try to help me overcome mine. One night when I was alone in Nacogdoches, Texas, with three little girls ages six and under, all of whom were sick, she called me and read 2 Timothy 1:7 to me: "For God did not give us a spirit of timidity, but a spirit of power, of love, and of self-discipline." I have held to that verse through many scary times and have quoted it to other frightened people.

Author and Jungian analyst James Hollis says that when we wake up in the morning, there are two gremlins waiting at the foot of our beds. One of those gremlins is lethargy, the state in which we cannot rouse ourselves enough to face the enormity of the day, and the other is anxiety. He says it is a heroic act simply to show up for our lives, go to work, pay our bills, care for our children, and then get up the next morning and do the same thing again.

I've also heard him say that we have two responses to the enormity of life, depression and anxiety. "If you have a choice, choose anxiety," he says, "because at least you are risking and acting in your life. Depression indicates that you have pressed down your energies."

But what about the sin factor?

In my childhood and adolescence, I came to believe a sin was something I did that was wrong like lying to my parents, cheating on my homework, or taking something that didn't belong to me. I heard gossiping was a sin, too, but all of the adults I knew did it. I knew murder and rape were the worst sins of all, but I didn't know anyone who did anything so heinous, and so those horrible sins made my little sins seem okay.

To say the new way of understanding Sin and sins revolutionized my life is an understatement. For the first time in my life, the issue of sin made sense to me because it was about everyday issues that cause conflict and heartache in everyday ways.

The most fundamental harm we can do to ourselves is to remain ignorant by not having the courage and the respect to look at ourselves honestly and gently.

—PEMA CHODRIN

The True Self is at the core of each of us, and the ego self is the false self, the *persona* we present to the world. We wear this persona because of an image we want to present. As we carry out different roles in daily life, we may present more than one persona. We do that not because we are phony or false, but because the ego self is an adapted self. The word "persona" actually comes from the Greek theatre in which an actor would wear or hold a mask in front of his face as he played various roles.

In a lecture on his book *What Matters Most*, Jim Hollis said, "The false self is not false intentionally, but it is adaptive rather than natural or instinctual and is an assemblage of behaviors, attitudes, and reflexive responses toward self and others to manage anxiety and get our needs met as best as possible."[2]

In my first series of group sessions in the spiritual growth groups, the others and I were asked to reflect on the four demons over the next week and see if we could identify which one was our biggest problem. Sometimes when I lead a group through this process, I ask participants to rank the demons in order of severity for them. These demons, remember, are the four Sins, the motivating causes that fuel our behavior.

Because it is sometimes hard to identify which demon gives us the most trouble, we were asked to look at some of the irritating or self-sabotaging behaviors in other people. "If you have trouble seeing your own masks," we were told, "look at what you don't like in others. Most likely, you'll be looking at one of your own masks!"

Here is the list I currently use to facilitate a process of identifying the behaviors that cause us trouble. It is expanded from that original list from the Yokefellow groups.

The Fig Leaves of Our Lives

(defense mechanisms, coping strategies, personas, masks, hideouts, cover-ups)

Must be right/first/best

Win at all costs

People pleasing

Goody two shoes

Critical attitude/nature

Negativity

Saccharine sweetness

Chief mourner

Polyanna attitude

Chicken Little/pessimist

Dominating attitude

Do-gooder

Playing dumb

Control freak

Authoritarian bearing

Professional helper

Playing helpless

Professional failure

Southern belle

Eternal child

Authority

On-going crises/chaos

Troublemaker

Victim

Princess

Rescuer

Religious rigidity

Problem child

Ultimate caretaker

Black sheep

Playing sick

The "different" one

Codependent

The drunk/the addict

Constant joking

Excessive sarcasm

Mr. Macho

Over-responsible

Party girl

Perpetual adolescent

Frat boy

Meddling/over-helping

"It doesn't matter"

Always grieving

Intellectualizing

Over-talkativeness

Miss Perfection

Withdrawing/stonewalling

Bully

Role rigidity/image bound

Habitual lying

Extremely pious/"holy, holy, holy"

Hypervigilance/worrying

Emotional rigidity/shutdown

Morality police

Judge and jury

Big Daddy

Big Mama

Raging

Eating disorders

All addictive behavior

Denial/avoidance

Justifying/rationalizing

Blaming others

Mad dog

Eternal pout

Superiority/inferiority complexes

Self-righteousness

Advice-giver (unsolicited)

Peace at any price

Conflict avoidance

Depression

Excessive shyness

Snobbishness

Nervous Nelly

Dark grandiosity

King Baby

Passive aggression

Poor pitiful pearl

Martyr

Hero

Scapegoat

Loser

Entertainer

Perpetual cynic

Perfectionist

Admittedly, it can be disconcerting to face your own *stuff,* to look at how other people see you and recognize the masks you wear, the scripts you play, and the ways you hide your True Self from others. Basil Pennington, the Benedictine monk who has worked with Thomas Keating to teach the simple, yet life-changing practice of Centering Prayer, says this: "Unfortunately, in seeing ourselves as we truly are, not all that we see is beautiful and attractive. This is undoubtedly part of the reason we flee silence. We do not want to be confronted with our hypocrisy, our phoniness."

Indeed, it is hard to face the fact that we are presenting a front or a façade to the world, and yet in doing this we can begin to dismantle the false self and allow the authentic and True Self to be revealed. Pennington goes on, "We see how false and fragile is the false self we project. We have to go through this painful experience to come to our True Self."

To begin this "harrowing journey," pick one or two of the "fig leaves" in the previous list that you think might be one of your behaviors or masks. Then ask, "What feeling might make me wear this mask or play this role?" Start with the behavior and track it back to the fire that keeps your behavior alive.

The following questions can open windows of awareness as well:

1. What are the masks or behaviors you most dislike in other people? Can you see that in yourself?
2. When people criticize you or confront you about your own behavior, is there a consistent "theme" about the criticism? In other words, is more than one person saying the same thing about you?
3. When you criticize yourself, what do you most often say? What do you criticize most about other people?
4. Are you able to hear others' criticism, and in the process, discern what is valid and what is not? Can you differentiate between what truly belongs to you and what is the other person's issue? Are you able to tell when others are projecting their material onto you?
5. When you identify a behavior significant enough that it bothers you or others, what *feeling* is behind or underneath the behavior? In other words, which "demon" is your mask hiding: (1) guilt/shame, (2) hate/anger, (3) feelings of inferiority, or (4) fear?
6. When someone criticizes or confronts you, what is your typical pattern for dealing with it? How is that working for you?
7. How does this behavior/attitude/habit keep your True Self bound?

8. If God is bringing to your attention an area that causes you discomfort or trouble in the outer world, what do you think God is trying to do?

9. What does 2 Timothy 1:7 have to do with this work of addressing one's demons?

THE WAY THROUGH

In reading the stories of Jesus' encounters with people in his earthly ministry, I am often struck by the way he could see through the outer husk of the person, the ego, the defenses, the persona, or the role, to the real person. It seems that in his interaction with individuals, he moved past the outer layers and touched the core of the person. Perhaps he called forth the True Self in each one so that transformation took place from the inside out. Transformation is part of the function of the True Self, after all.

In our Yokefellow group sessions each week, we would analyze ourselves, asking each other not for advice but for feedback and response. Always, the feedback was intended to help in the individual struggle to become free and to become who we truly were intended to be. Yoked together, as we had committed to be, there was the stated intention that we were also yoked to the Spirit of Christ, and so our work together had the focus of striving for the healing, transformation, liberation, and empowerment of each other.

As the group work was analysis, the personal quiet time each week was intended for synthesis. Through journaling, prayer and meditation, and reading, we would integrate what we had talked about, discovered, and learned with each other in the group. It was a sacred process, all of it, and I took it as seriously as anything I'd ever done in my life.

Drifting through life, when confronted with our flaws or failings, most of us either deny what is there, repress or suppress the feelings, or project them onto others. Sometimes we express our feelings in verbal outbursts or attacks or in physical violence, turned either in on ourselves or out on others. There is another way, the way that leads to emotional intelligence and the way, I believe, of becoming whole and healthy in everyday life.

I was stunned by the simplicity of the plan we were given for working with our discoveries. Resistant to formulae for spiritual growth and bumper-sticker theology, I was skeptical at first of a six-step plan for dealing with the thorny issues of my Sins and my sins, but I was told that what had worked for literally thousands of others might also work for me!

I remember vividly looking at the list the first time and thinking, "It can't be this simple." I was to learn that the plan was simple, but it wasn't easy, like so many things in life that work. These seven words were printed on a sheet we received: Awareness, Acceptance, Abandonment, Action, Practice, Persistence, and Patience.

This plan never fails to move me back to personal responsibility. It moves me from passivity to action, from blaming to responsibility, and from unconsciousness to conviction about what separates me from God, from my True Self, and from others. Using this plan is sometimes easier at some times, and with some issues, than at other times. On occasion, I've had to wrestle with my stubborn will, my complexes that have such a stronghold in my unconscious world and with God.

Awareness is the beginning point of any spiritual growth. Think about it. From the cross Jesus prayed, "Father, forgive them, *for they don't know what they are doing*" (Luke 23:34). In other words, they are unconscious. Out of unconsciousness, we are driven to do heinous and irritating things.

We become aware by choosing to pay attention to what we are doing, by listening carefully to what other people say to us and about us, and by noticing when something in our lives is out of sync, painful, or distressing. We stay unconscious because it is hard to take in so much data every day and because with consciousness comes a corresponding choice to make. We prefer to numb ourselves, medicate ourselves, and waste our lives in spectator sports, in an electronic haze, or in one addictive behavior or another.

To wake up is to wake up to pain. It is to see your flaws and know them as your own. Watch an infant struggle to emerge from the safe womb of sleep, struggling to pry first one eye open and then another, and you'll have a picture of how hard it is to become conscious, to wake up and to be aware.

The prodigal son, wasted in a pigpen, came to himself, the Scripture says in Luke 15, and we too are called to come to ourselves, to become conscious, and to know what we know.

Acceptance is an act of maturity, for in acceptance we say, "This belongs to me. I have this character defect. I am afraid, and I accept responsibility for this fear (or guilt, shame, etc.). I will not say you made me feel this way; I will accept the fact that I chose this feeling."

Indeed, there are times when people provoke a feeling response in us, either deliberately or unintentionally. However, I'm still responsible for that feeling and for my accompanying behavior.

There are times when feelings bubble up from the past, and there are times when I fall back into repetitive behavior. I'm still responsible, and when I can accept 100 percent responsibility for my actions, my words, and my attitude, I'm on my way toward becoming an adult.

Abandonment is the step of "turning it over." Recovering people talk about this step. In the Yokefellow model, the abandonment needs to be made in a specific way. "I abandon my fear," I say, with no hedging, no soft-pedaling, no excuses or rationalizations.

The crucial factor is that I am abandoning what is within me to God. I am not abandoning my pain or suffering, my flaw or my defect, into a vacuum, but into the heart and hands of God. This act of faith implies a belief, however small or great, in a God who is active and involved in our inner lives. It is an affirmation that the One to whom we consent in Centering Prayer really is there, present within us and actively engaged with us in the joint venture of becoming saved. In prayer, then, I abandon my afflictive emotion to God.

Having abandoned that feeling to God, I then take *action*. Nature abhors a vacuum, and so it is essential to begin putting new behavior in the place of the old. Slowly, then, I begin to make choices and behave in a way that is consistent with my decision. The new behavior may feel strange at first. It may feel hypocritical, but it is not. It is choosing to act in a new way, trusting that ultimately our feelings will catch up to our new behavior and the new behavior will eventually become as natural as the old, self-defeating way. "Fake it 'til you make it," one of the slogans of AA, is a helpful guide in making the transition from the old ways to the new ones.

It is also essential to ask God to fill the vacuum left by the afflictive emotion with love, courage, serenity, boldness, compassion, or whatever other emotion or attitude works best in that spot. This process has to be done repeatedly. My friends tell me about change, "You didn't get this way overnight, and you aren't likely to change overnight."

> *If we claim to be without sin, we deceive ourselves and the truth is not in us. If we confess our sins, he is faithful and just and will forgive us our sins and purify us from all unrighteousness.*
>
> —1 JOHN 1:8-9

Practice, over time, is the key, followed by *persistence* and *patience*. "Be as patient and as kind to yourself as God is," we were told, and so we ventured out, week by week, re-surrendering the afflictive emotion to God's forgiveness and mercy.

Slowly we inched toward wholeness, sometimes weeping and often laughing together at our human foibles and idiosyncrasies. Yoked together by a common commitment to each other's personal, spiritual growth in daily life, we mediated the grace of Christ to each other.

Throughout the process, which has continued throughout my lifetime, I have learned that when I "press down" the afflictive emotions, I also press down joy, hope, love, and the other feelings that add meaning to my life. In facing the dark side of my life, I move from either/or, good/bad thinking about myself and am far more comfortable with my imperfections and flaws. I still don't like it when some new weakness or defect comes roaring to the surface of my attention, demanding that I see something difficult in myself, but I am no longer surprised by the fact that I am always going to be a mixture of strengths and weaknesses, virtues and flaws, successes and failures, victories and defeats.

I have read that Golda Meier kept two pieces of paper in her pocket. On one was written the words, "For me the world was made," and on the other, "I am dust and ashes." Aware of the ways in which we humans tend to tilt too far in one direction or another, she would read whichever quote she needed to help her regain her balance.

Leafing through my worn copy of *The Ordering of Love* by Madeleine L'Engle, I find the words from "The Promise" again.[3] They greet me as she always did, with arms outstretched and a blessing in her eyes. On one particular morning, I needed words of mercy and grace.

> We fail you
> over and over again
> but you promised to be faithful to us
> not to let us fail
> beyond your forgiveness of our failure.

In the pre-dawn quiet, I turned off my reading lamp and sat in the stillness, letting Madeleine's words wash over me. I remembered John Claypool's words about how God's grace and mercy are bigger than any of our sins. "The way of forgiveness is the way of gratitude and astonishment," he said. "It lets the past become our teacher rather than our judge."

It is much easier to face your sins and your Sin when you are aware of the great cloud of witnesses, your balcony people, whose prayers for you are full of tender mercy.

NOTES

1. William R. Parker, *Prayer Can Change Your Life* (Englewood Cliffs NJ: Prentice-Hall, 1983).

2. James Hollis, *What Matters Most: Living a More Considered Life* (New York: Gotham Books, 2009).

3. Madeleine L'Engle, *The Ordering of Love: New and Collected Poems of Madeleine L'Engle* (Colorado Springs: Shaw Books, 2005).

Chapter 9

SURRENDER

When my daughter Michelle was four, I did something that displeased her. It was neither the first nor the last time that happened, but on that occasion, deprived of what she wanted, she stomped her foot and said, "You don't understand! I want what I want when I want it!"

At four, Michelle couldn't understand why we didn't give her what she wanted. Nor could she have known at age four how completely I actually understood that frustration!

Who doesn't want what she wants when she wants it? Michelle's attitude and behavior were appropriate for a four-year-old, and her dad and I were amused by it. Unfortunately some of us never grow beyond the gnawing, ever-hungry monster that makes us believe we are entitled to have our way. Some of us never become conscious enough to realize that the world does not have to conform to our expectations and that life is not obliged to deliver the outcomes we demand. Nor, it seems, is the Almighty inclined to answer all the petitions we make, no matter how fervently we pray or how much we believe that if we name it, we can claim it. What is cute on a four-year-old is not so attractive in an adult.

When I accepted Christ as my personal Savior at nine, that was easy. No one told me, however, that I would not find it so easy to deal with my self-will run riot, or that learning how to deal with the four-year-old within my inner landscape, the sometimes belligerent brat who wants what she wants when she wants, is part of what it means to "work out our own salvation with fear and trembling."

Fear and trembling indeed.

When I was the Teaching Director for the Community Bible Study in San Angelo, Texas, I attended a stress management workshop in Birmingham, Alabama. The workshop leader had developed a system for dealing with stress that at first seemed simplistic and formulaic; quickly, I discovered that he was teaching something that was simple but challenging enough to change my life. As my AA friends tell me, "The hard way is the easy way."

Stress, this man said, is caused by the thing my four-year-old daughter insisted she must have: what she wanted when she wanted it.

Think about it. When you're unhappy, isn't it because something isn't going the way you think it ought to go? Doesn't a lot of suffering stem from not being able to change circumstances, people, and events? Isn't it hard when you can't force or manipulate life to meet you on your terms or meet your expectations?

From the moment I learned Reinhold Niebuhr's Serenity Prayer, I have relied on it, prayed it, and shared it with others who, like me, struggle with hard times and with the problem of the self-will run riot.

> God, grant me the serenity to accept the things I cannot change,
> the courage to change the things I can,
> and the wisdom to know the difference.

It is a beautiful prayer, and I want to live it, but it is hard to live it. I often think there is surely *something I can do* to make things over in my image—some answer, some solution, some relief for whatever is disturbing my peace at the moment. Sadly, I often shrink back from changing the things I can change, and the truth is that sometimes even as I pray this prayer, I don't want wisdom nearly as much as I want my way!

Recently, I found myself feeling irritated with almost everyone close to me. Fortunately (for them and for myself), I have listened to Jim Hollis say many times, "If you are having trouble in several areas of your life or with several people at the same time, recognize that you are the one consistent person in all of those scenarios. Consider that the problem may be you!"

When you come to the edge of all the light you know, and are about to step off into the darkness of the unknown, faith is knowing one of two things will happen: there will be something solid to stand on or you will be taught how to fly.

—BARBARA J. WINTER

That orientation and attitude toward problems is not intended to remove responsibility from others, but it does precipitate a helpful internal change. Another person or persons may be problematic, but the only thing I can change is myself and my attitude and behavior. To begin exploring one's beliefs about a stress-producing situation is a part of "renewing of one's mind." I've learned to ask myself these questions:

- What about this situation produces stress for me?
- In what ways am I not getting my way in this situation?
- What is my responsibility in this situation? What is not my responsibility?
- Where am I clinging to my need for control?
- What makes me think I know the best way to handle this situation?
- What are the things I can change? What are the things I cannot change?
- What do I need to surrender?

Along with the blessing of choice, the giving of talents and abilities, and the drive to make things happen, we humans must also contend with the dark side of our freedom to choose—the need to control. We attempt to control other people and their attitudes. We manipulate to control events, other peoples' opinions, their perceptions, and life itself. Some of us are overtly and obnoxiously controlling, and others are more passive with our attempts to make other people and life conform to our ideas.

The reality is that we were given *dominion* over creation, but not *domination*. We are given the assignment to care for the world we inhabit and for each other, but there is sometimes a thin line between caring for another and attempting to control another.

We have a tendency to misuse freedom. We insist on the right to choose, and sometimes we think we are above the natural and logical consequences others must endure. The rub comes when we have to face the reality that we don't get to choose the outcome of our choices; we don't get to determine how other people will respond to them.

Because I wanted to work the Twelve Steps with a sponsor, I asked my friend Sandra Hulse if she would meet with me and walk me through them. As a recovering alcoholic with a longtime involvement with what she called "her fellowship" of Twelve Step followers, Sandra had reservations about working with me because I was not addicted to alcohol. Week by week, however, we met in a booth at the Crystal Confectionary, a favorite restaurant, and she did her best to help me integrate the steps into my life.

I know I didn't make it easy for Sandra, but I desperately wanted something I saw in her, qualities I now know were the result of her surrender to God and her dependence on God, one day at a time, for her sobriety. She showed me what it was like to live the surrendered life; in the language I knew, she showed me what it was like to "seek first the kingdom of God."

In this intimate relationship with a sponsor, working a Twelve Step program—a truly significant *joint venture*—I saw what it was like to live "the recovering life," and I observed the wonders of what Keith Hosey described as he talked about the wind stage of spiritual formation. Sandra would not want me to paint her as perfect, and I would not, but she talked about and lived the reality of a day-by-day reliance on the life-giving power of the Spirit of God who dwells within.

What's not to like about that? What was it about me that made it so hard?

More than once, Sandra held her head in her hands and said, in various versions and with varying strengths of frustration, "If only you were a drunk, I could help you, but until you can get _____ off the throne of your life, you aren't going to make any progress!"

Fill in the blank with any number of persons, a troubling situation, or an afflictive emotion (the problem of the week) that was filling up my head and wielding control over my inner life. All the while, I thought I was committed to a life with God as my center. I had a rotating circle of people who actually played the role of god in my inner life, each of them taking turns in running my schedule, controlling my emotions, or determining what behavior I would use to please this person or that person.

What I desperately needed was not to deny the validity of my childhood decision to accept Jesus as my Savior, but to make an adult decision to turn my will and my life over to God in adult ways. I needed to face the fact that my childhood decision, while it was sincere and authentic for my stage of development, was only a beginning and actually stood in the way of helping me face my egocentricity, my flaws and failures, my character defects, and my idolatries.

In a way, my "salvation experience" was ego-based, and it was based on pleasing my parents and doing what was right. It was appropriate for my stage of faith development when I made my initial commitment to Christ. For many of us, though, our religious practices become a hiding place. Carl Jung said man invented religion to protect himself from God, and while I did not know I was doing that, my religious life did form blinders to keep me from seeing myself as I really was. I was unable to face my character defects that somehow looked less offensive than the sins of others.

If anything, my months of working the steps with Sandra showed me how easily I could break the commandment, "Thou shall have no other gods before me" (Exod 20:3). With her, I learned how hard it was to surrender my ego (my way of being in the world or my way of understanding who I thought I was). I learned how challenging it was to move into the wind stage Keith Hosey had described. For those of us who are strong-willed and committed to our own self-reliance, it is no small order to "let go and let God" do anything. And for those of us who are part of a religious system that focuses on the rewards of the afterlife, it is ego deflating to come to terms with our sins of omission and our sins of commission, especially when those sins are of a religious nature or when we use our holy talk to cover our own hypocrisy, our prejudices and biases, our cruelties and our greed, and others.

Trust God from the bottom of your heart; don't try to figure out everything on your own. Listen for God's voice in everything you do; he's the one who will keep you on track.

—PROVERBS 3:5-6
(*THE MESSAGE*)

I continue to take seriously Scott Peck's book *People of the Lie*, especially when he states that religious evil is the most insidious evil of all.[1] What is done in the name of God, what we do as we hide behind religion, has a particularly terrible aspect to it.

To Sandra's credit, she hung in there with me, doing the best she could with my stubborn will and willfulness. It is to her credit that she confronted me when I wanted to make someone else's issue my problem and avoid taking a hard, fearless, searching inventory of my own darkness.

In no way do I mean to diminish the terrible struggle it is to give up an addiction to a substance or to change patterns of a lifetime in relationship to yourself and to the people in your family system, circle of associates or friends, or organization. I am amazed by those who have stood up to the horrors of substance addiction and are free of their hideous power.

Neither, however, do I want to discount or minimize the power of the addictions to care-taking, particular persons, people-pleasing, work, or religion, all of which are rewarded in our culture. For the most part, people cheer for the person who is trying to break an addiction to alcohol or drugs, gambling or sex. Part of what makes recovery from codependency, work, and religious addictions so difficult is that people who benefit from those addictions will often punish the person who is trying to save his or her life by recovering from addiction to what is, in and of itself, good.

The hard thing about surrendering your patterns of co-dependency is that you get rewarded for taking care of other people, putting them first, and putting yourself last. Then suddenly, the same people who have benefited from your caretaking want you to back off, get out of their business, or ignore what they are doing that is harmful to them! It's a complicated process to disentangle yourself from the webs of enmeshment and codependency.

Within our culture as well, work addiction is rewarded, and nowhere is that dynamic more insidious and perhaps damaging than with an addiction to religious work, "the church," or some religious practice.

In my struggle to surrender my will to God, I am comforted by knowing that Oswald Chambers, author of the classic *My Utmost for His Highest*, struggled with his own stubborn will.[2] I am also comforted by Paul's words in Romans 7:18b-19: "For I have the desire to do what is good, but I cannot carry it out. For what I do is not the good I want to do; no, the evil I do not want to do—this I keep on doing." Does anyone not understand that inner struggle?

Three scenes in Jesus' life that are meaningful to me reveal the humanity and vulnerability of Jesus as he struggled with the process of surrender, revealing to us that the process of transformation is a terrible dying to one reality and a wrenching letting go into another. Birth is a painful, bloody process, and so is rebirth. Our journeys are often fraught with terrible suffering. "Letting go and letting God" is not just a nice bumper sticker or a soothing bromide, but a difficult, painful, and sometimes unbearable yielding of oneself to the reality of what is and to the unknown.

Shortly after his baptism, Jesus wrestled with the Adversary, refusing the shortcuts to power, fame, and fortune, all paths that would have been ego-gratifying but soul-killing. In refusing the lesser ways, Jesus chose to fulfill the purpose for which he was born, and while some gloss over his struggle, the story belies the ease with which he made that choice.

Later, when it was evident that his choice had led him to the Garden of Gethsemane, his struggle was so great that it is described as shedding drops of blood. That we are allowed to see this depth of struggle and agony in Jesus is both terrifying and comforting to me. I am terrified because I see that surrendering is costly and painful. I am comforted because it shows me that surrender really is the only way to transformation and wholeness and that it really is something you have to do by yourself.

Hebrews 4:14-15 stuns and comforts me. I like Eugene Peterson's rendition in *The Message*: "Now that we know what we have—Jesus the great

High Priest with ready access to God—let's not let it slip through our fingers. We don't have a priest who is out of touch with our reality. He's been through weakness and testing, experienced it all—all but the sin. So let's walk right up to him and get what he is so ready to give. Take the mercy. Accept the help."

Is there any greater prayer of surrender than Jesus' prayer at the end of his battle with himself in the Garden of Gethsemane? "Thy will be done" is the model prayer.

On the cross, Jesus spoke the final words of his surrender as he committed his spirit to God, and that same declaration, "Into your hands I commend my spirit," is the one we are called to make if we are to surrender ourselves to God and move into what Keith Hosey calls the best stage of life, the wind stage when we are compelled by the Spirit of God who dwells within us.

Surrender, by definition, is the act of yielding to another person or giving up something to another. Surrender is not resignation or an act of weakness, but it may follow both a giving up and a struggle with one's own weaknesses. Surrender is an act of courage, a voluntary abandonment of oneself, one's way of being in the world, one's wishes and desires, or one's flaws and sins for the purpose of living in a new, healthier way. Surrender is a necessary and essential part of the work of salvation, just as it is necessary in recovering from an addiction.

Working the Twelve Steps, I have come to understand these things about the ongoing, arduous process of surrender:

1. True and authentic surrender is an inside job. It cannot be forced upon us, and it is not accomplished by repeating a formula or a plan, especially if we do it to please someone or gain admission to an organization.

2. No one can surrender for someone else, and no one can do another's recovery work for him, though some of us believe that if we work hard enough, we can "save" another person. Salvation and sobriety are processes that can be done only for onself. There are helpers and supporters along the pathway of this joint venture, but at some level everyone has to walk at least part of that lonesome valley by himself.

3. There is often a Big Surrender, the first one a person consciously chooses to make, either in an act of accepting Christ and choosing to become his follower or in beginning a recovery process. Surrender often happens when you've hit bottom or think you will die if you don't get relief from your problem or your pain. Once, however, is not enough, and that is why

the "one day at a time" approach to recovery is so powerful. Life is one surrender after another, isn't it?

4. Surrender involves giving up one set of beliefs and attitudes for another, and we must acknowledge that this is not easy. The beliefs we carry determine our behavior, after all, and our behavior, repeated over time, shapes our character and our destiny. By confronting the core beliefs that call the shots at an internal, often unconscious level, we are "transformed by the renewing of our minds."

5. There is perhaps nothing as important as examining one's God-concepts in the process of surrendering to God, for that concept may prevent the surrender of one's character defects and addictions and the gaining of what Jesus called "the abundant life." The third step for AA states that we turn our will and lives over to the care of "God as we understand him." Becoming conscious of how we understand God is vital, for some of our understandings of God keep us imprisoned in old, repetitive, self-destructive, and familiar patterns. Some of the ways in which we understand God actually make us sicker.

> *Therefore, continue to work out your salvation with fear and trembling.*
>
> —PHILIPPIANS 2:12 (NIV)

6. Surrender sometimes happens in layers, as if we cannot let go of something all at once, and sometimes it is agonizingly difficult to learn to take our hands off and let God take over. Sometimes it happens more easily than others, but always it is the action of God at work in us that empowers and liberates us to surrender to him, to life as it is, to love.

The third step prayer touches me deeply:

God, I offer myself to Thee—
To build with me
and to do with me as Thou wilt.
Relieve me of the bondage of self,
that I may better do Thy will.
Take away my difficulties,
that victory over them may bear witness
to those I would help of Thy Power,
Thy love, and Thy Way of life.
May I do Thy will always!

Some of the deepest, most complicated work is done at the level of one's God-consciousness, and some of that may sound like this:

- I surrender my belief that God is out to punish me, and I choose to believe God is merciful, forgiving, and gracious.
- I surrender my belief that God is distant and uninvolved, and I choose to believe God is with me always, in me, for me, and working with me in this present moment.
- I surrender my belief that God is an over-indulgent parent who will let me get away with my laziness, rebellion, and self-destruction, and I choose to believe I live under the same natural laws everyone else lives under.
- I surrender my belief that God has abandoned me because (my father, my mother, my friends, my spouse) abandoned me, and I choose to believe God will never leave me or forsake me.
- I surrender my belief that God wants me to conform to others' idea of who I must be, what I must do, and how I must feel, and I choose to believe my first responsibility is to be who God created me to be and do what I was designed to do in this life.

What about the images of ourselves that logically follow the God-concept we hold?

- I surrender my belief that I am a bad person, unworthy of God's forgiveness, and I choose to believe I can receive God's mercy, grace, and forgiveness.
- I surrender my belief that I am insignificant or inadequate, and I choose to believe I am made in the image of God.
- I surrender my belief that I am God's special pet and entitled to special privileges, and I choose to believe I am beloved by God, just as everyone else is.
- I surrender my belief that I am alone in the world and must make it by myself, and I choose to believe God is with me, often appearing through human instruments.
- I surrender my belief that I am obligated to any other human being or obliged to please him or her by sacrificing my authenticity, integrity, or authority, and I choose to believe that at the end of a day and the end of my life, I am accountable first to God.

7. Surrendering deep emotions can get to the root of our problems, but we are often scared to give up the emotions that keep us stuck and imprisoned in chains of our own making. It is as if our anger gives us power, our fear keeps us safe, and our feelings of inadequacy keep us from stepping up to the largeness of our lives.

Author James Baldwin says, "I imagine that one of the reasons people cling to their hates so stubbornly is because they sense, once hate is gone, that they will be forced to deal with pain."[3]

So we are called to more self-reflection in order to surrender yet another layer of deception, denial,

> *Be energetic in your life of salvation, reverent and sensitive before God. That energy is God's energy, an energy deep within you . . . .*
>
> —PHILIPPIANS 2:13
> (THE MESSAGE)

or duplicity so that we can live more in freedom. At any moment, any of these questions could be relevant to a current situation:

- If I give up my fear, might I have to act in courage and boldness?
- If I give up an attachment to my feelings of inadequacy, might I have to step out onto the razor's edge of risk without my loser's limp, my excuses, my rationalizations, and my justifications for why I can't do something?
- If I give up my guilt, who will I be? If I stop punishing myself and accept grace, how will that feel?
- If I give up shame, will I still be humble?
- If I give up my dependence on _____, will God fill the hole in my soul the substance, process, or person has filled?

8. Sometimes we must surrender our limited and limiting images of ourselves, our gifts, and our capabilities in order to step into the largeness of our lives. Sometimes we have to surrender our false pride and humility and assume full responsibility for the gifts we have and the gold of our greatness. It is scary to live up to our high calling; there's a lot of responsibility in choosing to live fully and abundantly.

9. Surrender means we sometimes accept things as they are, as hard as they are, giving up the fight to make them over in our image.

Acceptance is the answer to all of my problems today. When I am disturbed, it is because I find some person, place, thing or situation—some fact of my life—unacceptable to me, and I can find no serenity until I accept that person, place, thing, or situation as being exactly the way it is supposed to be at this moment. . . . Unless I accept life completely on life's terms, I cannot be happy. I need to concentrate not so much on what needs to be changed in the world as on what needs to be changed in me and my attitudes.[4]

Early in the morning, I sit in study and pray the Prayer of Abandonment, a prayer I was given many years ago at my first silent retreat at Wellspring, the retreat center of the Church of the Savior, in Washington, DC. The prayer is a version of the Our Father, written by Charles de Foucauld. It has become so much a part of my inner world that sometimes when I wake up in the night, I am praying it, and it comforts me.

Father,
I abandon myself into your hands.
Do with me what you will.
Whatever you may do, I thank you.
I am ready for all; I accept all.
Let only your will be done in me,
and in all your creatures.
I wish no more than this, O Lord,
Into your hands I commend my soul.
I offer it to you with all the love of my heart
for I love you, Lord,
and so need to give myself,
to surrender myself without reserve
and with boundless confidence,
for you are my Father.
Amen.

In the opening line, I substitute many other things for "myself" in surrender. I abandon (yield, surrender) my relationships, a loved one, a problem, or an afflictive emotion to God. I abandon myself to God, and also my work, my gifts and abilities, my time, and my decisions. When I wake up at night praying this prayer, I often remember when I sat on the banks of the Concho River on a warm spring day and felt that God wanted me to know that he had abandoned himself to me as well.

In working with individuals and using this prayer, either on retreats or in spiritual direction, sometimes I find that they are resistant to using the name "father" for God, and some stumble on the word "abandonment." One person said to me, trembling, "My father was cruel to me, and then he abandoned me, and so I can't pray this prayer for stumbling over these words."

I never discount that resistance, and I take seriously the pain underneath the resistance. Transforming our God-concept and experiencing healing of the pain of abandonment may be the most important thing some of us do as we work out our salvation at the deep, inner level of our souls.

Sometimes I substitute other names for God and words such as "give, release, let go, yield" for "abandon." Often, resistance is our issue, and sometimes the process of working through it takes a long time.

Surrendering completely to love, be it human or divine, means giving up everything, including our own well-being, or our ability to make decisions. It means loving in the deepest sense of the word. The truth is that we don't want to be saved in the way God has chosen; we want to keep absolute control over our every step, to be fully conscious of our decisions, to be capable of choosing the object of our devotion.

—PAULO COELHO

The process of surrender and the working out of our salvation takes place over time. Such prayers as these, taken from my journals over many months, reveal an inner shift in my process:

• God, I cannot bear this pain, but I cannot let it go. Please help me. Please be bigger in my mind than this problem!
• God, if I'm honest, I want my way, but I know I should want your way. The best I can do today is tell you that I want to want your will, but right now it feels as if you are silent and distant and unconcerned. Can't you see how hard this is? Why won't you help me?
• You could change this if you would. Don't you part the waters and roll away stone? Why are you so silent? Why won't you do something? How can I trust you if you won't act?

- How can I keep trusting you without something to go on, some break, some sense that you hear me, see me, notice me?
- God, please do in me what I cannot do. Please remove my resistance to your work within me. I cannot seem to give it up, even though I know that is the only way out of this struggle. If you could just help me push my own self-will out of the way!
- God, I give this to you. I give you my willfulness and I give you the situation. I give you everything related to this mess, the things I know and the things I don't know. I give them to you, and please don't tell me you want them back! I don't even know if you hear me or not, but I'm asking you to take this and do with it what you will. I'm scared you won't take it, but I can't carry it any longer.
- You heard me. Nothing's changed, at least not yet, but I know you heard me. I can't prove it, but something inside my body has shifted. Let it be. Let it be.

So it is that in the gift of the constant, loving presence of the Holy Spirit that lives and moves among us, between us, and in us does finally make that presence known, though the movement may be as gentle as a slight breeze.

Isn't it the breath of God within us, the wind of his Spirit, that is there all along, waiting to be acknowledged, accessed, expressed, and lived?

The knowledge and experience and awareness of God-who-dwells-within becomes the Source, the wellspring, the light, the guidance system, the life force, the ultimate reality that gives the love, joy, peace, patience, kindness, and self-control we need to live the life to which we have been called. God within inspires and supports us as we live the one wild and precious life we've been given.

NOTES

1. M. Scott Peck, *People of the Lie: The Hope for Healing Human Evil* (New York: Simon & Schuster, 1983).

2. Oswald Chambers, *My Utmost for his Highest* (Grand Rapids: Discover House, 1935).

3. James Baldwin, *Notes of a Native Son* (Boston: Beacon Press, 1984) 101.

4. Alcoholics Anonymous, *The Big Book*, 4th ed. (New York: AA World Services, 2001) 417.

Chapter 10

PRIESTS TO
EACH OTHER

The words on the front cover of the June 7, 2010, issue of *Time* magazine, emblazoned over a photograph of the back of a person who appears to Pope Benedict, grabbed my attention: "Why Being Pope Means Never Having to Say You're Sorry."

Grabbing the magazine from the pile of mail, I stuffed it into my carry-on bag as I left the house for a trip to the Passion Play in Oberammergau, Germany. On our tour bus through Switzerland, Germany, and Austria, that issue of *Time* was the subject of several intense conversations.

I hurt for the wonderful Catholics writers, friends, and teachers who have introduced me to the life-changing practices of spiritual direction and contemplative prayer. Because they are members of a denomination that is frequently in the headlines, I ache for those for whom the recent scandals in the Catholic Church have caused hurt and embarrassment. I lament for all of us within the Christian world as the brokenness among us comes roaring to the surface, publicly and privately. It is easy to forget that when one part of the Body of Christ hurts, we all hurt.

I come from a religious tradition that embraces and sometimes argues about the doctrine of "the priesthood of every believer," and for the most part, I like that doctrine. I like the idea that every one of us has direct access to God and that none of us need a mediator in order to communicate with God or for God to communicate with us.[1]

The dark side of that doctrine is that it can lead to spiritual arrogance and isolation. Often I listen as ministers tell me of their terror of struggling alone with demons that the rest of us have. Their great shame is accompanied by the pressure to appear to have it all together. Far healthier are the priests and pastors I know who have found a soul companion or a group with whom to share their struggles.

I live with the belief that God is present within me and around me, alive and active as the center and circumference of all things. I experience God as the animating, life-giving force of all that is, never confined to

Because of the Lord's great love we are not consumed, for his compassions never fail. They are new every morning.

—LAMENTATIONS 3:22-23A

any one place but present in all places at all times. "There is never a place you can go where God is not," I've told my daughters, trying to reassure them of God's constancy, only to hear back from them that sometimes that all-present God was a bit of a burden, especially when they couldn't get away from people who knew their parents!

There have been times in my life, however, when the grace, mercy, and love of God, mediated through another person, have literally pulled me out of that "slimy pit of mud and mire and gave me a firm place to stand" (Ps 40:2). I have needed to hear the voice of forgiveness coming through a living instrument of Christ who sits before me. I have needed the tenderness of mercy communicated through presence and participation in my suffering.

At times, I have needed a human being to confront the fig leaves of my defenses and help me remove them. I have needed people to remind me that I am more than my failures, my wounds, and my heartaches. I am more than any label anyone has ever put on me, greater than any role I play, and more than my Sins.

Sometimes I have needed someone to unwrap my death cloths of guilt and shame, inferiority and fear, hate and anger. I've needed someone who could stand the stench of those death wrappings long enough to wait as I struggled to come up out of the grave of loss, sorrow, and failure. I've needed someone to walk me out into the fresh, clean breezes of a new day.

For the priests in my life, lay and professional, who have been willing to mediate the presence of Christ to me, I am forever indebted and eternally grateful.

As far as I can tell, this joint venture, this journey we call life, is a lifetime venture, and on the path of it, we both learn a lot and we are always beginners.

Like the confused and dismayed disciples on the road to Emmaus after the wrenching experience of the crucifixion of Jesus, we walk along together, and now and then the Living Christ appears between us and with us, and when we recognize that Presence, our hearts, like the disciples', are strangely warmed. We then have the courage and the capacity to be what Carlyle Marney called "priests to each other," a phrase that challenges us with the capacity each of us has to extend God's love to each other and the courage required to step into that role.[2]

I can think of nothing more practical in the spiritual life than the act of coming clean in confession. If I had my way, which I do not, I would reinstate the confessional booth, not as an obligatory ritual, but as a way of providing an opportunity for us to confess our sins. There are few things more profoundly life-changing than knowing the forgiveness of God.

The brokenness within organizational structures of the church demands to be acknowledged, addressed, healed, and liberated. Unfortunately, instead of doing our own inner soul work, we in the church are more prone to projection, scapegoating, and pointing fingers of blame outward to whoever the current enemy of the day happens to be.

The *Time* magazine cover is shocking, but it stirs me to ask if any human is above having to say he or she is sorry? Could it be that even the idea or belief that someone is above that humiliating act is possibly the cause of suffering for others?

How many times could one family's tragedy have been different if each person in the family could have owned his or her part in a problem? When one member of a group won't own his fault, who carries it? Whose projections get shuffled onto others, and what bitter fruit does that produce?

Is it any wonder, then, that when I asked for an answer to a perplexing dilemma, my analyst would say to me over and over, "Consciousness, consciousness, consciousness," letting me know that I was responsible—painfully, unendingly, and always responsible—for my part in a problem. Awareness, he told me, was the key to getting loose from the shackles of my shadow, my character defect, and my lack of responsibility!

"The burn you feel is the unchaining of your soul," a wise friend said about her own coming to consciousness about her character defects.

The truth is that every one of us frail and fallible human beings must ultimately face our own culpability and sin. The process of owning up to what one has done that has hurt another person or oneself isn't easy for any of us; no one enjoys having to admit the wrongs done to others, and yet sometimes that wrenching process brings us to restored life, repaired relationships, and rekindled hope.

As a child, I remember hearing adults talk about the sins of omission—failing to do the things you know you should have done—and the sins of commission—doing the things you should not have done. Sometimes we do hurtful things out of ignorance, and sometimes we do them out of willfulness, and sometimes we are complicit with evil systems either because we don't know what to do or we are afraid to do what we know to do.

A poster of a dancer on a beach at sunrise hung on my wall for years. The words from Psalm 23, "He restores my soul," graced the poster. Restoration of the soul and the restoring of one's relationship with one's inner being, with God, and with others is grace at work. Having received forgiveness, surely an appropriate response is to dance.

However, admitting we're wrong, saying "I'm sorry" for the least offense, or owning our part in the breakdown of something seems hard for most of us. The willingness to say, "I was wrong, "or "I hurt you, and I ask for your forgiveness" is rare. Often I hear or read something that is more along the lines of "I'm sorry if I hurt you," or "I didn't mean to offend you," which not only is an avoidance of responsibility but also a missed opportunity for experiencing the blessing of forgiveness.

It is hard to admit we've done something wrong or hurt someone. It's hard to admit our character defects, and the truth is that for some, it is so hard that they cannot do it, even if it might save their lives. It is easier to blame someone else, blame "the illness" or the devil, spin out justifications, rationalizations, and excuses than it is to say, "I did it, and I take responsibility for it," or "I did it, and I will do what I can to repair what I have broken."

When my grandson Matthew was four, he picked up a metal bucket at his Montessori school and banged his cousin Madeleine on the head with it. Of course, Matthew's action set off a chain of events and conversations and created quite a buzz in the classroom. On the way home from school, my daughter Michelle said to Matthew, "I heard that you hit Madeleine on the head with a bucket today. Did you do that?"

Matthew responded, "I did."

Perhaps Michelle was hoping that Madeleine had provoked Matthew's aggression toward her, which would explain such an act and maybe even excuse it a bit. However, Matthew offered no reason for what he'd done and didn't seem interested in justifying why he had done it,

"Why did you do that, Matthew?" Michelle asked, and he replied simply, "I just did it."

Of course there was a reason, but there was something rather healthy about his simple admission of guilt. As adults, we might learn from Matthew's example, but we also live with a responsibility to become more conscious and figure out why we do what we do.

It is worth noting that Matthew didn't go the next step and say he was sorry for what he did, and maybe he wasn't. Being sorry, I suppose, will have to come later as his sense of moral consciousness evolves and matures.

He will learn that being sorry he got caught and punished is not the same as being sorry he did something wrong.

When our family gathers now, there are seven grandchildren, and six of them are under six years old. Someone is always doing something to provoke, irritate, offend, or even injure someone else. Inevitably, one of the children comes running in to tattle on another one, and one or the other of my three daughters, "the mothers" as Madeleine calls them, says, "Is this my problem or is it yours?"

On the one hand, I think these little cousins are young to have to figure that out, and occasionally I suggest that they might need a little help with discernment. Now and then, as well, I step in where neither fools nor angels should tread and take up for whichever little one I think is being played as a scapegoat. Sometimes children have a hard time pulling out of a downward spiral and need an advocate, a comforter, or a friend.

Primarily, though, I am impressed at the way these children are learning to set boundaries, say I'm sorry, and get along with other children. I'm impressed with my daughters' parenting, and I am impressed with the Montessori schools some of them attend and the ways in which my grandchildren are learning how to live with other people.

We all like sheep have gone astray, each of us has turned to our own way . . . .

—Isaiah 53:9

I've learned a lot about owning my behavior, examining myself, making confession, and making amends over the years, and I hadn't expected to have to do that. Growing up, I thought and assumed that since I had invited Jesus to come into my heart, my sins were covered. Perhaps there is no more damaging illusion within my particular part of the church than this, but it is countered by another damaging part of the whole "salvation story." We need to rethink it. On the one hand, we are taught from an early age that we have a black stain in our hearts, and only Jesus can rub it out with his blood. On the other hand, we are given the assurance that if we have accepted Jesus as our personal Savior, our sins are covered and our salvation is assured in the sweet by and by. In the meantime, what do we do about the messes we make, the fears we harbor, and the angers we nurse in our earthbound existence?

I've heard others talk about how they worried as children about committing the unpardonable sin. I've heard my Catholic friends talk about straining to come up with something they could confess to the priest so that they could receive the Eucharist, and this misunderstanding about our nature and God's nature has not, I think, made us better people overall. Perhaps the fear of doing wrong has kept some of us out of trouble, but if you refrain from doing something out of fear, are you really "good"?

When we moved to Houston in 1992, I was aware of two things about the city. At the time, this magnificent city had two or three of the largest mega-churches in the country, and the rest of the city was literally filled with smaller churches. On the other hand, the city also had the highest crime rate in the country. As I drove through the city in those first few weeks and months, I pondered the disconnection between the easy availability of churches and the terrible crime rate.

Now, eighteen years later, I am even more troubled by the statistics that show the high percentage of children who go to bed hungry in this state every night and reveal that this city is a major crossroads for drug and human trafficking. This city has produced some of the biggest white-collar criminals and some of the most corrupt politicians in the country.

What, I ask, is the problem?

As a lifelong member of a local church in a denomination in which leaders once bragged about big numbers, I lament the turn my people have taken in the last thirty years. As a group, we have become a symbol of hypocrisy and arrogance; some of that is earned, and some of it is hyped up by those who need a scapegoat. I do know, however, that much of the dissension and trouble within my expression of the church is the result of projecting our inner darkness onto someone else. What we need is what I discovered in the world of recovering people: to admit our failures and defects, to surrender to God, to take a moral inventory, to make confession, and to make amends. Collectively, we need to be priests to each other!

Yet, could it be that our theology and doctrine—the black stain and the belief that all we have to do is say yes to Jesus—keeps us locked in self-righteousness and unable to deal effectively with our brokenness? Does it keep us pointing our fingers outward at the current designated enemy, offering simplistic slogans and solutions to the deep sufferings of people, and losing members by the thousands?

As I write this chapter, novelist Anne Rice's statement on leaving Christianity has grabbed the headlines. "I quit being a Christian. I'm out," she wrote on her Facebook page. "I remain committed to Christ as always, but not to being a Christian or to being part of Christianity. It's simply impossible for me to 'belong' to this quarrelsome, hostile, disputatious, and deservedly infamous group."

My eyes filled with tears as I read the rest of her words: "My conversion from a pessimistic atheist . . . to an optimistic believer in a universe created and sustained by a loving God is crucial to me. But following Christ does not mean following his followers."

I sucked in my breath and held it as I read the indictment against organized religion and, in Anne Rice's case, her own experience of "church," ever mindful that there are enormous differences in the institutionalized church, the hierarchy, the various denominations, and a local church. Anne Rice's experience within the Catholic Church, her experience of Christianity, is far different from my experience in an autonomous, free Baptist church in which we say we are free from hierarchical structures, but she strikes a valid blow at the awfulness of contemporary cultural Christianity. I hope we all wake up and take note of what she has said.

The following week, in his comments about Rice's words, *Miami Herald* columnist Leonard Pitts referenced the trending down of the number of people who call themselves Christian in this country and the increase of those who claim no religious affiliation.[3] Ironically, the trend downward, Pitts says, seems to have been aided and abetted by religious zealots who carried a message not of hope, mercy, and love, but of condemnations, exclusivism, and strife. Yet, at the end of his column, Pitts delivers his own message of hope in the form of piercing questions that we who serve within a local church must face and ponder.

"What of those who are not atheists?' Pitts asks. "What of those who feel the blessed assurance that there is more to this existence than what we can see or empirically prove? What of those who seek a magnificent faith that commits and compels, and find churches offering only a shriveled faith that marginalizes and demeans?"

I've read Pitts's column over and over, and each time I think, "It's come to this." If this column and the announcement by Anne Rice are not wake-up calls for us, what is?

As a columnist myself, I wanted to rush to my keyboard write my own op-ed piece about the big difference between organized religion and the living organism known as "the church." I wanted to elaborate on the differences between Rice's experience within a hierarchical structure and mine in a free church, a free and flawed community of faith, a body of believers who share a common commitment to Christ. I want to differentiate between being a church member and a follower of Christ; I want to make the point that in my experience, salvation isn't through the church but through a commitment to Christ that is lived out on the hot anvils of life, challenged on the razor's edges of risk and difficulty, and realized in moments of grace here and there, now and then. I want to write in bold letters that

> *If we claim to be without sin we deceive ourselves and the truth is not in us. If we confess our sins, he is faithful and just and will forgive us our sins . . . .*
>
> —1 JOHN 19

there is more to "being a Christian" than having your name on a membership roll, being baptized either as an infant or an adult, and showing up for a service now and then or every week!

I weep for how the Body of Christ has lost its way. I weep for the ways in which the denomination I serve and what many call institutionalized religion have become more about self-preservation than healing the wounded and liberating the captives of addictions and brokenness. I cringe when I realize that we within the church have often given bumper-sticker answers to questions people aren't asking while the wounded, lost, and lonely have to seek help outside the church walls. And I continue to go back to the basic and practical practice of confessing one's own sins. We in the church need to get on our knees and confess our sins.

I've come to understand the teachings of Jesus to be profoundly sound and life giving. In fact, I'm pretty convinced that healthy spirituality is the same thing as healthy psychology. After all, the word *psyche* in the Greek means *soul*. Psychopathology is about the suffering of the soul. Psychology is the study of the soul. Who more than Jesus reveals what happens when people are changed, healed, and transformed at the soul level?

From the beginning, I learned from my Twelve Steps friends that I cannot change anyone but myself, but that I'd better work on myself. I keep wondering why on earth the people who lead these grand churches and denominations have not heard the good news of the power of the middle steps. Framed at the beginning by the first three steps of surrender, "I can't; he can, and I'm going to let him," and at the end by the last two, "I'm keeping conscious contact with God and I'm giving away what I have," are the seven steps that will transform your life if you work them.

From the first moment I read these steps, I knew in the deepest part of my soul that they were biblically based, which was important to me. I knew that if I worked through them, they would ease the suffering in my soul that I could not yet name but was always there, pushing up from my unconscious mind to get my attention. Whereas some people recoil from this process, I ran to it and run to it now when I am in an emotional knot or a conflict.

Jesus said it like this: "Do not judge, or you too will be judged. For in the same way you judge others, you will be judged, and with the measure you use, it will be measured to you." Matthew recorded these words what we call the Sermon on the Mount (Matt 7:1).

That profoundly sound psychological principle is a foundation of both the Yokefellow Spiritual Growth Groups that formed my early spirituality and the Twelve Steps of Alcoholics Anonymous.

"You can't change anyone but yourself, Jeanie," my friends in AA told me over and over when I wanted to blame this person or that one. "Work on yourself," they would say. "You're going to find that that is a full-time job, and you're never done."

"You can't do anyone else's moral inventory," a wise, weathered woman told me, "but you'd better do your own if you really want serenity and peace."

Rabbi Jesus' knowledge of projection and his depth of wisdom are evident in these homespun words from Matthew 7:3-5: "Why do you look at the speck of sawdust in your brother's eye and pay no attention to the plank in your own eye? How can you say to your brother, 'Let me take that speck out of your eye,' when all the time there is a plank in yours? You hypocrite, first take the plank out of your own eye, and then you will see clearly to remove the speck from your brother's eyes."

In Matthew 13:24-31, Jesus' parable about the enemy who sows weeds among a man's good wheat reveals a truth that seems lost in contemporary Christianity. The owner's servant asks if the owner wants him to go to the field and pull up the weeds, and Jesus says the owner responds, "No, because while you are pulling up the weeds you may root up the wheat with them."

After I spoke at an event about my book on Job, a man came up to me to respond to my description of Baptists' denominational war, which I likened to a kind of Job experience and an ash heap of suffering. He recounted a conversation he had with one of the leaders of the group that has led the purging of our convention. The man said, "In this denominational war, careers have been destroyed, reputations have been ruined, trust is all but non-existent, churches are split, families have been broken. Friendships have been forever ended. People have had health crises and there have been deaths attributed to the stress of this. Longtime ministries have been cut and, worst of all, the children of these people who have been destroyed by the purge have either left the church altogether or have left us to go to a place where there is no fighting."

"For what?" the man finished, weeping. "Why?"

It seems to me that those who felt that they were right and righteous have pulled up the good wheat with what they saw as weeds. We are a broken, wounded group of people, and all of us are standing in the need of grace. *But some of us think the problem is those sinners out there.*

What if, instead of going after all the enemies out there, each of us would tend the soil and the weeds, the rocks and the pests in our own gardens? What if, instead of blinding others with our criticism, judgment, and censure, we worked on the planks in our own eyes?

I have heard Jim Hollis say on many occasions in his classes at Houston's C. G. Jung Center that we are under a moral obligation to clean up the toxic waste dump of our inner lives and, instead of being narcissistic to do our inner work, we would actually be doing an act of kindness to our family, friends, and colleagues. All of us, it seems, are standing in the need of a moral inventory!

Early in my friendships with members of the recovering community, I heard about the "two-step" that many people do. "We love to take a first step and admit we are powerless over whatever substance, process, or practice has us in its grips," my friend told me, "and we love to go out and bring in someone else (following the twelfth step). Those are the easy steps."

It didn't take much for me to connect the dots in my religious world. We have a two-step as well. We want to be saved, and we are taught to go out and bring in someone else, but there is a lot of working out one's salvation that should go in between. When I saw the ten steps

Lord Jesus Christ, have mercy on me . . . .

—THE JESUS PRAYER

between the first and the twelfth, I knew they were a vital link in becoming whole, healthy, and saved.

These steps provide a way to deal with our character defects, to clean up the toxic waste dump of our inner lives, to own our defects and darkness, to admit our failures, and to make things right with the people we have harmed. Are they easy? No. Do they work? Yes!

Here are the Steps that may make you weep and gnash your teeth, but they also can liberate you.

1. We admitted we were powerless over alcohol—that our lives had become unmanageable.
2. Came to believe that a Power greater than ourselves could restore us to sanity.
3. Made a decision to turn our will and our lives over to the care of God as we understood Him.
4. Made a searching and fearless moral inventory of ourselves.
5. Admitted to God, to ourselves, and to another human being the exact nature of our wrongs.
6. Were entirely ready to have God remove all these defects of character.
7. Humbly asked Him to remove our shortcomings.
8. Made a list of all persons we had harmed, and became willing to make amends to them all.
9. Made direct amends to such people wherever possible, except when to do so would injure them or others.
10. Continued to take personal inventory and when we were wrong promptly admitted it.
11. Sought through prayer and meditation to improve our conscious contact with God, as we understood Him, praying only for knowledge of His will for us and the power to carry that out.
12. Having had a spiritual awakening as the result of these Steps, we tried to carry this message to alcoholics, and to practice these principles in all our affairs.[4]

Over the course of these years, I have found incredible healing in the experience of writing down my shortcomings, wrestling with them in prayer, confessing them to another human being, and attempting to make amends. This process has become part of my daily life, and probably no other spiritual discipline I do has more practical and immediate effect than working these steps.

Being known as I am by another human being has helped me know myself. Being heard without judgment or censure or even evaluation or interpretation has liberated me from the emotional knots of a lifetime. Being blessed by words of forgiveness has transformed what I thought would kill me into something that has helped me become stronger and more compassionate. Strangely, allowing myself to admit my shortcomings has given me the eyes to see my strengths and claim them. Admitting my weaknesses has made me stronger. Accepting my flaws and failures has changed the way I live. Allowing myself to know that I am imperfect and incomplete has given me courage to access, develop, and express strengths and abilities I didn't know I had.

All of this has helped me bear with more grace the problems I cannot solve, the dreams I've had to relinquish, the mistakes I can never repair, the time I cannot get back, and the wounds I have inflicted on others. For another human being to sit with me in infinite patience and tolerate my insufficiencies, inabilities, and weaknesses has freed me to accept those things in myself and be more patient with myself than I ever dreamed I could be.

My friend Tim Blanks is the facilities manager of Laity Lodge, a retreat center in the Hill Country of Texas that has been a sacred space for me for four decades. Tim is also a recovering alcoholic, a reality he wears with gratitude and joy—now. One morning as we waited on the porch for the bell to announce that it was time for breakfast, he and I chatted about the way recovered alcoholics try to keep their alcoholism a secret.

"It's strange to me that when we're using [alcohol or drugs] and running over parking meters and falling down drunk," he said, "we aren't concerned about who is seeing us like that, but when we get into recovery and get sober, all of a sudden we are concerned about our anonymity!"

It is ironic, isn't it?

Tim went on to talk about the freedom of living clean and sober, out in the open, unafraid of others knowing that he is a recovering alcoholic.

"It's really my biggest strength," he said. "My strength comes from my weakness. To be free of that junk in my life, to be able to talk about it openly and know that what happened in me can help someone else . . . ." Then Tim stopped. I think he must have stopped because the magnitude of forgiveness and grace simply overtook him.

Truly, there are no words to express such a miracle as God's amazing grace, mediated through human beings as we are priests to each other.

In my religious culture, we might find our way back to what really matters by following the practices of our recovering friends. We might find our way out of the wilderness we have created by falling on our knees and confessing to another human being, especially those we have harmed. Perhaps we might find peace if we could do what the Bible counsels us to do—since we say we believe the Bible—and confess our sins to each other.

But why am I writing in the editorial "we" when I have just stated that I can't change anyone but myself? I cannot take another's moral inventory, and I cannot confess another's sins, but I must do that for myself. I cannot make amends for anyone but myself, but I must do it for myself, and when I have harmed someone I must do what I can to repair what I have broken.

Working the Twelve Steps over these years, I have learned that there is another side to this process and other truths that must be woven into the fabric of my spirituality.

I've learned that while it is true that I cannot do another's inventory, I need to be aware of the ways in which other people who don't or won't do their work project their darkness onto me. I need to be aware of the times and the people who might make me a scapegoat or use me in a way that is harmful to me, thus avoiding facing their own darkness.

I've learned that while I may work on one of my own defects of character, sometimes other people may try to maneuver me into playing the role of persecutor, rescuer, or victim in their life dramas to avoid taking responsibility for their own flaws of character.

I've learned that there are times within a family when everyone may be organized against seeing and knowing and telling the truth about something, but that doesn't mean I have to do others' work for them or that what I perceive to be true is wrong.

I've learned that pronouncing "my truth" to others may not be the smartest thing to do. Sometimes I'm showing off or strutting my advanced spirituality. Sometimes I'm trying to gain power, and sometimes I'm trying to manipulate others by my superior consciousness, which nearly always isn't quite as superior as I would like to think it is. While I may know what's going on, if I impose it on others, I'm apt to get feedback I don't want.

I've learned that there are situations and systems in which other people are willing for me to carry the blame for something, but that doesn't mean I am to blame. It may mean that other people won't do it and I'm conditioned to do it.

I've learned that there are times when forgiveness and reconciliation are not possible, but that doesn't mean I have to continue beating myself up.

Forgiveness is a process that involves the offender and the offended. It must be asked for. It can be given, but it's a two-way street. I can be willing to forgive, but it takes two to complete the process.

God can work in all things, however broken and blocked they are, to bring about good, but I have noticed that God seems to work most effectively when there are open hearts, open minds, open hands, and eager spirits to live in love, grace, and tolerance together.

We all are broken people, and we all stand in need of prayer. All of us need compassion—both to give it and to receive it. Forgiveness is a way of life, a lifestyle that leads to peace among people. I cannot change another person, and no one else can change me, although other people affect us all the time.

Forgive us our sins, as we forgive those who sin against us . . . .

—LUKE 11:4

Leonard Cohen's mysterious anthem "Hallelujah" ends by declaring that "ours is not a victory march," but is instead a "cold and a broken hallelujah." Yet it is still a hallelujah. He seems to know the grace and mercy of God that are available to us in spite of our failures. Hear this statement of grace in the midst of failure from that song:

> And even though it all went wrong
> I'll stand before the Lord of Song
> With nothing on my tongue but
> Hallelujah.

These words always take me to the image of Jesus, naked and dead on a criminal's cross. Surely, in that moment it must have seemed that everything had gone wrong. Who among us has not had those terrible moments? Even so, we affirm that in the midst of that, there is a hallelujah!

In "Anthem," another acknowledgment of our imperfections, Cohen gives meaning to the broken parts of ourselves. The song offers grace in these lines:

> The birds they sang
> at the break of day.
> Start again
> I heard them say.
> Don't dwell on what has passed away

Or what is yet to be . . .
Ring the bells that still can ring
Forget your perfect offering
There is a crack in everything
That's how the light gets in.[5]

Is there any clearer gospel than that?

It is through our broken places that the Light gets in.

We must admit and then lament our losses and grieve our failures, but we do not have to stay there. We must weep and sometimes wail about the things we have done and the things we have left undone, but then we are to rise up from our ash heaps and begin again. And then begin again. And then begin again.

NOTES

1. It is important to differentiate between the official function of ordained priests and the function of friends, sponsors, therapists, and analysts who mediate the love, grace, and mercy of God to us. In this chapter, I am speaking of the latter.

2. Carlyle Marney, *Priests to Each Other* (Greenville SC/Macon GA: Smyth & Helwys Publishing, 1991).

3. Leonard Pitts, "An Evil with Many Masters," *Miami Herald*, April 7, 2010.

4. Alcoholics Anonymous, "The Twelve Steps of Alcoholics Anonymous," Service Material from the General Service Office, http://www.aa.org/en_pdfs/smf-121_en.pdf (accessed 9 April 2011).

5. Leonard Cohen, "Hallelujah," *Various Positions*, Sony, 1994; "Anthem," *The Future*, Sony, 1992.

Chapter 11

GUARDING
YOUR HEART

"You have to walk your talk, man," a friend of mine told his buddy who was new to Alcoholics Anonymous. "It's not enough to talk it. Talk's cheap," he continued, speaking out of long years of his own recovery from an addiction. "You have to walk your walk and talk your walk, and you have to do it every day."

The new member of AA shook his head, as if he couldn't imagine the day-by-day discipline and consciousness that was going to be asked of him.

"For the rest of my life?" he asked.

"Yep," his new sponsor said to him, not giving an inch, "but the good news is that you can't do it but one day at a time, and every day you get a brand new day."

Walking the talk of the Christian life might be easier if all of us were put in Twelve Step groups, and, in fact, my friend Keith Miller has proposed and encouraged such a thing. The fact is that it isn't easy to give up an egocentric life and begin to live from the kingdom that is within. It seems to me that we might all be better off if we had a sponsor with whom we could check in when life gets complicated and we want to revert to our old ways of being in the world. There have been times when I have wished I were required to attend a meeting every day for ninety days so that I would be accountable to others for walking my talk!

Indeed, it is true that people are slaves because freedom is hard and slavery is easy, whether you are a recovering addict, an ordinary flawed human being, or an active church member. Following Jesus' teachings and his example of living a fully authentic life is hard, given the pressures and constraints of the culture in general and our individual families, friends, and coworkers. I want to live with integrity and authenticity. I want to love and forgive like Jesus did, but my own complexes and defects often interfere.

"I thought I'd taken care of this!" the man said, despairing of the fact that he was back in the grips of a problem he thought he'd solved forever.

"Haven't we been here and done that before? Why do we have to keep repeating the same old thing?" a woman asked me. Frustrated with herself and the pull of her old patterns of behavior, she was discouraged and disheartened by what she called the weakness of her will and the strength of her addiction. "I'm so tired of this problem! It is so boring!"

> *Above all else, guard your heart, for it is the well-spring of life.*
>
> —PROVERBS 4:23

My mentor in writing, Madeleine L'Engle, used to say, "It's not one thing after another that gets me, but the same damned thing over and over!"

Who doesn't understand that?

One of the most seductive temptations I have faced is thinking that with all I know, with all I have learned, with all I have experienced, I should be further along the road of life than I am. I should be more on top of things than I am, and I should be better/more sane and serene/less afraid/whatever than I am!"

Listening to Jim Hollis lecture on the necessity and power of persistence, I gave up my idea that I would be zapped with enlightenment at some point if I only worked hard enough. There in class, I had to surrender my fantasy that someday, somehow, on some enchanted evening I would finally arrive, solve my big problem, and be free forever of what bothered me at the time. In that moment, I realized that while I might have an increased understanding of my problem and increasingly inspiring insights from my attempts to learn and understand, I was in a lifetime process and truly, the journey itself was the destination.

Quoting Carl Jung, Jim Hollis talked about how "the greatest and most important problems of life are all fundamentally insoluble. They can never be solved, but only outgrown," or, as Jim said that night, "We can learn to live with them in a different way."

In some ways it is a relief to know that, but on the other hand, knowing that simply makes me want to wring my hands and wail!

Persistence and perseverance are necessary qualities on the path of wholeness, and the reality is that spiritual growth is not a linear process or a ladder of success we climb toward some goal of perfection. Instead, our growth is more circular. We circle back and around the same issues for most of our lives, but hopefully we gain insight and a deepening sense of wholeness as we make that circuitous journey.

I have come to understand that the joint venture I am on is filled with uncertainty, imperfection (the world's, other people's, and, most painfully and certainly, my own), disorder, disease, and chaos. Carl Jung also said, "Nobody, as long as he moves about among the chaotic currents of life, is without trouble," and then he pushed even more on my resistance and said, "Man needs difficulties; they are necessary for health."

As I read the Bible, sacred stories of God's involvement with human beings are filled with victory and defeat, failure and loss, wars and battles, blood and guts, and that reminds me that trusting God with my whole heart and counting on the assurance of a heavenly home someday does not exempt me from the vicissitudes of life here on earth. I do believe Jesus saves, but I do not believe in a simplistic view that says we are saved from the perils of living in this plane. Jesus saves, and I believe that means the Spirit of God works within us to make us whole and healthy—if we cooperate in the process! Jesus may be the answer, but we have to know what the questions are, and sometimes we may have to learn how to live with unanswered questions, unresolved pain, broken dreams, misunderstandings, and dots that never connect.

Accepting that life is difficult for all of us, learning how to trust God and myself, and accepting the reality of the nature of life is an ongoing process for me. Living one day at a time, trusting moment by moment in the belief that God is at work in my life, and letting go of my need to control events to manage my anxiety calls for an ongoing recovery process.

Rainer Maria Rilke's words quoted in the introduction express a way of life in which God is a Verb, the one whose spirit blows freely here and there and cannot be captured in a fixed idea or in one place.

The famous writer "Anonymous" counsels, "In order to get from what was to what will be, you have to go through what is." How I get from what was and through what is can be easier when I make guarding my heart a priority and when I lift the concept of "seeking first the kingdom of God" off the pages of the Bible and integrate it into my daily life.

I am convinced that the intention of the Spirit of God, working from within and in our individual and collective lives is to heal, transform, liberate, and empower us to be who we are created to be and to do what we are sent here to do. In the Gospels, Jesus walked into peoples' lives with that same intent. He said almost nothing about the afterlife, but he spoke much truth about how to live this life now.

The Twelve Steps of Alcoholics Anonymous provide a pattern for daily life that those who attempt to live in a joint venture with God can use. Working the steps calls for a daily surrender of oneself to God, and as participants in recovery groups say at the end of each meeting, "Keep coming back. It works, if you work it."

"If you work it" matters.

"The reason we have slogans," I was told by a friend who had been in AA for many years, "is that they are like anchors for us when we begin to drift away from sobriety or from our program. When I was a child, I was told that the memory verses I learned

> *Let us run with perseverance the race marked out for us. Let us fix our eyes on Jesus, the author and perfecter of our faith . . . .*
>
> —HEBREWS 12:1-2

in Sunday school would help me someday, and indeed they have. At some of the most difficult moments of my life, those sacred Scriptures I learned as a child have bubbled up from the archives of memory to speak hope, comfort, encouragement, and inspiration *from within.*"

As I began working the Twelve Steps, I was drawn to the eleventh step, "We sought through prayer and meditation to improve our conscious contact with God, praying only for the knowledge of God's will and the power to carry it out."

Quickly, I began to see that although working all the steps is important either in recovery or in living the joint venture of life with God, the eleventh step is key in making the other steps work, and so I was drawn to the contemplative life and contemplative prayer. Soon, John 15 became my favorite passage of Scripture, and the guidance in it to "abide in Christ" became one of my anchors, a goal for my life and a visual image of how our life with God should be. Indeed, we are as intimately connected to God as a branch is connected to a vine, and the life of God flows into us as naturally as the life of the vine flows into the plant, producing the fruit that is already in the plant. I think there is no better image of the intimacy of our relationship with God than that of the vine and the branches, and the implications of abiding in Christ moment by moment, one day at a time, are practical and transforming.

Many of us live in fear; the Gospel writer John records that Jesus invites us to live (abide, dwell) in him. Some of us live in anger, or we are motivated by guilt or shame, and the more we dwell on those afflictive emotions, allowing them to take charge of our inner lives, the more we create the "fruit" that is the logical result of dwelling (wallowing, marinating) in the emotions.

The writer of Proverbs was right in suggesting that we are to guard our hearts, and it is true that whatever is at the heart of a person will be acted out (Prov 4:23). The heart, in Hebrew thought, is the innermost part of a person. More than the muscle that beats away in the chest, the heart is best understood as the part of us where the mind and emotions and the will come together.

There is nothing in my daily life that is more important than the practice of abiding in Christ, maintaining conscious contact with God, and guarding my heart. Perhaps another synonym is "walk your talk," and that spiritual discipline requires conscious effort and consistency if I am to live the life I'm intended to live and do the things I was sent here to do. That practice, also called practicing the presence of Christ, is the way in which the Divine Therapist who dwells within me heals me, liberates me, empowers me, and transforms me. It is the way I cooperate with God in this joint venture of the abundant life.

Over the years, I have developed many ways to keep myself abiding in Christ, and teaching these methods in workshops, retreats, and one-on-one spiritual direction sessions has helped me most of all. For my own well-being and spiritual growth, as well as for the benefit of those I teach, I have explored and learned many different and varied ways to strengthen our connection to the kingdom within.

No experience has been too unimportant, and the smallest event unfolds like a fate, and fate itself is like a wonderful, wide fabric in which every thread is guided by an infinitely tender hand and laid alongside another thread and is held and supported by a hundred others.

—RAINER MARIA RILKE

In recent years I have attended five eleven-day silent retreats at the Benedictine Monastery in Snowmass, Colorado, and I have been trained to facilitate Centering Prayer workshops, studying the work of Thomas Keating who, with Basil Pennington, developed the method of Centering Prayer and the training for facilitators.

"I can't do this!" a friend said to me one day as we walked down the hill from the retreat center at Snowmass for the evening prayers at the monastery. "I've prayed intercessory prayers for others for so many years that when I try to be still and know the presence of God, my mind automatically starts pleading on others' behalf."

Indeed, it takes a long time to change a lifelong habit or thought patterns. Others have said to me that they feel that spending twenty minutes in silence twice a day is selfish or self-centered. I remind them of the speech we who fly in airplanes can recite by memory now: "If you are traveling with a small child, put on your own oxygen mask first."

Over the years, I have also struggled with what to pray for others. How do I know that what I am praying is not me imposing my own will? How can I presume to know how to pray for another person, or, frankly, even for myself? I know what I want, and I've been prone to dictate my laundry list of desires to God, but who am I to assume that I know God's will for myself or for another human being? Do I, with my requests for others, pray amiss? Might I, by my intercessions, run the risk of binding another person in a way that is counter to the will of God, or are intercessory prayers that powerful? Is what I want for another person and my supplication in harmony with what God is trying to do, or am I working against God's intent and purpose? Does what I pray for another really make a difference or not?

On an early walk around my neighborhood one morning, the High Priestly prayer of Jesus in John 17 suddenly came to me. I knew I had found a way to intercede for others and pray for myself in a way that was consistent with God's will.

Jesus was intimately involved with his followers, especially the disciples, Mary and Martha, and Mary Magdalene. He had a deep bond with his mother; how heavy his sorrow must have been at the thought of his earthly life coming to an end. I am struck by the idea that he must have been burdened with the awareness that no matter how he had tried to communicate a whole new way of living with God, his followers had not quite gotten it. I can imagine that Jesus' love for his friends and his enjoyment of life with them must have made the idea of leaving them almost unbearable to him.

As I read John 17, I can almost see Jesus drawing apart to a room adjacent to where his followers might have been gathered around him. I can imagine his

> *I urge you to live a life worthy of the calling you have received.*
>
> —EPHESIANS 4:1B

saying to himself, "What can I say to them to help them live this new way? How can I give them something that will sustain them when I am gone?"

Every time I read this prayer in John 17, I am struck by two things. First, as a person who has been taught to put others first, I am amazed that Jesus begins by praying for himself. Second, in John 17:3, Jesus gives the definition of eternal life: "This is eternal life: that they may know you . . . ."

The Greek word for "knowing" in this verse does not indicate intellectual knowledge or a cognitive awareness, but rather the knowledge that comes from intimacy with God that is born from experience over time. This knowledge transcends facts, ideas, and doctrines and expresses the radical, life-altering truth: it is possible to have an intimate, personal, dynamic love relationship with the Creator of the universe. Eternal life is about our primary relationship with the Source of life; it is not so much about length of life or the afterlife, but the quality of life.

> *He who began a good work in you will carry it on to completion until the day of Christ Jesus.*
>
> —PHILIPPIANS 1:6

The goal, then, of spiritual growth is to strengthen the connection between oneself and God. The point of the process is to stay connected to the vine, the source of life and nourishment!

After Jesus prayed for himself, he prayed four specific requests for his disciples and "for those you have given me." Later in the chapter, after praying specifically for his disciples, he prays "for those who will believe." I am assuming that these prayer requests are for those of us who attempt to be Christ followers, and I believe the sequence of the requests is significant. In Romans 8:26, Paul writes about our mysterious connection with the Living Christ/the Holy Spirit. He says, ". . . the Spirit helps us in our weakness. We do not know what we ought to pray for, but the Spirit himself intercedes for us with groans that words cannot express." Is it too much of a leap to believe that the Living Christ/the Holy Spirit intercedes for us with these four petitions in Jesus' earthly prayer? And if these petitions are straight from the heart of Christ, are they not useful for us as we pray for our loved ones and for ourselves?

First, Jesus prayed for unity in John 17:11: "May they be one as we are one." Previously Jesus made radical claims about his own oneness with God, and he repeatedly said that whatever he did was guided by the Father's intent. In John 14:20, he speaks of this intimacy when he says, "I am in my Father and you are in me, and I am in you." These claims were threatening to the religious establishment of his day!

Here Jesus is praying that we have the same kind of unity with God that he has with God, and the implications of this are mind-boggling.

I know what it is like to feel fragmented, split, and pulled in many directions by competing claims and commitments. I know what it is like to feel broken and maimed by life, and I know what it is like when my inner life is in conflict with my outer life. I know what it is like to feel lonely and be distant and alienated from loved ones, from God, and from myself. I am acutely aware of what it is like to want one thing, but be unable to have it or bring it about; I know what it is like to have to wrestle with competing conflicts between my outer world realities and my inner world longings.

I am familiar with the terrifying moments in life when the silence of God is deafening, the seeming absence of God is overwhelming, and the gap between what I know I should do and what I cannot do feels like the great spans of space in the Grand Canyon.

As if my own inner wars were not enough, I am almost unbearably aware of the brokenness in the Body of Christ, both in the larger understanding of "the church" and within my experience of church. Having experienced the fracturing, devastating blows of denominational conflicts for more than thirty years, I know what distrust, rumors, lies, and power plays do to create strife and disunity among followers of Christ.

There are those within the Body of Christ who have tried to force uniformity on the church, insisting that one isn't a "real Christian" or a "true believer" unless he says he believes in a certain dogma, recites a particular creed, or "does" Christianity their way. We must note that the prayer of Jesus for his disciples is for unity and not uniformity. Within the church, we are to be united in our common love for Christ, but it seems clear that our unity is kept strong by our diversity. Jesus chose a diverse and what some have called a ragtag group of people as his followers, and Paul the apostle guided the early church to affirm and celebrate the diverse expressions of gifts that would make the church vibrant and effective.

Mercifully, I know what it is like to return to this simple prayer Jesus prayed for his disciples and pray *with him* for unity with God, and because I believe what Jesus said about the kingdom of God being within, I trust that when I seek first that kingdom, God is going to reconnect me with himself. If sin is separation from God, and I believe it is, then this prayer is the step back toward reunion, reconciliation, and restoration.

When I am feeling, lost, confused, afraid, or conflicted, I pray this prayer. When I do not know which direction to go, I start with this prayer. When I do not know what to pray, I start with, "Make us one," and when I am resisting God's work within my inner life or in the outer world and cannot yet pray "Thy will be done," I can begin with "Make me one with you." My plea is an acknowledgment that unity with God, the Source, is made possible by the action of that Source of life, working from within my mind and heart.

Though I would love to believe I know best how to pray for my husband and children, I have learned through the years that the safest prayer I can pray for them begins with "Make him/her/them one with you," and when I can pray the prayer Jesus prayed, I surrender my will for others and take my hands of control and manipulation off their lives, allowing God do to with them what God wills. (Sometimes I even think I hear God breathe a huge sigh of relief when I finally hand over the steering wheel of control into his hands!)

What is required of us is that we love the difficult and learn to deal with it. In the difficult are the friendly forces, the hands that work on us. Right in the difficult we must have our joys, our happiness, our dreams: there against the depth of this background, they stand out, there for the first time we see how beautiful they are . . . . Perhaps all the dragons in our lives are princesses who are only waiting to see us act, just once, with beauty and courage. Perhaps everything that frightens us is, in its deepest essence, something helpless that wants our love.

—RAINER MARIA RILKE

I do slip back into wanting to control others, and I let others control me from time to time. Praying my agenda for another human being can be one of the most insidious forms of control and manipulation. I may be right, *from my point of view,* but if I hand God my list of what he must do to please me, I set myself up for turmoil if God doesn't see fit to honor my requests, or for arrogance if somehow things turn out my way. Insistence that God answer my prayers for others as I want them answered indicates an arrogance of spirit and reveals my confusion about the nature of God and the purpose of prayer.

Unity with the Father seems to be Jesus' primary prayer request for his disciples. The second prayer request indicates Jesus' next priority for them and for us. In John 17:13 Jesus prays, *"that they have the full measure of my joy within them."* It is important to note that this joy, his joy, is the result of unity with the Father.

Early in my adult journey of faith, my West Texas friend Travis Perry gave my husband and me a beautiful decorative piece with a quote of Teilhard de Chardin. "Joy," Teilhard asserted, "is the most infallible sign of the presence of God."

Joy is a deep, inner quality, the second fruit in the list of the fruit of the Spirit in Galatians 5:22-23, following only love. It seems to be laced with love and peace and the other fruit of the Spirit.

Happiness can be faked, if necessary, but joy is an authentic expression that arises from within. Happiness is dependent on external realities, but joy is the result of the connection with God who dwells within, and it can be present in the midst of some of the deepest suffering. Joy cannot be earned, for it is a gift of grace, the result of the presence and action of God at the innermost level of one's life.

Now and then, I lose my connection with that wellspring of inner joy, but it is always available to me. Getting absorbed in daily life, I may forget about it; when I get too hungry, too angry, too lonely, or too tired, I may lose my way and become depleted and discouraged and even depressed, but what is different for me now is that I know my way back to the Source. Even better, I am confident that because I have turned my will and my life over to the care of God, somehow God reminds me that I've lost my way and wandered off into one pigpen or another. God is always present, and when I return to that awareness, the Waiting Father always welcomes me home, extending the deep, abiding joy that is the result of abiding in him.

Jesus' third request for his disciples indicates his awareness of the nature of human beings. In John 17:15 he prays, *"My prayer is not that you take them out of the world but that you protect them from the evil one."* Jesus' request is for protection, but it seems to me that his prayer is directed at anything that would break the unity of his people and the inner unity and harmony of his individual followers. Knowing how people are threatened by authentic joy, Jesus prayed for protection against the forces that would rob a person of his joy.

My father used to weep over any human being, especially little children or women, in whom "the lights had gone out of their eyes." Indeed, there is such a thing called "soul murder," an abuse so heinous and insidious that it is as if the soul of a person has been silenced or flogged away by criticism, physical or verbal or emotional violence, or religious abuse.

In an era in which Christians have gathered together in holy huddles to protect themselves against the forces of the devil who always seems to be "coming against them" through the media, the secular humanists, the liberals, or some other designated enemy of the day, Jesus' prayer is not that we escape into religious bunkers, but that we remain as salt and light in the world. Granted, we all feel safer if we are with people who think like we do, talk like we do, sing the same songs we do, and dress like we do, especially if there are large numbers of us beating time to the same music, but feeling safer and being safe are not the same.

Forgetting what is behind and straining toward what is ahead, I press on toward the goal to win the prize for which God has called me heavenward in Christ Jesus . . . . Let us live up to what we have already attained.

—PHILIPPIANS 3:12-15

We must ask ourselves if being safe is the point of the Christian journey. I think not, and history would not indicate that it is. As I understand this prayer and attempt to pray it for my loved ones, it is an act of faith for me to stop obsessing over the terrible things that might happen to my loved ones and pray simply that nothing will destroy their unity with the Father. I know life is going to happen to my loved ones, no matter how hard I work to protect them and attempt to prevent bad things from happening to them. My children have been and will be hurt by others. My husband will be affected by disease and distress; I will face loss and suffering, for that is life, and it is part of the abundant life. I can and must and do pray for protection for that innermost prayer closet, the soul, that place where the branch of my life is attached to the Giver of life.

I grew up on the great Baptist anthem "To the work, to the work, we are laborers for God. Toiling on . . . toiling on."

I have to smile when I think about how long it has been since I've heard that old hymn or the one about bringing in the sheaves and working until

Jesus comes. In this era of religious entertainment and sensationalism, hologram preachers and easy believism, those songs don't sell. In my world, we didn't much believe in grace, but we acted as if we had to work hard to earn the mansion in the sky with a crown of glory. We thought we were assured those things only if we were good enough, pure enough, and saintly enough and if we followed the rules well enough and *had enough faith.* Working out our own salvation with fear and trembling wasn't about becoming whole as much as it was about earning brownie points with God.

It is interesting to me, then, that the fourth and last request Jesus prayed for his disciples was for *usefulness. "Sanctify them (set them apart)," he prayed, "by the truth."* In other words, make them useful for my work. This request seems to be the result of unity with Christ, the joy that flows from that unity, and the protection of both the joy and the unity.

There is perhaps nothing more satisfying in this life than meaningful work and rich, deep love. Work is made meaningful by what we bring to it, and when it flows from a sense of calling that is based on unity with Christ, it is intensely satisfying and rewarding.

What if a big part of working out your own salvation is finding the work you are intended to do and doing it "as if unto the Lord"?

The last line of the short version of the Serenity Prayer is a request for the wisdom to know the difference between the things we can change and the things we cannot change. My life experience over these decades indicates that such discernment happens over time, and there is always something new to learn. There is always a new challenge to working out my salvation and participating in the joint venture of life with others as they work out theirs.

Marcel Proust says, "We do not receive wisdom; we must discover it for ourselves, after a journey through the wilderness which no one else can make for us, which no one can spare us . . . ." And yet, the One who made each of us is in us, attempting to work for good in steering us along the way of the individualized journey. He seems to be interceding on our behalf, praying for unity, joy, protection, and usefulness for us along the way.

As I have experienced the process of depth analysis, I have come to understand that the Self, as Jung called the part of us that is the most authentic, original part, is intimately connected to God, and so the abundant life is possible when I can shift my focus from my ego-outer world attachment and go deep within, seeking the kingdom of God. The prayer for unity with God like Jesus had seems to me to be a prayer for a connection with the True Self within. Praying it is a way of guarding my heart and keeping it going in the same direction that God is going.

The True Self is like an inner GPS, and sometimes I am led from within into situations that are intended to bring about my own growth and development, though those situations may appear as crises, difficulties, and challenges too big for me to handle with my present level of faith. The Self/God within knows what it is doing, however, and its purpose, God's purpose, is transformation and the fulfillment of the purpose for which I was made.

If you're going through hell, keep going.

—WINSTON CHURCHILL

I can attest to the fact that living from the inside out, answering to the God who dwells within, and being the authority of my own life is both challenging and life-giving. Writing my own life script, guided from within instead of acting and reacting to another's agenda or script for me, and living from my own Self-chosen values bring about a deep, abiding joy that defies description.

I can also attest to the fact that it is far easier to conform to outer-world expectations, to worry about what others might think, and to obsess about meeting standards of success than it is to live one's calling. The ego dies hard if it dies at all, and the complexes have an unusual and oppressive power. Eternal vigilance and prayer for the protection of the True Self is a vital part of communicating with God. The forces that would push and shove you back to accommodations, adaptations, and conformities are relentless, but the intention and the energy of the Self are relentless in accomplishing its goals.

On a cold January day I walked out on my deck and gasped. My Don Juan climber was blazing with gorgeous red roses, blooming out of season. I was so astonished that I said out loud, "What do you think you are doing, blooming like that in January?"

The rose bush felt no obligation to answer me, and if it had, it would have scared me to death, and yet it did answer. The blooms, big and beautiful and full of life, announced the presence of the life force surging through the stems of that bush, blooming blooms that were consistent with the nature of the bush and giving me a gift of beauty and grace that I have never forgotten. Did the rose bush care that it was blooming out of season?

How do we know that, from the bush's perspective, it was out of season?

Later, I rummaged through my large CD collection for my copy of the soundtrack to the film *The Rose*. I stuck it in my car and let Bette Midler sing it for me over and over as I drove across Texas to lead a retreat about rebirth and restoration in the dreary days of winter. I am always haunted by the image of the life force buried in the snow, waiting for the right time to bloom, and the memory of that Don Juan climber, bursting with blooms in January.

Guarding your heart, then, is tending the life force in whatever ways are meaningful to you. It is doing daily the spiritual practices that keep faith alive. As my friend Roger Paynter says, "We must learn to keep the faith . . . and let it keep us."

Even now, years later and with miles of trying to walk my talk under my belt, I return to the words of "The Rose" and let them encourage me to keep on keeping on.

> When the night has been too lonely and the road has been too long,
> and you think that love is only for the lucky and the strong . . .
> Just remember in the winter, far beneath the bitter snows
> lies the seed that with the sun's love
> in the spring becomes the rose.

In *The Message*, Eugene Peterson renders 1 John 1:3 in this way: "What marvelous love the Father has extended to us! Just look at it—we're called children of God. That's who we really are." Underneath the personas, the masks, and the ego lies who we really are.

The love of God, working deep within our depths, brings forth the True Self.

God does God's work. Our task is to guard our hearts and our feet, our hands, our minds, our bodies, our very lives.

We are, after all, the temples in which God dwells.

Let it be. Let it be.

Chapter 12

KAIROS TIME, SYNCHRONICITY, AND OTHER MYSTERIES

"You can't make this stuff up," my friend says to me when I tell him a tall tale that also happens to be true.

When I look back on the events of my life, I sometimes shake my head in wonder. I couldn't have made up the stuff of my life, but somehow through the twists and turns of it all I can see a pattern. As much as I resisted particular events, I can see that God was working for good in them. I can also see how my resistance to the flow of life has made my life harder; I can see that when I was able to relax and yield to reality, my life went much more smoothly. Sometimes, too, there have been surprises and synchronicities that have given me a deep, blessed assurance that God was with me.

Along the way I have pleaded with God to get me out of some situations and get me into other ones, and sometimes the silence of God before my requests and petitions has been deafening. I have protested and railed against misfortunes and difficulties of others and myself. I have fussed and whined about how hard it is to wake up from the luxury of denial and avoidance and participate fully in my life.

I have asked God to guide me and have found that sometimes the only guidance I got was for the next small step in the darkness of confusion. "I just get to trust God and do the next thing indicated," my friend Catherine Darden says, and I am always stunned by her faithfulness to that simple and hard way of being in the world.

My friend Vaughn Counts introduced me to the poem by Rainer Maria Rilke "The Man Watching," in which Rilke observes how we are shaped—

formed, reformed, or perhaps deformed—by the various events, moments, and relationships that occur in our daily lives. These lines from the second and third verses leap out at me every time I read them:

> What we choose to fight is so tiny!
> What fights us is so great!
> If only we would let ourselves be dominated
> as things do by some immense storm,
> we would become strong, too, and not need names.
>
> When we win it's with small things
> and the triumph itself makes us small.
> What is extraordinary and eternal
> does not want to be bent by us.[1]

Later in the same poem, Rilke draws on the idea of the Angel wrestling with Jacob in the Old Testament:

> Whoever was beaten by this Angel
> (who often simply defined the fight)
> went away proud and strengthened
> and great from that harsh hand,
> that kneaded him as if to change his shape.

These lines remind me that I work out my own salvation in wrestling with what seem to be unbearable inner opponents, and it is a lifelong process that is often done with fear and trembling. Jacob was wounded by the wrestling, but in many ways our wounds can become the means through which we are healed. If we are willing, the wounds we think will break us become useful for others. Wounded healers are, after all, the most effective healers of all. In fact, being wounded is probably a prerequisite for being an effective healer.

On this joint venture, we need friends who understand that wrestling with an angel often feels like wrestling with a dragon or a demon, but in standing up to our biggest fears, our tenacious and dif-

The wind blows wherever it pleases. You hear its sound but you cannot tell where it comes from or where it is going. So it is with everyone born of the Spirit.

—JOHN 3:8

ficult character defects, and our deepest wounds, we are able to step into the largeness of the one wild and precious life we've been given.

Vaughn ends every e-mail with these last words from the last verse of Rilke's poem:

Winning does not tempt that man.
This is how he grows: by being defeated, decisively,
by constantly greater beings.

Every time I read this, I am reminded not only of the great power of redemption, but that I have a friend, a fellow traveler on this journey called life. In that moment, reading these words from a friend, it is as if God breaks into my ordinary world with a flash of light, reminding me in the moment that God is at work below the surface.

In the culture in which we live, winning is one of the ultimate goals. Competing and defeating, being the biggest and the best, having the most, and getting there first are rules of our daily lives. Whoever comes out on top, whoever gets the power seat in a restaurant, and whoever accumulates, acquires, and accomplishes the most is deemed "the winner," no matter what his life is like at home when he shuts the door behind him.

In the outer world, it is easy to measure success, and it's often done by the dollar sign, but wholeness is the goal in the inner world, and that is hard to measure. It's difficult for us to live with our focus on the journey rather than the destination.

This summer, in lectures on "The Love Song of J. Alfred Prufrock" and other poems from T. S. Eliot's early years prior to his conversion, Jim Hollis discussed the gap between what we want, what we can imagine or see, and our ability to attain what we want. As Jim lectured, I felt deeply the angst and heaviness of my personal gaps, and as I left class I felt a heaviness about the things I have not been able to change in my life.

There is a lingering sadness and frustration about being able to see how things could be different in your life, but not being able to transcend the gap between reality and that vision. There is a yawning ache when you realize you could have done something that would have made a difference in your current state of being, but didn't, either because you didn't have the resources or because of a failure of nerve, a lack of courage, or doubt in your abilities.

"Leap and the net will appear" is a quirky slogan emblazoned on bumper stickers and art objects. It is intended to foster courage and belief in the power of taking action. For those of us who have leapt only to find that the net did not appear, it is sometimes hard to leap again. When we don't have the courage to leap, we wonder and wallow around in the pit of "what if" and "if only."

One day at the C. G. Jung Education Center, Jim lectured about T. S. Eliot's poem, "The Journey of the Magi." I was reminded of how much courage it takes to leap into the abyss of recovery, take the journey of self-actualization, reach for an impossible goal, or overcome what seems to be an insurmountable obstacle or problem. I was also reminded of the wonder and mystery of *kairos time*. Kairos moments and synchronicities are ways that God breaks through ordinary time; some say it is the way God winks at us. I like that.

Listening intently to Jim read and discuss "The Journey of the Magi," I suddenly realized that I was not only hearing the poem, but I was experiencing it at three levels.

Most of the time we think of time and our lives as happening in a linear way. We think we begin at Point A and travel logically and systematically toward Point B, Point C, and beyond. We measure life with calendars and clocks and we perceive one day following another, chronologically. Ancient Greeks called this *chronos* (or *kronos*) *time*.

At any given time, a song, a memory, a conversation, or something that seemingly pops up out of the blue can transport us back in time, and sometimes people have premonitions that are powerfully helpful, if only they will acknowledge and honor them. Dreams, too, aren't concerned about linear time or space; they seem illogical, but only to the person who refuses to explore beneath the surface and mine the gold within the symbols and images of the dream.

Kairos time is another way of experiencing time, and it seems to fit better when we're talking about the mysterious ways of life and perhaps the way God sees. In kairos time, there is no beginning or end, but life is seen as a whole and, indeed, as Eliot said, time past, time present, and time future are all happening at the same time. It's hard for our logical, rational minds to fathom, but during Jim's lecture I had one of those kairos moments in which I perceived things on more than one level.

In the New Testament, kairos time connotes "the fullness of time" in which events come together in an extraordinary and purposeful way, as if God is breaking through and entering into those events in order to bring about a particular purpose. Kairos time is sometimes described as a defining moment, a dramatic turning point, a moment of unusual mystery. Kairos time cannot be captured in a calendar, for it transcends our understanding of seconds and days. It is fluid, moving, and, in my experience, one of the ways God has healed and transformed me.

Kairos moments happen when it seems that God breaks into an ordinary moment with extraordinary grace. I have learned that while we cannot force those moments to happen, we can be available to them by our spiritual practices that help us keep our minds and hearts open to the invisible yet persistent movement of the Spirit of God.

I remember hearing Madeleine L'Engle talk about kairos time as the mystery that penetrates or breaks through kronos time when a child is at play, a painter is at his easel, a person is at prayer, friends are in communion around the dinner table, and lovers are making love. Kairos moments are transcendent, holy moments when it seems as if you lose track of time and enter into another sphere. My experience of kairos time can best be expressed by saying that it is when the Holy One moves toward me, almost as if in an embrace or a kiss, and I know I am different

> *The Self is relentless in accomplishing its purpose.*
>
> —CARL G. JUNG

because of the encounter. In a kairos moment, the separation between God and me is bridged, and I live in union with my soul/True Self/Christ within. In those kairos moments, the emotional wounds of a lifetime can be healed.

It was a healing moment for me as I sat in class that night, pondering the meaning of Eliot's magi and their journey. I could feel the real-life journey of the magi who went to see the newborn Jesus, a journey that gets sentimentalized in our Christmas pageants. Eliot crashes through that sugar-coated version of the birth of Jesus from the beginning by stating that it was "Just the worst time of the year for a journey, and such a long journey."

Still engaged with the biblical journey of the magi, I listened as Jim told us Eliot wrote this poem as he was on the cusp of his conversion experience. I could feel the turmoil of that liminal, in-between time when he was no longer where he used to be but had not yet arrived at the place where he wanted to be. How often on this journey we, like Eliot's magi, "travel all night, sleeping in snatches, with the voices singing in our ears, saying that this was all folly."[2]

Indeed, the journey of faith is going to be tested, and sometimes it feels as if the fire of that testing will burn you to a crisp! Along the way, self-doubt, the voice that says it is all folly, sets up a racket in our heads that clamors and clangs and makes us question the journey, God, ourselves, and our own sanity.

On yet another level, that night in class I was identifying deeply with my circuitous journey over the many decades of my life, and when Jim read these lines I almost wept with understanding:

> There was a Birth, certainly,
> We had evidence and no doubt. I had seen birth
> and death,
> but had thought they were different; this Birth was
> Hard and bitter agony for us, like Death, our death.

Many times in the process of depth analysis, I had cried out, "I don't know if I'm being born or if I'm dying," and my analyst had said each time, "Yes, you are."

The process of rebirth, resurrection, and renewal often feels like a death, and it is—a death of the old ways. Rebirth feels like a birth, and it is—the birth of greater, deeper, more intense consciousness and responsibility, and it is hard, laborious, and bloody. Sometimes people are stillborn. No wonder Nicodemus quaked at the idea of being born again!

I sat with friends Chris and Sylvia Drake one night and heard Chris say, "When we were kids, we were told that the Christian life is easy, and that was a lie! It isn't easy; it's hard!"

It's hard if you take it seriously. It's hard if you try to follow the path of Christ. It's hard if you believe salvation is more than staying out of hell and getting into heaven!

The spiritual journey of becoming who you were intended to be—of being saved from who you aren't supposed to be and restored to who you are meant to be—is not easy. Eliot said it well: it is "hard and bitter agony for us, like Death, our death."

There I was, then, sitting in class, engaged with Jim's lecture and yet also engaged with the wise men and with Eliot, when suddenly I was propelled back in time to the moment I stepped into Poet's Corner at Westminster Abbey, looked down to see the name T. S. Eliot beneath my feet, and burst into tears.

It was 2004, and my trip to England was not a mere sight-seeing trip, but a pilgrimage I'd wanted to take since I was eight years old when an uncle returned home from World War II with an English bride. I adored that aunt who told me stories about England and the queen and brought me a book about the queen's coronation at Westminster Abbey. For decades I wanted to go to England and Westminster Abbey so much I could taste it; I yearned for England as if it were my native land, and in many ways it is.

Constrained by time and schedules on the day we toured the great Abbey, I felt rushed, making my way around the building. Knowing we had to meet our friends at a particular time, I became more and more agitated, trying to see everything and fearing that I would not have enough time to sit and savor Poet's Corner. Finally, Martus, sensing my distress, went on ahead of me, and then returned to say, "You're almost there! Keep walking!"

Martus knew how much this trip meant to me and how long I had wanted to be in Westminster Abbey, so he was shocked when I burst into tears. Embarrassed, I moved to the far side of Poet's Corner and sat down, looking up at the names of the writers and poets I'd studied and loved my whole life. "Why are you crying?" he asked me, and all I could say was, "Ann Miller's class."

For my thoughts are not your thoughts, neither are your ways my ways, declares the LORD.

—ISAIAH 55:8

When I was nineteen and a sophomore at Baylor University, I dated someone who didn't make it on my mother's approved list. The young man was older than I. He was from a different part of the country and, worse, he had grown up in another religious denomination.

To understand fully the implications of this, you have to understand that I am a third-generation Baptist minister's wife. I sometimes say it is the family illness; we pass it down from generation to generation. I'm not sure why it was such a big deal for me to date this young man, but my dating someone who was outside our family's tradition threw my family into an uproar that got worse as the fall semester edged toward the end of the year.

Finally, when I was home for Christmas vacation, I endured what felt like unbearable and terrible pressure from two family members who finally resorted to shame and guilt to get me to conform to their ideas about what I should and should not do. To this day, the memory of the long night in which they berated and lectured me makes me shudder.

After Christmas vacation, I went back to school, took my finals, and broke up with this young man. Most likely, I would have broken up with him anyway, but as things unfolded and with the words that were said to me, what happened wounded me at a sensitive, tender place in my young heart.

The wounding was harder for me than it might have been for another more spirited and confident person, but the experience was a repeat wound that had as its source a deep, lifelong fear of being abandoned, rejected, and wrong. The terror I felt at the threat of being abandoned if I did not conform to these family members' agenda shook me at the core of my being. Furthermore, the wounding was exacerbated by the fact that, essentially, my freedom to choose was taken away from me. Much of my journey in life has been spent retrieving that primary, God-given freedom from the ash heap where it was tossed.

Going back to Baylor for the spring semester of my sophomore year, I was several pounds lighter and less sure of myself. I had enrolled in Ann Miller's class for the second half of sophomore English, and I was both scared to death of her and eager to prove to my family that I could rise above the circumstances that had consumed the previous semester.

Ann Miller was known as the most demanding professor on campus, but one of the most interesting and challenging, and something (the Self?) in me wanted that challenge. She was beautiful and classy, highly intelligent and articulate, and so I showed up in her class, wanting to please and wanting to pull myself up from the pit of self-condemnation.

On the first day of class, Ann Miller told us that we would answer the roll each day by quoting a line of poetry, and so I returned to my dorm room to scour my textbook for a line of poetry that was meaningful to me. For reasons I still do not know, I chose lines from "The Four Quartets" by T. S. Eliot.[3]

Time present and time past are both perhaps present in time future
and time future contained in time past.

—T. S. ELIOT

At the next class, I sat with fear and trembling, hoping and not hoping to be chosen, and then I heard my name. My face flushed, as it always did in those days, and my voice quivered, but somehow I spoke Eliot's words.

Ann Miller lifted her eyes from her roll book and pierced mine. "What does that mean, Miss Ball?" she asked, and I clearly and articulately said what I had no way of knowing I knew: "I think it means that in one way, all of time is the same." Without realizing it, I had given a tip-of-the-iceberg definition of *kairos time*.

I will never forget the smile that spread across Ann Miller's face or the blessing she pronounced on my wounded soul when she said, "*Very good, Miss Ball!*"

She had no way of knowing that the smile she beamed across the classroom felt like the sun coming out after a long, dark, dreary winter.

That blessing, as it turned out, spoke a turning point into my life, pulling me up from the mirey depths of self-doubt and setting me into a new era of personal freedom, though even I didn't know it. In the moment, I simply received her words as a sign that I had pleased her, but when I stepped into Poet's Corner—*decades later*—and looked down to see T. S. Eliot's name on the stone marker under my foot, I was suddenly caught in a profoundly significant kairos moment in which I suddenly realized how important and crucial Ann Miller's smile and blessing had been for me at a terribly vulnerable point in my life.

So I wept in Poet's Corner on that warm spring day because I realized for the first time how much Ann Miller and the poets whose words and work she offered to us meant to me. I realized that in her smile, she had redeemed me in a way, buying me back from an extremely wounding experience. That day in Poet's Corner, I realized as well how long and hard and tedious my spiritual journey had been, and yet in that same moment in the wonder and mystery of kairos time, something healed that long-ago wound and the earlier, original one at an even deeper level. In kairos time, I felt the power of the Spirit of life working from within to liberate me from those old memories and set me free, empowering me and transforming me. As I wept, the old was washed away.

Eliot's poem about the magi ends with this line: "I should be glad of another death."

Later, in an e-mail to Jim Hollis in which I expressed my gratitude for his class and his lecture on "The Journey of the Magi," I said, "I really understand wishing there could have been another way, an easier death, a journey only in springtime. Frankly, I would have preferred to have been somebody's arm candy."

But not really.

Along the way, mentors and friends, teachers and fellow pilgrims, strangers and enemies have shown up at just the right times, making their imprint in my life, participating in the joint venture of spiritual growth in a myriad of ways, and all I can do is fall to my knees and give thanks for the ways in which others have helped me bear my own burdens and prayed for me.

In this rational, logical world in which I live, it is countercultural to talk about kairos time, synchronicity, or the numinous energy of God. When I talk about the way the Dream Maker offers up amazing images and disturbing plots, I wonder if some people think I'm nuts, but the power of my dreaming has been so great that I no longer concern myself with what people might think. I am careful how and to whom I tell my dreams, but I know for sure now that they are viable and reliable, though often mysterious and cryptic, messages from the depths of my soul.

I've learned to enjoy and even laugh about the times when God acts as the Trickster, appearing as a slip of the tongue or a quirky turn of events that flips things upside down and upsets the status quo. When I say that sometimes God winks at me in the strange, inexplicable moments of life, I feel a bit strange, but less so than I used to feel, for I have learned that God does work in mysterious ways to bring about what he wants.

Several years ago I was a co-leader at a retreat center that I have loved for many years, Laity Lodge in the Hill Country of Texas. The retreat didn't go well, and somehow all that happened there stirred up feelings and memories from the past, so that I was both at the retreat, feeling bad, and also reliving earlier experiences of rejection from the past, which made me feel worse.

I have learned that when something in the present moment stirs up painful memories from the past or puts me into a complex, God is at work attempting to heal some wound in my soul that likely goes way back in my history.

After the retreat I was scheduled to spend several days in solitude and silence at the Quiet House, a sacred stone waystation perched on the canyon walls above the retreat center at Laity Lodge. My assignment for those days, apparently, was to deal with all the stuff that had been stirred up and brought to my conscious mind during that awful, painful retreat.

I cried a lot and tried to remember that tears are the body's way of praying. I read some and journaled a lot, and periodically I went outside and walked in the hot sun among the gnarly cedar tress and hill country rocks.

On one of those walks around the house, my eye caught for the first time a crudely built cross leaning against the wall. It was made of small tree branches, and under it lay a pile of rocks. Something on one of those rocks seemed to sparkle. Shading my eyes, I walked toward the house. Words written in a beautiful calligraphy with stars all around on a rough rock seemed to be just for me: "I am my Beloved's, and my Beloved is mine."

I have no idea how that rock got there or who wrote the words on it, but I grabbed it, weeping. It was just what I needed at that particular moment in time. I have many treasures from a lifetime, but this rock is one of my most precious treasures.

Pittman McGehee introduced me to the concept of *anamnesis,* the capacity humans have to remember, to bring meaningful moments back from the archives of our memories. Anamnesis is the opposite of amnesia, and by the act of anamnesis, we can re-experience an exchange, a moment, or a relationship from the past, reviving it through the mystery of imagination and remembering. Anamnesis makes it possible for a memory to be available to us in the present moment.

> *God moves in mysterious ways, his wonders to perform.*
>
> —WILLIAM COWPER

So it is that our ritual processes, such as the observance of the Lord's Supper (as it is called in my religious tradition) or the receiving of the Eucharist or the sharing of Communion, provide us a way to reenact and remember the time when Jesus, at dinner with his closest, most beloved friends, shared bread and wine with them as an act of communion. With his understanding of the power of anamnesis, Jesus said, "When you get together, do this *in remembrance of me.*"

There is nothing I love more within the life of the Christian community than the taking of the bread and wine, touching and tasting the elements, and *remembering* Jesus' words, "I am with you always."

I love that moment when everything else stops and I can pass the plate if I am at my church, or go to the altar and kneel if I am worshiping with my children, and the Extraordinary breaks through the ordinary and reminds me that, in fact, God is present all the time. Every moment has within it the reality of being a kairos moment.

Sometimes God is more dramatically present than at others, it seems, and sometimes I'm more available for that numinous, mysterious wink from the Holy One who reminds me, "I am with you always."

Moment by moment, the joint venture unfolds, sometimes aided by a friend's lines of poetry at the end of an e-mail, often propelled by a problem, and frequently enhanced by the experience of sharing the bread and wine of Communion with my fellow pilgrims, my brothers and sisters in Christ.

Robert Browning says it well: "God uses us to help each other so, lending our minds out."[4]

We also lend our hearts and our hands, an e-mail, a funky rock that appears mysteriously up against a ragged cross, a class lecture, and sometimes a smile of grace.

In another poem, "At Communion," Madeleine L'Engle writes of the inexplicable mystery of life when "Time and eternity are face to face" and "Infinity and space meet in this place."[5] For her, God was so great and so intimately present that we who listened to her speak and sat with her in prayer could almost experience that numinous presence emanating through her.

The last lines of her poem speak to me:

In mystery, Break time, break space, O wild and
lovely power. Break me; thus am I dead.
Am resurrected now in wine and bread.

In Communion with each other, we are resurrected over and over again.

In Communion we remember the Living Christ who comes to us again and again.

Of all things, this joint venture is Mystery and mysterious, and we can live, for a moment, in kairos time, eternal time. And God winks.

Let it be.

NOTES

1. Ranier Maria Rilke, "The Man Watching," *Selected Poems of Ranier Maria Rilke: A Translation from the German and Commentary by Robert Bly* (New York: Harper & Row, 1981) 105.

2. T. S. Eliot, "Journey of the Magi," *The Complete Poems and Plays 1909–1950* (New York: Harcourt Brace & Co., 1967) 68–69.

3. T. S. Eliot, "Burnt Norton," *The Four Quartets* (New York: Harcourt Brace & Co., 1971) 13.

4. Robert Browning, "Fra Lippo Lippi," *Victorian Poetry and Poetics*, 2d ed. (Boston: Houghton Mifflin Co., 1959) 213 (ll. 305–306).

5. Madeleine L'Engle, *The Ordering of Love: New and Collected Poems of Madeleine L'Engle* (Colorado Springs: Shaw Books, 2005).

Chapter 13

CARRYING THE MESSAGE

"You have to give it if you want to keep it," my friends in recovery tell me about the importance of carrying the message of hope and healing to others. "It's not really yours unless you give it away," they say.

As a lifelong teacher, I know I learn best when I am teaching. When I began teaching at age twenty-two, I thought I had to know everything about a topic before I could teach it, but I have learned that is not true. I teach what I know, but I also teach to learn.

A recent incident with two of my grandchildren illustrates that we all both teach and learn from each other, but we also all learn from a particular context, and all of us teach imperfectly.

Watching the opening scenes of the movie *The Sound of Music*, three-year-old Dylan was intrigued by the nuns in the convent, dressed in their black habits. His context is informed by an obsession with superheroes. "Who are they?" he asked his big sister Madeleine, who was almost six at the time.

"They are nums, Dylan," she said.

"What are nums, Maddie?" he asked. "Are they the good guys or the bad guys?"

It is important, after all, to be able to differentiate between the good guys and the bad guys, but the truth is that we all see through a glass darkly, and we need to be careful whom we choose to be our teachers. As my friends in AA say, "Stick with the winners; the losers will get you drunk." Sometimes when you learn "nuns" as "nums," it's hard to relearn it right.

I learned from my friends in recovery the importance of carrying the good news of recovery to another person, sponsoring another person, and continuing to share the principles, traditions, slogans, and one's personal story with others.

Perhaps the sharing of one's personal story is the crucial element in the effectiveness of recovery groups. When a recovering addict says, "This is how I used to be," or "This is what happened to me because of the program," there is an authority and strength to the message that is sometimes missing in evangelism programs within organized religion.

At the memorial service for his father, my friend Jackson Wise delivered a loving, humorous, and honest eulogy. At the end of his eulogy he spoke bold and courageous words to a sanctuary packed with individuals who had gathered to mourn the tragic death of their friend and celebrate the wonderful things about him. With his three sisters standing behind him in solidarity, Jackson took a "twelfth step" with dignity and vulnerability, acknowledging the grief, but making himself and his family available for the hope and healing of others.

> *Having had a spiritual experience as a result of these steps, we tried to carry this message to others and to practice it in all our affairs.*
>
> —TWELFTH STEP,
> ALCOHOLICS ANONYMOUS

"We are grateful to God that he had mercy on my dad, and that he has now given all of us the chance to move forward and make something positive out of this tragedy," Jackson said. "We want each of you to know that if you or someone you know is or might be suffering from alcoholism or some other addiction, it is never too early or too late to try to find help. We have been through this, we have compassionate ears to listen, and we know the right people to call to get help. We will be here for you night or day, as you have been for us today."

What clearer way could the message be given that there is hope and help and a way through to a better life?

If you had the cure for a great disease, you wouldn't keep that cure to yourself. If you know a way to sobriety, you are under a divine imperative to share that cure with another who struggles with addiction. And if the good news of Jesus' life, the miracle of authentic salvation, the process of being made whole is real, then we must share what we know in a way that has integrity and is respectful of others' freedom to choose.

Because of my personality and temperament, and perhaps even more because of the beliefs, experiences, and values I hold, the techniques of evangelism programs of my part of the religious world have never worked for me, and yet I know that when something life-changing has happened in my life, I want to tell it. How, then, do I tell the good news I have experienced? How do I carry the message of my spiritual awakening and spiritual journey to another? Do I carry it in order to share it without my preconceived expectations about how the person should respond, or do I try to force agreement from her?

Because I am so convinced that salvation is about more than staying out of hell and getting into heaven and mostly about a living, dynamic, love relationship with the Mystery of God whom I know in Christ, I cannot reduce the process to a one-time event.

Because I am confident that salvation is about becoming whole and healthy and authentically who we are intended to be, I cannot reduce that holy process to stating a formulaic prayer. Being transformed is more than right belief, more than being baptized, more than reciting a creed or four spiritual laws, more than attending church and having your name on the membership roll, doing good deeds, or receiving Communion. Salvation is a lifelong process.

At a recent meeting of the Cooperative Baptist Fellowship in Charlotte, North Carolina, Dr. Bill Leonard, Baptist historian and former dean of the Divinity School at Wake Forest, began his speech to our group by asking us to close our eyes. "How many of you have been embarrassed about being Baptist?" he asked, and of course the crowd laughed. I raised my hand, and peeped enough to know that many people around me did not raise their hands.

"The rest of you are lying," he said, and we laughed even more, but it was nervous laughter. Whether it was laughter at the thought of getting caught lying in public or the uneasy laughter of discomfort at admitting that what we love and serve, being a Baptist, sometimes causes us embarrassment and discomfort.

I do cringe when I read an embarrassing thing that Baptists have done. I am quick to criticize us, but I don't like it when outsiders do. I lament our failures and flaws, but I also have been blessed by our strengths. I don't like it when Larry King interviews only one Baptist who presumes to speak for all Baptists; I don't like it when one group leaves some of us out because we see differently or hold other opinions. I lament and regret all of that because, out of my rich and multi-textured religious heritage, I got some spiritual nourishment that has served me well.

Growing up Baptist, I got good Bible teaching from people who loved the sacred stories and believed that if you lived by the principles in the Bible, life somehow went better. There was always an open Bible in my home when I was growing up, for my father was always studying for a sermon and my mother was always preparing for one of the Bible study classes she taught until she was eighty-six. In college, I had excellent professors for survey courses in Old and New Testament, and for decades I have listened to my husband's good sermons and excellent Bible teaching. From him I built

> *Now it is required that everyone who has been given a trust must prove faithful.*
>
> —1 CORINTHIANS 4:2

on the solid foundation of biblical knowledge and understanding from my childhood and young adulthood, and I have loved teaching the Bible and writing curriculum for Bible studies for most of my adult life.

From my Baptist heritage, I have a sense of concern for the global community and a strong sense that ethics matter in daily life. I have a keen sense of responsibility to other people, both to those with whom I share life and those who are less fortunate than I, and a love for the community of faith known as the local church. In the churches of my lifetime and at Baptist gatherings throughout my life, I have heard some of the most beautiful music in the world in the great hymns and anthems of the church.

More than anything else, I value the teaching my father called "the centrality of Christ" that is at the core of my spiritual life. I grew up hearing about my father's dramatic conversion experience when he was twenty-six, but I also saw him live out his life in a dynamic relationship with the Living Christ. From him I learned that it is possible to have an intimate, moment-by-moment love relationship with the Mystery we call Christ. It is probably because I watched him express his deep love for Christ, talk about how his relationship with Christ had transformed his life, and minister to others in the name of Christ that I, too, came to love the Living Christ. For the past thirty years, I have studied and taught various aspects of the life of Jesus and have written two books about his encounters with people during his earthly life.

My internal grounding frees me to explore beyond my tradition and follow what I believe to be the guidance of the Holy Spirit, working through my authentic Self, to the contemplative world and to the world of depth psychology. By following the path that has made sense to me, I have come to understand that while the Bible records that Jesus said, "Go into all the world and make disciples," it also gives other imperatives. It is interesting to me that we who declare our love for the Bible sometimes leave out large ideas, and in doing so we create an incomplete and unbalanced religious system.

Jesus also left these imperatives. It seems to me that they are as important as "go and tell."

Abide in me.
Love your enemies.
Love one another.
Feed the hungry.
Forgive—seventy times seven.
Go into your closet to pray.
Let your light shine.
Judge not.
Do not be afraid.
Let your yes be yes, and your no, no.
Do not worry about your life.
Seek first the kingdom of God.

I cannot do door-to-door evangelism or buttonhole a waitress or a friend and ask if she knows where she would spend eternity if she should die, and I'm not going to distribute tracts, though I always remain open to the prospect of others using those methods. I cringe at Jesus yells and holy Scriptures emblazoned on billboards and bumper stickers, and when I saw a woman wearing a T-shirt with the words "Jesus Chick," I wanted to cry. I'm for reinstating the Jewish practice of refusing to utter the name of God; I am offended by the tackiness with which the holiness of God is treated and the ways in which we so easily take God's name in vain.

That's what I don't like, but what *do* I like? What does have authenticity for me? How can I carry the message of the life-changing Mystery, the kingdom of God within me, and the joy of my salvation to others in a way that has integrity and authenticity? If something has healed, transformed, liberated, and empowered me, how do I share that with other people in a way that is respectful of their experience and autonomy?

A few months ago, I received an e-mail from my longtime friend Jenny Eubank, in which she told about her grandson Christian's "inviting Jesus into his heart." Since I've known Christian's dad since he was a newborn, this message touched me deeply. It also carried me back to my own experience of inviting Jesus into my heart.

I didn't understand what it meant to be a follower of Christ at the time, but with a child's heart and a child's understanding of mystery, "inviting Jesus into my heart" made sense to me, and so I gave as much as I knew of myself to as much as I knew of God, and my father baptized me. As he lowered me into the baptismal waters he said, "I baptize you, my little daughter," and as he raised me out of those waters, he said, "and I raise you, my sister in Christ."

I find it remarkable, looking back, that he didn't say a word about washing away the black stain in my heart that so many of my Baptist friends heard about. Instead, his words indicated a new relationship, transformation, a possibility of maturing, a new position in the community of faith.

Looking back, I now understand that the words "inviting Jesus into your heart," while symbolic, set me on a pathway of knowing that my relationship with him was an *interior* experience and that it was *my experience.* No one could take that inward relationship away from me, and it was totally not dependent on the church, any rite or ritual, doing good works, or following set rules and practices. Over time I even began to see that checking the squares on my offering envelope had nothing to do with my inner connection with the Living Christ.

> *Preach the gospel always, and when necessary use words.*
>
> —FRANCIS OF ASSISI

Often, when I'm listening to Jim Hollis or Pittman McGehee lecture on the teachings of Carl Jung, I think about my parents and smile. While the language is different and the approach to "the kingdom within" is certainly different from what they learned in seminary in the 1940s, what my dad lived and preached was in harmony with the teachings of Jung. While my parents would never have gone to a Catholic monastery to learn how to meditate, they lived as contemplatives. They practiced the presence of Christ in daily life.

Recently I was sitting with a woman who had been to a funeral at a Baptist church. A lifelong member of a church within the liturgical tradition, she recounted hearing a Baptist preacher tell about his experience of accepting Christ as his personal Savior. She was intrigued by what she had heard and by the power that experience had had in his life.

At four o'clock the next morning, I woke up with what felt like the blow of a two-by-four to my head, remembering the words of the jailer who'd been shaken up by the earthquake in the prison that held Paul and Silas. As recorded in Acts 16:16-34, all the prison doors flew open, and everybody's chains came loose. About to kill himself because he feared that his prisoners had escaped, the jailer fell trembling before Paul and Silas and asked, "What must I do to be saved?"

In the pre-dawn hours, I realized that in my fear of making salvation so simplistic that it had no power and in my fear of being perceived as trying to impose my understanding of salvation on someone from a different tradition, I had missed an opportunity to talk about the wonder and mystery of "inviting Jesus into your heart." Sometimes I am hesitant to carry the message of the Living Christ because I don't want to be identified with either street corner evangelists or televangelists. My wake-up call reminded me that part of the purpose of spiritual direction is to discern where the Spirit of God is moving in a person's life.

That morning, I made my way to my computer and sent an e-mail, describing my childhood experience of inviting Jesus into my heart. I wrote, "No matter how much I learn about what it means to be saved, I have somewhere deep within me the knowledge and belief and experience of Christ dwelling within my heart."

Because of that early experience, it is not hard for the child who still lives in me to know that the Living Christ is always with me. The adult in me may try to intellectualize it. The cynic in me may have moments of doubting, and the doubter in me sometimes begs for evidence and proof on my terms. The narcissist in me wants God to perform for me in a way that is special, and the rebel in me sometimes wants to throw the baby of my denominational life out with the bathwater.

I do not believe in shaming people into the kingdom of God, which I believe is the kingdom of Love. I don't believe in scaring people down the aisle. I'm opposed to childhood evangelism or any evangelism that counts heads and puts up statistics as a sign of their dominance, prominence, or power. I don't like evangelistic campaigns or crusades, but I do believe these things:

• God meets each of us at the point of our need, and sometimes what works for me works for others, and sometimes the method I cannot do is what another needs.

• There are many different ways to say "yes" to the spiritual journey, yes to Christ, and yes to recovery.

• Carrying the message that is mine and delivering it in ways that have integrity for me is a necessary part of my working out my salvation.

• I did invite Jesus into my heart when I was nine. I do that again every time I sit in the silence, doing Centering Prayer, and consent by my word and my intention to the presence and action of the Holy One in the deepest depths of my innermost being.

• Every time—*every single time*—I experience the Presence of the Living God in my life, it is another advent, another second or hundredth coming of that Mystery into my life.

• (This one makes some people nervous.) If it turns out that it is all a hoax, if the Jesus story is just a fiction, if God is the opiate of the people and there is no heaven, then what I have experienced in this life on this plane in this small span of history has been so magnificent that I will be okay.

• And what I have experienced on this plane is so magnificent that I cannot believe it's all a hoax. Something deep within me believes with all my heart. The child in me believes all the time; the adult in me believes almost all the time.

Listening to Marcus Borg lecture in 2010 at St. Paul's United Methodist Church in Houston, and reading his books, I am struck by how we in the Christian community need regularly to update our perception of who Jesus is at different times in our lives. We need to revisit our definitions of the language we use to convey deep spiritual truths. In an era of cultural Christianity, we need to think and talk deeply about who we understand the historical Jesus to be, how we experience the Living Christ, and what it means to be a follower of Christ.

As you go, make disciples . . . .

—JESUS

As politicians and wannabe political celebrities use, misuse, violate, and sometimes desecrate what is sacred for their own gain, defining "Christianity" in ways that will gain votes, sway elections, prejudice the ignorant, and offend the informed, we need to reflect on what it means to be saved, what it means to be the church, and what it means to "know Christ."

My childhood experience of "inviting Jesus into my heart" has evolved and enlarged over time to include such mysteries of the spiritual life as abiding in him and knowing him. Now and then I get a glimpse of understanding about what Paul meant when he said, "Christ in me, the hope of glory," and those glimpses are enough to keep my hope, faith, and trust alive and active (Col 1:27).

Carl Jung believed Christ was the symbol of the True Self. People who hear that for the first time sometimes have a knee-jerk reaction and reject the statement without reflecting on it simply because it doesn't sound like anything they have heard before. Jung also taught that at some point, around midlife for sure, we have to turn from our attachment to the outer world and make the connection with the True Self within us.

For me, it feels true that the True Self and Christ in me are the same, and following Jesus means following his way of becoming not like him so much as doing what he did so I can become my authentic Self. For me, it fits that Jung's idea of establishing the ego-Self axis is the same thing as turning to the kingdom within. Abiding in Christ and Christ's abiding in me is about living from the inside out—informed, guided, inspired, led, and sometimes pushed by the Holy One who dwells within.

I believe in the historical Jesus, and I believe in the Christ who lives within me, though I cannot prove either one of those assertions from a rational, logical perspective. My parents taught me those things, but the beliefs come from my life experiences that have been so large and powerful that I no longer need intellectual proof. At a deep level of my life, I have been grasped by a love that will not let me go, a love so great that when I sing these words from an old hymn, they ring true in every cell of my body:

> He lives, he lives. Christ Jesus lives today.
> He walks with me; he talks with me along life's narrow way.
> You ask me how I know he lives. . . . He lives within my heart.[1]

I love teaching the Bible, and I love guiding people into the experience of Centering Prayer and other forms of contemplative prayer. I love leading retreats and workshops on the spiritual life, and those are forms of carrying the good news of my spiritual awakening and healing to others. Sometimes I delude myself into thinking that my public pronouncements are enough, but carrying the message of salvation is multi-faceted.

The proof of my belief is in how I live every day, and never is that proof more evident than when I fail and am given the strength to try again. It is never more real to me than when I treat a loved one with disrespect but am forgiven, when I tremble in fear and am given courage, and when I am depressed, discouraged, or defeated and somehow, through the mystery of the Holy Spirit, I am lifted out of what the psalmist called the mirey clay and inexplicably given hope to begin again.

The proof of Christ in me is the presence of inexplicable joy in the midst of unbearable pain, peace in the midst of turmoil, and love instead of power and control. Christ in me pulls me out of the patterns of victim behavior and sets my feet on the solid rock of courage and confidence and *life.*

Now and then, I have the opportunity to say to another child of God, no matter how old she is, "Trust him. Invite him into your heart and see what happens."

The child in us gets that, but we may have to tell the adult in us to sit down and be quiet.

If I had my way, which I do not, every person would be in a group like Alcoholics Anonymous that moves through the Twelve Steps. All of us would receive the nurture we need from a community of faith, and all of us would be required to work through programs of faith, recovery, or whatever, for I have noticed that in fellowship with others and in communion with others, we learn how to live. It is my opinion that small groups based on the principles of Yokefellow Spiritual Growth Groups and/or Alcoholics Anonymous are the way in which we nurture faith and transmit it to each other. I know from experience that some of the deepest curing comes through the caring extended within the safe and nurturing circle of fellow pilgrims.

Because of my religious culture, I understood witnessing and evangelism from a narrow framework that I could never quite do. The AA approach and the Yokefellow Spiritual Growth Groups approach make more sense to me, especially as I have observed and experienced the power of the group meetings in which living, present-tense stories were told about real-life despair and defects, amazing interventions by God in daily life, and struggles to work through a process of healing.

You are the light of the world! Don't hide your light under a bushel. Let your light shine.

—JESUS

Part of the reason I entered the training program for spiritual directors was that I believed deeply in the power of being companions on the way, walking with each other through life, and delivering the message one on one. The necessity of having a sponsor and being a sponsor in a recovery program caught my imagination, and I bought into the idea that I was temperamentally more at home with that kind of sharing than with any other method of spreading the good news of what has happened to me.

I am convinced that if we in the church would get back to what matters most and become true followers of Christ and not just cultural Christians or church members, then our evangelism—our telling of the good news— would happen naturally, spontaneously, and authentically as we go about our daily tasks. As we go about our lives. As we go.

At the end of his earthly life, Jesus admonished his disciples to go into the world and carry the message of life and hope and redemption to others. "Love one another," he said, "as I have loved you" (John 15:12). He asked us to be salt and light, change agents, friends of his, and friends to each other. He asked us to teach his Way to others, making disciples (disciplined followers) as we go about our daily lives.

What if our primary assignment as human beings while we are on this earthly plane is to learn how to love? What if love is what we are meant for, and without learning how to love and to be loved, we are missing everything? What if loving is the most important lesson of all, and what if it's true that without love, nothing else matters?

What if our homes are intended to be laboratories of learning how to love, to give, and to forgive? What if one of the main purposes of the home and family or the tribe or group to which one belongs is to provide experiments in learning how to love? What if that intention is verbalized among the adults so that they can model and teach the children and each other what it means to live in loving relationships?

What if our power issues with each other could be transformed into learning opportunities? What if our conflicts could be lessons for learning conflict resolution, listening skills, and forgiveness?

What if everyone could discover what he or she loves to do and then do that as a gift of love to the world, either as a volunteer or as a paid worker? What if more of us believed and lived by the truism that "work is love made visible"?

What if someday we find out that all along our religious institutions or communities are charged with the daunting tasks of providing laboratories of learning about loving God? What if those organizations saw themselves as healing agents in a broken world, agents of reconciliation and restoration, and mediators of compassion, tolerance, and forgiveness?

What if the purpose of the Christian church today is not to indoctrinate, but to provide a place in which we can learn how to love those who are different from us, those with whom we have conflict, and those who are struggling to get through life? What if the reason we are to gather together in the name of Christ is not to get each other saved so that we can go to heaven together when we die, but to become saved and live more peacefully together here?

What if being Christ to each other means we are to participate with the Living Christ in helping each other become free of the chains that bind us and free for the abundant life we are intended to live? What if we are meant to encourage each other instead of straighten each other out? What if we are intended to share in each other's sufferings, bear each other's burdens, and help each other figure out the problems we all encounter?

What if being Christ in the culture means not that we are to get our candidate elected, but that we are to love our own wild and precious lives that the Creator designed and brought forth into this world so much that we want to be whole, free, and fully actualized?

As I have imagined a world in which loving and being loved is taken as seriously as making a living, winning a championship, achieving, acquiring, accomplishing, and accumulating, I am reminded once again that Love is the meaning of Easter, and I am an Easter person. I am committed to the reality not of life and death, but of life and death and *Life*!

The story of Easter begins with the giving of a love that heals, transforms, liberates, and empowers human beings to become whole and healthy and to live an abundant life. Easter illustrates the power of going the ultimate distance to reveal the kind of love that can change the world. Easter is about Love that is fierce and strong and faithful all the way to the end. Easter isn't a soft, sentimental love; it is Love filled with courage and boldness.

Easter is about the triumph of love over hate, courage over cowardice, authenticity over hypocrisy, and faith over doubt. It is the revelation of love made visible and active, alive, and dynamic throughout creation. It is the symbol of the Source of life, a Source that continues to be life giving, morning by morning, and it is the victory of life over death.

The only significance of life consists in helping to establish the kingdom of God . . . .

—TOLSTOI

"I don't buy that Easter story," a man told me. "It's unbelievable, and I don't believe anything that is not provable by hard, scientific data."

"Really?" I responded. "And how's that working for you?"

"You're a Romantic and a flower child of the '60s," another person said to me when I proposed my ideas about life and love. Maybe so. Or maybe not.

Maybe I'm actually a Realist, and maybe I have seen enough of life devoid of love to know that road leads where nobody needs to go. Maybe I've lived through enough Good Fridays and Resurrection Mornings to know what is Real.

What if the joint venture we are in together is the grand adventure of loving one another?

How are we doing? Let's do it better.

Let's live it better, this gospel of freedom and grace. Let's love better, each other and our enemies, so that it can also be said about us, "See how they love one another."

I live with these challenges and within this joint venture of faith as a full participant in life, attempting to discern and cooperate with the intention of the One whose name is love in carrying the good news and the hope expressed by Teilhard de Chardin: "The day will come when, after harnessing space, the winds, the tides, gravitation, we will harness for God the energies of love. And on that day, for the second time in the history of the world, man will have discovered fire."

And with the psalmist I add my prayer: "Hasten, O God, to save us; Oh, Lord, come quickly to help us" (Ps 70:1).

Between now and then, in this in-between time and sometimes in the meantime, I intend to keep asking, seeking, and knocking. I will remain a pilgrim and a wonderer/wanderer about the things that matter most, the things that don't have right or wrong, either/or, good/bad answers. I will continue my quest to know myself and the mysteries of life; I will continue to seek God with all my heart, confident this joint venture matters. I will continue responding to the Voice that invites, "Come to me, you who are weary," and the Voice that sings, "Come home, come home."

As long as I have breath and consciousness, I'm on the quest with seekers like T. S. Eliot and others who have beamed the light of life and love in my path.

> We shall not cease from exploration
> And the end of all our exploring
> Will be to arrive where we started
> And know the place for the first time.[2]

Ah, home. Home—that place in which you know your one wild and precious life and what you must do with it.

Home—that state of being in which you know that God dwells within your heart and that you dwell in the heart of God.

NOTES

1. "He Lives," words and music by Alfred H. Ackley.

2. T. S. Eliot, "Little Gidding," *The Four Quartets* (New York: Harcourt Brace & Co., 1971) 49.

Chapter 14

BLESSED ASSURANCE

On a crisp spring morning almost six years ago, our family gathered at Palmer Episcopal Church for the baptism of our granddaughter Madeleine. Dressed in a long white baptismal dress that her Aunt Amy had made, she was only six months old.

My daughter Julie and her husband Darrin had asked all four grandparents to gather at the baptismal font at the appropriate time as stand-ins for Maddie's godparents, and of course we agreed to do that.

The service was at nine o'clock, and so Martus could be at that service and then leave immediately after Maddie's baptism to rush to our worship service at River Oaks Baptist where he would preach the morning sermon.

This was a first, a brand-new experience for our family, and I trembled all over. We stood there, all four of us grandparents. Frances and Jack Schlegel are lifelong Catholics. Martus and I are Baptist preachers' kids. We have a lot of religious history and heritage among the four of us and a deep, abiding respect and affection.

On that particular Sunday morning, one of the bishops stood beside the rector at Palmer, Jim Nutter, who had been unusually sensitive and kind to our family and especially to Martus. When he took Madeleine in his arms, he turned her toward all of us and then stood there, glasses perched down on his nose, with his free hand resting on the edge of the baptismal font. It seemed that he stood there forever. I wondered what he was doing.

Overhead, above the altar, the gorgeous stained-glass window was filled with the morning's light, streaming through Jesus' image.

Suddenly Jim beamed those laser eyes of his across the baptismal font and said to Martus, "Do you want to do this with me?" The whole world seemed to tilt, and time stood still.

I looked up at Martus. I knew he had struggled with this moment, given our lifelong belief in believers' baptism. In that split second, I didn't know if he would refuse or not, but then I heard his strong, deep voice say, "Yes. Yes, I do," and Jim said, "Then come up here with me."

My eyes met Julie's, and we both began to cry. As Martus moved to stand beside Jim at the baptismal font, everyone else had to shift positions ever so slightly, even the bishop.

Deeply thoughtful, Jim stood for another minute, holding Maddie. "Here's what we're going to do," he said to Martus. "You're going to put your hand on mine, and we're going to go down in these baptismal waters together and then we are going to baptize your baby granddaughter." And they did.

I've heard that there was not a dry eye in the house. I cannot speak for anyone but Julie and myself, since I was filled with gratitude and blessing and the enormity of that moment, but my own tears flowed so profusely that I thought I might have to have Gatorade to replenish my fluids.

Was it possible that the light emanating through Jesus in that stained-glass window brightened just at that moment, filling the nave with light and love and splendor, or was it just my imagination?

Through the years I have witnessed Martus's asking various relatives who were also ordained ministers to baptize their own loved ones, but this was the first time that generosity had been returned to him. Frankly, it overwhelmed all of us.

> *I'm absolutely convinced that nothing—nothing living or dead, angelic or demonic, today or tomorrow, high or low, thinkable or unthinkable—absolutely nothing can get between us and God's love because of the way that Jesus our Master has embraced us.*
>
> —ROMANS 8:38

Afterward I said to Jim, "That was one of the most generous and kind things I've ever seen. It was a moment when grace triumphed over the law." He responded that he'd thought about what others might think. "Then," he said, "I decided that I work for Jesus, and it seemed to be the right thing to do." Our family will never forget that moment of grace.

Indeed, grace moved through us all that Sunday morning, and when I tell the story I make the point that for that to happen, all of us—clergy, parents, and grandparents alike—had to shift positions.

God, the Verb, moves. Sometimes we have to move, too, to make space for grace. As we ride the rapids of change, adapting, flexing, and adjusting to a world we sometimes don't understand, what holds strong? Where is the Center that holds? What can we count on given this wild ride of life?

On a spectacularly beautiful Colorado morning, I walked from the retreat house at the Benedictine Monastery in Snowmass to the chapel. I tried to take it all in: the big sky, Mt. Sopris, the fields of hay, the clean, cool air, dancing aspen leaves, mountain aromas, birdsong, and the sound of the bell calling us to prayer.

The Monastery Chapel is a simple room made sacred by the prayers of the faithful monks and the countless pilgrims who, like me, have found something unspeakably beautiful and powerful there. On Sundays the chapel is full because people from the community crowd in for Mass. For me, the gathering is different in almost every way from my worship experience of a lifetime. What I love and crave there is *the silence.*

On this Sunday I was early enough that Brother Chuck was still doing the last-minute preparations that included setting up his chair and music stand. I watched him take a guitar out of the case and I smiled; I didn't know he played the guitar!

Father Thomas Keating, the great monk and teacher, came in and took his place in the circle of chairs, and one by one, other monks joined him, some of them coming in from their chores on the ranch. Over time I learned some of their names; some of them talked to us after prayers, but in the chapel they made no eye contact. It is as if we were invisible.

Abbott Joseph. Brother Raymond. Father Charlie. Father Micah. Brothers Thomas and Benito. Father Theophane. They had gathered each day to lead us in prayer in the Benedictine manner—ancient, deep, powerful.

"Ever so gently" is the way Father Thomas has taught us to introduce our prayer word when we do Centering Prayer. "And when your mind wanders, simply begin again with your prayer word—*ever so gently,*" he counseled us. "The prayer word is not a fly swatter or a baseball bat. Just return to it *ever so gently,* as if you are placing a feather on a cotton ball."

Brother Chuck began to sing ever so gently, strumming softly, almost as if he didn't want to interfere with the silence of the chapel. The song, his voice, and the tender strumming all began to weave a kind of holiness around me, and then the words to Enya's "How Can I Keep from Singing?" knocked my socks off.

> My life goes on in endless song
> Above Earth's lamentation
> I hear the real though far-off hymn
> That hails a new creation.[1]

Somehow that last line got me, and I could feel myself getting still, almost as if I thought that if I moved, the moment might vanish.

Was there still a song in me, a song that was above and beyond my lamentations? Was there to be a new creation, a turn in the road, a new beginning? Was hope still alive in me, springing up from within some deep, inner well?

Another song from a moment earlier in the year popped into my mind. It happened during an unexpected moment when a line from an Elton John song had jumped out of my CD player, moving around the corner to the room where I was getting ready for the day. "Thank God my music's still alive," Elton John sang. I stopped, hairbrush in my hand, and held my breath. Somehow, a seed of hope had stirred. Now, at the monastery, I knew for sure that my music was still alive. The True Self that had almost gotten buried beneath role constraints, life's wounding, and too many losses in too brief a time was warming up, strumming my heart softly with new life.

By the time Brother Chuck got to the next words, I could not stop the rush of tears.

> No storm can shake my inmost calm
> While to that rock I'm clinging
> Since love is Lord of heaven and earth
> How can I keep from singing?

Embarrassed by my tears, I tried to stop them until I remembered again that tears are the body's way of praying, and so I went with it. I let the tears flow as silent prayers without having to give words or meaning to them. I didn't need to know why I cried; I just needed to cry.

Brother Chuck's song was a gentle and sweet reminder to me that Sunday morning, a blessed assurance that I had not been left to face my perils alone.

Later, Theophane said to me, "I noticed that song got to you."

It had seemed to me that he was oblivious to anything but whatever was going on in his inward, secret room of prayer. That he noticed my tears reminded me how we are all connected at a deep soul level just as all the aspens are joined beneath the soil in one enormous underground root system. It also reminded me that God is nearby, always watching us.

A couple of years after that tender moment, I settled back in my seat on an airplane. Preparing for a long-awaited trip to Ireland and Scotland, I'd been reading about Celtic spirituality and hoped I would experience one of those "thin places" in which the veil between the invisible world and the visible one was, as they say, "very thin." I knew enough to know that I could not plan or manipulate a moment of encounter with the inexplicable, numinous presence of God, but I hoped I could be *available*, just in case God might want to let me know he was present and active.

My son-in-law had loaded my new iPod with music, and so I put on my earphones and hoped I could go to sleep. I'd almost zoned when an exuberant, celebrative, joyous sound suddenly split through my daze. Instead of the calm, quiet voice of Enya or Brother Charlie singing "How Can I Keep From Singing?" it was Eva Cassidy belting out that same song to a different beat and with a lively choir.[2] This rendition wasn't intended to soothe a troubled soul, but to raise the roof and shout a glad hosanna to the reality of the innermost Self/soul that goes on and on in endless song, regardless of tyrants and trouble.

I've listened to that song countless times since I experienced that holy, thin place up in the air, and every time I lament Eva Cassidy's early death from cancer. I always imagine that the free-hearted anthem she sang was a fist in the face of anything that would defeat her, a joyful alleluia to life and to her life, and to the part of her—the unique song within her own wild and precious life—that goes on and on and on. Perhaps hers is Leonard Cohen's broken hallelujah, but it is a hallelujah that lifts my spirits every time I listen to it.

Early in my adult journey, I attended an event at which author and speaker Joyce Landorf spoke. Inspired by her speech, I wrote something on my yellow legal pad. I could not have known then how important the idea of "singing your own song" was going to be in my life or that my mission and purpose would be to call forth the music in others.

At the end of the evening, I tore my poem from the legal pad, and in an uncustomary blaze of courage I took it to Joyce Landorf and thanked her for what she had said that night. I had no way of knowing that she would put it in her book *Balcony People*, but she did, and through the years I've heard from many people who heard the call to sing their own song or to be a balcony person, an encourager to others who had forgotten the song placed in them by the One who made them.[3] Here is that simple free verse I wrote.

> I wrote my purpose into you . . .
> It is my song you have to sing . . .
> I gave it to you with love.
> In your fear,
> You think you have your own song . . .
> that the idea to sing is your own
> and that the music depends on you.
> You are My precious child,
> And before you were even born,
> I had you in mind—
> And I am the One who wove the
> lyrics and the melody
> into the fabric of your life.
> So, My child, sing My song.
> Let the music flow through you with freedom . . .
> as My love
> and power
> flow always through you.
> And don't forget . . . . The song in you is My Idea.

It puts a different spin on this spiritual journey to acknowledge that it is not some egotistical venture to become your own True Self, but a sacred responsibility and a partnership effort with God himself. It changes your perspective when you see the task of doing with your one wild and precious life what you are designed to do as participation with God in a joint venture of love. Doesn't it change your idea of yourself to recognize that the gift that is in you is the stamp of God, originating with the Creator?

Several years ago I was asked to give two separate Lenten meditations at St. Matthew's Episcopal Church in Austin, Texas. The theme for the Lenten series that year was *gratitude*, and in the year between accepting the assign-

Live to the point of tears.

—ALBERT CAMUS

ment and delivering those meditations, I both researched the topic of gratitude extensively and made an intentional journey into a more deeply focused practice of gratitude. The process forever changed something in me.

At the time gratitude was "in," but I had been brought up in a home in which gratitude was part of our daily life. We would not have thought of eating a bite of food before a meal without "offering thanks." I knew that a habit of gratitude was a good thing.

In my research, however, I found out how important the practice is. It is so important and vital and practical that textbooks have been written about it, as well as countless articles and books designed for ordinary readers. Cultivating an attitude of gratefulness seems to have an impact on brain function. It is a way out of the blues. Gratitude can change your life.

My friend Victoria Harrison, a therapist and teacher in Bowen Family Systems Theory, visited New Orleans and the Gulf Coast after Hurricane Katrina ravaged that area. In her seminars on dealing with the impact of such a disaster, she heard over and over again stories attesting to the power of gratitude. Those whose natural reactions included gratitude were better able to undertake the difficult tasks of recovery.

Among other reactions, the practice of gratitude—consciously, intentionally, repeatedly—is a powerful help in healing wounded spirits, transforming tragedy into something positive and hopeful, and liberating people from despair and for the daunting tasks of rebuilding their lives. Gratitude mysteriously and yet unrelentingly empowers people to overcome incredible obstacles and sing their own songs once again.

In my life, the discipline of gratitude has repeatedly been the way out of darkness and into the light. Saying thank you has on multiple occasions given me the strength I needed to say yes to hope, yes to life, yes to taking the next step, yes to the joint venture of life with God.

Gratitude is one of my practical spiritual disciplines. It helps me keep the song alive.

It's one thing for me to give thanks when I am sitting in Colorado, savoring the mountains and blissing out in the warm womb of the meditation hall. I find it easy to give thanks when things are going well and going my way and moving and not getting stuck. It's one thing for me to give thanks on the mountaintop. It's harder to do it when I'm in the valley, but most of my life is lived in plain events, in ordinary time, in everyday places that are simple, flat, and level.

In my quest for wholeness, the quest to know God more deeply and intimately and myself more fully, I have stumbled and faltered. Now and then I have had breathtaking encounters with the numinous energy of God that leave me spellbound and longing for more. Working out my salvation has been a mixed bag of experiences.

In my journey toward freedom and fulfillment, I have sometimes soared and I have also often sauntered with pride, only to be returned to the path I'm supposed to be on by some humiliating moment. The spiritual journey has not been what I expected it to be, and one of the things that has surprised me most is that there is no destination, at least not on this side of heaven. There's no heavenly high seat for God's special pets, and assuming to ascend to that high post is a guarantee of being plunged to your knees. "The higher they fly," my mother used to say, "the flatter they fall." That's funny . . . unless I'm the one who falls.

In fact, the journey really is the destination.

Wanting to "be spiritual" has not exempted me from suffering or from conflict, and perhaps it is true that it has plunged me more deeply into both.

On the hot anvils of life, I have learned that every one of us has access to a power greater than ourselves and that sometimes all we can do—even those of us who presume to talk about God and spirituality—is cry out, "Help!"

Thanks be to God, I have learned that if that is all I can do, it is enough.

Life is hard for Christian or atheist, believer or cynic, Muslim or Jew or nothing—and the truth is that it seems to be harder for some than for others. Perhaps that is why we sometimes want to run away, pulling the security blankets of denial and avoidance over our heads. But we can cry out for the One who said he would never leave us or forsake us. Mysteriously, difficulty and the assurance of God's presence somehow go together, and faith may be defined as living in that paradox.

As I write these words, an e-mail has come from a friend who is in desperate physical pain, suffering from cancer. I stare at my screen, knowing that nothing I can say will take away his pain or his agony over the possibility of dying and leaving his beloved family. I feel the absolute frustration of not being able to do anything to help him. In biting, painful empathy with my friend, I feel the darkness and blackness of hopelessness and helplessness, but then once again the hope, the Light of Christ within me, stirs. I write him back, offering prayers, support, and encouragement. My friend and I are in a joint venture, too, walking through this dark night, crying out to God. Sharing his sorrow and suffering, I am changed and changing. I pray for him, and then I return to my manuscript, but with the apostle Paul's affirmation that nothing can separate us from God shimmering beneath the conscious level of my attention as I write.

Recently, I spent the afternoon listening to what was on that day one heartbreak after another. At the end of the day, I felt as if I were carrying people's stories of suffering and of life's seemingly immovable puzzles in my

body. Toward bedtime, I turned to music once again, and this time, the song
"Calling All Angels" and the haunting voices of k.d. lang and Jane Siberry
touched something deep within my heart, perfectly expressing my own need
and desire, but also reminding me how fragile and challenging life is for
everyone.

> But if you could . . . do you think you would
> trade in all the pain and suffering?
> Ah, but then you'd miss
> the beauty of the light upon this earth
> and the sweetness of the leaving.

And then these last words of the song became my own prayer and my
prayer for others:

> Calling all angels, calling all angels
> walk me through this one . . . don't leave me alone . . . we're tryin' we're
>   hopin'
> we're hurtin' we're lovin' we're cryin' we're callin'
> 'cause we're not sure how this goes.[4]

And isn't that the human condition? We live in the midst of mystery, trying,
hoping, and hurting, and there is some deep longing in all of us that cries
out for the angels, all of them.

I am challenged to face whatever I'm facing head on and to walk into it
and experience it as it is, hiding neither in religious escapism nor in psychological denial.

Sometimes I would like to trade in all the pain and suffering. But it's
also true for me that while the exquisite moments of grace and beauty don't
make me forget the suffering, they infuse that suffering with beauty and light
and love. The presence of the Living God may not take away the ugliness,
the agony, or the suffering, but somehow that Presence breaks through just
as I think I will break and lifts me out of the pit. Sometimes it seems as if
God waits too long to reach for me, but perhaps that is my perspective.

In Isaiah 55:8 God declares to the children of Israel, "For my thoughts
are not your thoughts, neither are you ways my ways."

Sometimes I'm happy about that, and sometimes I'm not, but my happiness either way doesn't change the reality of God's sovereignty or mystery.
When I keep my mind open, I finally know I can trust God's ways, but fear

and terror can slam my heart and mind shut. God is an expert, though, at prying open minds and hearts, tight fists, and clenched arms.

Over and over I am brought back to this thought: I am grateful, and I am grateful that I can still say "thank you."

I started this book by declaring that life has not turned out as I thought it would. I would be remiss if I did not say I have been profoundly blessed beyond anything I could have imagined. I have had enough sorrow to know God's mercy, but I have had more blessings than I can count.

I've made the point that salvation is a process, and that it has to do with how we live life on this plane. I'm content to leave the afterlife in God's hands.

I've made the point that all of us live under the imperative and the opportunity of answering the question, "What will you do with your one wild and precious life?"

Over the years I've lived into some hard questions and forced into consciousness (or were they forced on me) some troubling

Fear not, for I have redeemed you.
I have summoned you by name; you are mine.
When you walk through the fire, you will not be burned . . .
For I am the Lord your God, the Holy One of Israel, your Savior . . .
Since you are precious and honored in my sight,
and because I love you . . .
Do not be afraid, for I am with you.

—ISAIAH 43:1-5 (SELECTED)

paradoxes, ironies, and ambiguities. I've learned that the dots sometimes never connect and that there are few straight lines between those dots.

Sometimes when I'm slammed against a reality I cannot bear and a puzzle that doesn't make sense to me, I still rail at God and demand an explanation. When suffering goes on too long, when people lose too much, and when there are no answers, no relief, no solutions, I make it clear to God that I'm frustrated because I can't do anything about that suffering. Sometimes, after I have poured out my lament, I remember how my father used to sing while he was shaving, though never in public. Sometimes he sang "Farther Along," and when I hear it now I think about his life and the hard things he overcame, but mostly I remember his eternal optimism and deep faith.

Tempted and tried, we're oft made to wonder
Why it should be thus all the day long;
While there are others living about us,
Never molested, though in the wrong.

Those words always remind me of something my husband said in a sermon: God has a lot to answer for. The whole idea shocked me, and yet it made sense to me. Just knowing that the Almighty might give us reasons at some point is comforting. Perhaps the anonymous writer of "Farther Along" had come to the same conclusion.

Farther along we'll know all about it.
Father along we'll understand why.
Cheer up, my brothers, live in the sunshine,
We'll understand it all by and by.

Sometimes "father along" and "by and by" don't come, and yet the hope that God is in the midst of it all keeps me committed to the journey.

Through it all, I am guided by an inner *knowing* that I learned at my mother's knee, a knowing that no one can take that deep knowledge away from me. With the gift of memory I hear the simple, childlike melody and words my mother sang to me, words I sang to my own children as I held them close to my heart and rocked them to sleep.

Yes, Jesus loves me.
Yes, Jesus loves me.
Yes, Jesus loves me.
The Bible tells me so.

Thanks be to God, she did not leave me there in that vital but self-centered affirmation. She also sang this song to me.

Jesus loves the little children,
All the children of the world.
Red and yellow, black and white,
They are precious in his sight.
Jesus loves the little children of the world.

In those sweet, simple songs that were appropriate for me at that earliest stage of my spiritual formation, my mother taught me that life is indeed a joint venture. God extends love to us, and we join in grand participation, loving each other. Our loving is lived out in the everyday, ordinary pathways of our lives, out beyond the limited circles of those who look like we do or talk our language.

She and my father also taught me, by their words, their actions, and mostly by their lives to love Jesus. I have had to come to falling in love with Jesus my own way, but my parents started me down this path of knowing him, loving him, and wanting with all my heart to follow him.

Last Sunday I joined my daughter Julie and her family for worship at their church, Palmer Episcopal Church. I sat beside Julie, who sat beside six-year-old Madeleine. I watched Julie hold the Bible during the Scripture readings so that Maddie could read along, and hold the hymnal so she could sing, which she loves to do. When Maddie got restless, her dad simply took her small hand in his strong one and held it close to him. Madeleine and I walked to the Communion rail together, and we knelt together. I thought my heart would burst when she knelt between her mother and father when we returned to our seats. It's a different worship service from my parents', and it's different from my usual one, but as I knelt with my family—my daughter, my son-in-law, my granddaughter—I gave thanks for the ways in which faith and love for God are passed down from generation to generation.

I did smile through Jim Nutter's homily, though. What he preached could have been straight out of my childhood or my church, River Oaks Baptist. In no uncertain terms, Jim Nutter, priest and rector, told us that Jesus matters and we are to be about the business of loving Jesus and following him. My Baptist minister father would have loved it, and so did I.

Hearing that sermon about Jesus stirred my own faith; being with others who believe in Jesus strengthened me, fed my soul, gave me courage, and built my hope.

At the end of that Sunday, I received an e-mail from my longtime friend Tim Edwards, telling me about his morning at Meadowcreek Nursing Home in San Angelo, Texas, where he and his wife Georgia Alice Edwards lead Sunday morning worship once a month as part of a ministry of Southland Baptist Church. Tim is a Baptist preacher's kid like I am, and he, too, has wrestled with the same things that have bothered me in being "a Jesus person." You won't ever catch sentimentalism or spiritual bromides coming out of his mouth.

He described the service he led that morning, and then he said, "Every time we go there the highlight is us leading them in the singing of 'Jesus

Loves Me' just before the benediction. Even those who have slept through the whole thing wake up and sing. A psychologist might be able to figure that out. Myself, I just think that Mr. Jesus speaks to those folks through 'Jesus Loves Me.' Amen and amen."

What is it about this Jesus that makes us love him?

Life is abundantly full of joy, and it's full of pain and suffering, but this joint venture is a holy venture, and we who are made in God's image have the privilege of calling all the angels and God himself to our aid. He who has initiated it all is in the joint venture with us.

I believe. I believe in Jesus, and I believe in the Holy Spirit. My belief, though, is not mere mental assent, though it is that. My belief is more like love. With my heart *I believe.*

Thanks be to God for that belief and the assurance that nothing can take it away from me.

I trust this God I've met on the mountaintop, in the valleys, and on the long stretches of the flatlands to help my unbelief.

Thanks be to God for the fellow pilgrims on the way who remind me when I forget.

My mother often sang the old hymn "Blessed Assurance," sometimes as she prepared lunch on Sundays, and when we sing that song and others in church, I can almost hear her strong alto voice as if she were standing beside me, singing her faith. Those moments planted seeds of faith in my tender, young heart, and the memories make me stronger. When I sing that song, the child in me remembers: Jesus is in my heart. Jesus is mine. I am his. And he loves all the children of the world. All of that is true and real, and singing helps me remember.

Around us all is such a great cloud of witnesses. Around me are those who have let me lean on their faith, assuring me that there is nowhere I can go where God is not and reminding me to sing the song I'm intended to sing and to encourage you to sing the song you're meant to sing. Around me, too, are the fellow pilgrims

There is a sacredness in tears. They are not the mark of weakness, but of power. They speak more eloquently than ten thousand tongues. They are messengers of over-whelming grief . . . and unspeakable love.

—WASHINGTON IRVING

who lean on my faith, for there is a holy reciprocity, a shared life together that keeps the music playing.

We are in a joint venture of hope and faith and love. And we are not alone.

That is a blessed assurance. It is my story. It is my song.

Let it be. Let it be.

NOTES

1. Enya, "How Can I Keep from Singing?" *Shepherd Moons* (Reprise, 1991).

2. Eva Cassidy, "How Can I Keep from Singing?" *Eva by Heart* (Blix Street, 1997).

3. Joyce Landorf, *Balcony People* (Waco TX: Word Books, 1984).

4. k.d. lang, "Calling All Angels," *Recollections*, Nonesuch, 2010.

Made in the USA
Lexington, KY
13 June 2014